In Search of Dr. Jekyll and Mr. Hyde

In Search of
Dr. Jekyll and
Mr. Hyde

Raymond T. McNally
&
Radu R. Florescu

RENAISSANCE BOOKS
Los Angeles

In memory of the great Gothic scholar, our friend, Sir Devendra P. Varma, of Dalhousie University, Halifax, Canada, author of *The Gothic Flame.*

Library of Congress Catalog Card Number: 00-108764
ISBN: 1-58063-157-6

10 9 8 7 6 5 4 3 2 1

Design by Jesús Arellano

Published by Renaissance Books
Distributed by St. Martin's Press
Manufactured in the United States of America
First edition

Acknowledgments

The authors wish to acknowledge the help of Arthur Morey, managing editor; Kimbria Hays, associate managing editor; Jim Parish, editor; Abbey Park, assistant editor; Allan Taylor, sub editor; Sheila Rudy; Fernando DiFino; Scott Richard Stets; Gina Florescu; Kevin Gibson and Carol McNally; our research assistants; Stephen Vedder of the audio visual department at Boston College; Dr. Elaine Greig, curator of the Writer's Museum in Edinburgh, Scotland; and Dr. Andre Huis, head archivist at the Royal Palace (formerly the Amsterdam City Hall) in Holland. A travel research grant from Boston College permitted one of the present authors of this book to study in Edinburgh and Amsterdam.

Contents

Prologue

Our discovery of the historical Dracula (*In Search of Dracula,* 1972, revised edition 1994) became a bestseller that is still in print today, and it inspired us to go in search of the background of other horror figures. We were interviewed about Dracula on nationwide television, including *The Today Show,* A&E *Biography* with Peter Graves, *The David Frost Show,* the Discovery and Learning Channels, and a Halloween special with George Hamilton, as well as on French, German, and Austrian television. *In Search of Dracula* was published in more than a dozen foreign editions, including Swedish, Japanese, Portuguese, and Serbo-Croatian. Using similar literary-sleuth techniques, we embarked upon the search of the real Frankenstein, the prototype of Mary Shelley's Victor Frankenstein, publicized nationwide by the ABC network documentary that accompanied Kenneth Branagh's 1994 feature film *Mary Shelley's Frankenstein.* In each instance many fans wrote us that the original models we discovered were often more engaging than their fictional counterparts.

The popularity of the original archetypes in these novels and the hundreds of adaptations produced since, added two words to our language associated with evil: "Dracula" the blood-sucking vampire and "Frankenstein" the man-made monster (actually the name of the medical student who made the creature). In retracing the history of the many plays and films about these Gothic twins, we noticed that there existed an uncanny similarity between them and another familiar figure in popular mythology. When people speak of a "Jekyll and Hyde," we understand them to mean a person with two distinctly dissimilar aspects of personality. The concept obviously resonates. Many more movies have been made on this theme by major actors such as John Barrymore, Fredric March, Spencer Tracy, Jack Palance, and Kirk Douglas than on the Frankenstein monster and Dracula.

In addition, we noticed that the book, the *Strange Case of Dr. Jekyll and Mr. Hyde*, "a shilling shocker" written in 1886 by Robert Louis Stevenson, sold 40,000 copies in Britain within six days and more than a million in the United States by the turn of the twentieth century—far more books than *Dracula* and *Frankenstein* combined after their publication. How can we account for the extraordinary success of this novella?

The obsession of the author with the themes of the story may have given it unusual power. The historical person who inspired Stevenson, William Deacon Brodie (1741–1788), led a double life and his legend fascinated Stevenson from childhood on.

But the subject of double identity, which haunted Stevenson during his youth in Scotland, did not spring exclusively from his nightmares. Upon being asked by a friend as to the source for his famous novel, in a moment of sincerity, Stevenson acknowledged: "I believe Dr. Jekyll is quite willing to answer to the name of Stevenson." The author had, in fact, written a short essay on the double life of Brodie when he was barely age fourteen. The catalyst that fired Stevenson's imagination was provided by his nanny, Allison Cunningham. While the sickly boy was bedridden, she pointed to a beautiful chest in his bedroom and told him it was built by one William Deacon Brodie, whose legend and real-life story of dual existence lived on in the folklore of the city of Edinburgh, Scotland, sixty years after his execution in 1788.

Brodie's story is undeniably fascinating. He was a wealthy businessman and lived in a Georgian mansion in the fashionable part of the old town. He was always impeccably attired, a public figure—head of the incorporation of Wrights (meaning carpenters and woodworkers), as well as a member of the Governing Board of the City of Edinburgh. Brodie never married and led an overtly respectable moral life during the day, worthy of such a member of the elect of the city. At night, however, whether through drink, drugs, or potions, as was the case with Stevenson's Jekyll, he donned a black garb and "became a man until morning." (The phrase means that he gave free reign to his secret and repressed longings.) Brodie's Edinburgh by night was the old, unfashionable, slummy inner-city of pimps, thieves, and whores. In separate humble abodes, he kept his two mistresses, Anne Grant and Jean Watt, and fathered five illegitimate children.

Brodie's life mirrors that of the great literary figure Macheath of *The Beggar's Opera* by John Gay (1685–1732). (Gay's play was the basis of *Three Penny Opera,* a brilliant Weimar-era drama set in the London underworld by Bertholt Brecht and Kurt Weill, which contains the famous song "Mack the Knife"). For Macheath, excitement, not financial gain, was the principal motivation for crime. Brodie was eventually arrested and sentenced to death by hanging in one of the most famous trials in British history. Brodie tried to cheat the hangman by having a French surgeon wire him to avoid jerking, inserting a tube through his throat to avoid strangulation. According to rumors, he was able, thereafter, to prolong his double existence in America. Like the historical Dracula whose tomb was opened and found empty, Brodie's tomb located in the cemetery of the Duke of Buccleuch in Scotland was excavated and found to contain no body. The mystery of his vacant grave persists to this day.

We don't know Dr. Brodie's motives for crime or his drug of choice. But Dr. Jekyll's instrument for shifting from one nature to another has a painful contemporary ring evoking our modern drug culture. Drug abuse was also familiar to members of Victorian society who toyed with opium and laudanum for mood swings and literary stimulation, as did Lord Byron and Percy Shelley. Stevenson uses eleven different terms to describe Brodie's "potion or drug" and stresses the complexity of mixtures needed to transform the respectable Dr. Jekyll into the evil Mr. Hyde. Such metamorphosis in a laboratory by way of "powders" recalls Victor Frankenstein's efforts in creating a big man at Ingolstadt. Though never described in detail by Mary Shelley, this metamorphosis has been reenacted many times on the screen. Stevenson had, of course, read Mary Shelley's novel printed in 1818. For both writers, physical monstrosity demonstrates a troubled spirit or psyche. Using such terms as "troglodytic," "dwarflike," "apelike," and "with cornered hairy hand" to describe the monster Hyde, Stevenson lays, therefore, an emphasis upon the physical aspects of the personality change, in essence a man/beast transformation, a universal theme extant in the mythology of all nations. For Stevenson, however, the physical ugliness of Hyde had a connotation it could not have had for Shelley. In 1859 Charles Darwin had published *The Origin of Species* followed in 1871 by *The Descent of Man,* which laid out the evolutionary theory of man's descent from apes. Darwin refers to *atavism,* a reversion to the beast form, and this theory, which deeply shocked late Victorian society, spills out in other Stevenson writings such as *Arabian Nights* (1882).

Our search into the inspiration for *Jekyll and Hyde* focuses on the city of Edinburgh, which, unlike Victorian London in which Stevenson's celebrated novel was set, provided the real home for Jekyll and Hyde's prototypes: both Robert Louis Stevenson and

Deacon Brodie. In describing Edinburgh, Stevenson makes note of this ideal framework: "half capital and half country town, the whole city leads a double existence." Moreover, the Scots, who venerate their history and legends, have admirably preserved most of the major landmarks of our story.

By coincidence, a recent Frankenstein tour ended in the cemetery of St. Peter's Church in Bournemouth on the Isle of Wight, England. This happens to be the place where Mary Shelley (1792–1851), the author of *Frankenstein,* is buried, as is Mary Wollstonecraft (1757–1797), an early feminist. Percy Shelley's (1792–1822) heart, which survived his cremation, is buried here as well. Tourists expressed an interest in visiting the nearby site of Skerryvore, because that was the location where *Dr. Jekyll and Mr. Hyde* was written in 1885. Was this an augury to send us off in search of the historical inspiration for Jekyll and Hyde? Or does it confirm, as we believe, that Jekyll and Hyde has a hold on the human imagination as powerful as Frankenstein's monster and Count Dracula?

In Search of Dr. Jekyll and Mr. Hyde

Introduction

The fire burned in the grate: a lamp was set lighted on the chimney shelf, for even in the houses the fog began to lie thickly; and there, close up next to the warmth, sat Dr. Jekyll, looking deadly sick. He did not rise to meet his visitor, but held out a cold hand and bade him welcome in a changed voice.

—Robert Louis Stevenson, *The Strange Case of Dr. Jekyll and Mr. Hyde* (1886)

Dr. Henry Jekyll holds out a cold hand to his visitor Gabriel Utterson in Robert Louis Stevenson's classic horror story, the *Strange Case of Dr. Jekyll and Mr. Hyde,* first published in January 1886. Jekyll acts much in the way that Count Dracula welcomes his visitor, Jonathan Harker, with a hand that "seemed as cold as ice," some ten years later in Bram Stoker's novel *Dracula,* which appeared in print in 1897.

In Stevenson's tale it is an important moment, because it occurs just after Jekyll has experienced the shock of having metamorphosed first into the sinister Edward Hyde and then back into Jekyll. Jekyll's voice has changed, because he speaks like Hyde, and he cries out to his visitor Utterson in desperation,

"I have had a lesson—O God, Utterson, what a lesson I have had!"

When most readers hear or see the words *Jekyll* and *Hyde,* they often assume that the words come from some old legend like the vampire or the werewolf. Though the idea of two persons in one body is very old, it is Stevenson who described the phenomenon before Sigmund Freud and other psychologists had developed their theories of the relationship of the conscious to the unconscious self or had written about patients with split personalities.

Muriel Spark, in her bestselling novel, *The Prime of Miss Jean Brodie* (1961), set in Edinburgh, has her heroine, Miss Jean Brodie, claim William Deacon Brodie as one of her ancestors. No one, however, has comprehensively described and analyzed this historical prototype behind Stevenson's classic horror tale. Nor has anyone traced the historical development of the many theatrical and movie adaptations from as early as 1886 to the present.

Robert Louis Stevenson was born in 1850 and bred in Edinburgh, Scotland. He married an American, however, and spent a good deal of his mature life in the United States. Most readers know little about the historical background of Scotland and its influence upon Robert Louis Stevenson, but the popularity of the Mel Gibson movie *Braveheart* (1995) has at least brought some limited attention to Scottish history.

Stevenson was heavily influenced by his Scottish history. He was proud to be a descendant of the Gaelic speaking Celts, called *Scotti* by the Romans, who had emigrated to Scotland from Northern Ireland from the fourth to the sixth centuries and had given that country its name. These Celts were renowned for their highly imaginative literature of fantasy and fancy, and this trait is embodied in Stevenson's the *Strange Case of Dr. Jekyll and Mr. Hyde.* Stevenson could tell a good, believable story in which one could not discern fact from fiction.

As a Scotsman, Stevenson also felt the danger of being swallowed up by the English to the south of their territory. He had an ambivalent attitude about writing not in his native Scottish language, but in English. In fact, the English had been trying to dominate Scotland since at least the thirteenth century. In 1299 the forces of William Wallace, the great Scottish patriot, popularly known as Braveheart, temporarily defeated the English at the Battle of Stirling Bridge. Thereafter, Wallace was betrayed and captured. His body was emasculated, drawn and quartered, and finally hanged and burnt by the English in London in 1305. These tales of high adventure and heroism clearly influenced Stevenson stories such as *Treasure Island* and *Kidnapped.*

But the religious history of Scotland also affects much of Stevenson's work. *Jekyll and Hyde* is a moral tale about the risk of expressing the pure indwelling evil that exists under the surface of even the best of men. In Scottish religious tradition, human nature is seen in black-and-white terms. One must at least give the appearance of absolute rectitude.

Anyone who has traveled within Scotland and knows its people is easily convinced of the double aspect of the Scottish national character. The twin personality of the Scot is best exemplified when he imbibes the traditional "Scotch," which has enriched his country for centuries. Unlike the French who will openly admit, even to their children, their fondness for wine, a typical Scot would never be seen drunk tottering through the streets of Edinburgh for fear of being consigned to eternal damnation imposed by his Calvinist creed. He would have, however, no qualms slipping a "bribe" when ordering his groceries for a certain bottle of spirits well hidden in the vegetable basket. The Protestant Reformation in the person of John Knox, an admirer and former pupil of John Calvin, emerged in 1559 when Knox delivered a fire-and-brimstone sermon in which he solemnly denounced the Pope and the Church of Rome. Knox was more successful in turning Scotland into a Presbyterian, Calvinist stronghold than Calvin had been in his native Geneva, Switzerland. By 1560, the Scottish parliament formed a Presbyterian Church independent of both the Pope and monarchy. Young Stevenson was brought up in this severe Calvinist creed, though he soon rebelled against it.

In the centuries that followed, religious differences continued to spawn civil wars in Scotland. Scottish Protestantism was split between the ardent Presbyterians, on the one hand, who hated all rituals and church hierarchies, especially the traditional role of bishops in the Episcopal Church of England (also known as the Anglican Church) and, on the other hand, the moderate Scottish Calvinists who were close to Anglicanism. Calvinism in Scotland, however, spawned its own peculiar heresy: Antinomianism— the doctrine that God's grace is the only force capable of saving sinners. It is a radical interpretation of Martin Luther's "salvation by faith alone." In practice this sometimes was taken to mean that, because one cannot achieve salvation by good works, faith bestows immunity from the traditional moral law. Stevenson himself considered this belief hypocritical.

In the year 1637, while the dean of St. Giles Cathedral in Edinburgh was reading aloud the English *Book of Common Prayer*, which was a symbol of the episcopacy, an Edinburgh greengrocer named Jennie Geddes threw a stool at him in protest; this incident touched off long-lasting local riots. Angered by the high-handed interference of the king, more than five thousand people gathered in Greyfriars Church in Edinburgh to sign a protest that was eventually signed by some 300,000 people across Scotland during the following year. In November 1638, the General Assembly of the Church of Scotland met and denounced Charles II's *Book of Common Prayer* and the Episcopalian reforms. Under the leadership of the Earl of Argyll, these self-proclaimed Covenanters, who derived their name from the two covenants of 1638 and 1643, reaffirmed their Protestant faith and the Presbyterian organization of the Scottish Church in contrast to the Anglican Church controlled by bishops.

The Covenanters, ancestors of Robert Louis Stevenson, rejected the Restoration policies of King Charles II in the 1660s, which attempted to bring back the power of bishops. Ultra-Calvinists, who hated any reversion to popery and to church rule by bishops, such as existed in the Anglican Church, continued to oppose state intrusion into their religious beliefs and practices. In turn, the state persecuted them as extremists. After the battle of Bothwell Bridge in the west of Scotland in 1679, some 1,200 Covenanters were rounded up by the government and held captive in Greyfriars Churchyard under such deplorable conditions that most of them soon died. Stevenson's nanny, Cummy, would tell him about this rebellion and imprisonment when he was a youngster.

In 1745 Charles Edward Stuart (Bonnie Prince Charlie), the son of James Edward Stuart (the Old Pretender to the Scottish throne), traveled from France to Scotland to claim the throne for his father. The forces of Bonnie Prince Charlie were initially successful but were resoundingly defeated at the Battle of

Culloden in 1746. Dressed as a woman, Bonnie Prince Charlie fled into exile. After that the English government forbade any private armies, the wearing of kilts, and the playing of bagpipes in Scotland.

During the second half of the eighteenth century the New Town of Edinburgh to the north of the main Old Town was built. It was where the wealthy—Stevenson's family among them—fled to live. By the time King George IV formally opened the New Town of Edinburgh in 1822, the dividing line between the rich and the poor had been sharply drawn. And a fire in Old Town in 1824—which destroyed St. Giles Cathedral—made the contrast even sharper.

Stevenson's Edinburgh and London shared fog-shrouded streets. Edinburgh, nicknamed "Auld Reekie," was well known as a stinking, rotten place, due to the heavy smoke from numerous chimneys. Between the years 1841 and 1844, G. W. M. Reynolds published his personal account which portrayed the squalor and cruelties of underground London, with its labyrinth of slums, including Soho where Stevenson had his Hyde live. The sewage system of London flooded twice each day by the Thames tide; excrement and filth ebbed through the streets wherever one walked. The ex-playwright and journalist Henry Mayhew detailed this in his volumes dedicated to the London workers and poor. He gave vivid descriptions of the filth and ceilings overrun with "hangings of putrid matter like stalactites three feet in length." In his novella, Stevenson blended elements from his native Edinburgh, which he knew well, with features of London, which he did not know as well.

CHAPTER ONE

The Double Life of
William Deacon Brodie—
The Inspiration for *Jekyll and Hyde*

---

*Even the fortune of 10,000 English pounds
William Deacon Brodie had inherited was not
enough to finance his recklessness, and so he turned
to crime using his knowledge of Edinburgh society
and business to carry out a series of minutely
planned burglaries.*

—Ian Ansdell, *Strange Tales of Old Edinburgh*
(1975)

Just over a decade before the birth of George Washington
(1732), and close to the events that preceded the American
Revolution, there was born on September 28, 1741, William, the
eldest of eleven children, to one Francis Brodie and his wife Cecil
Grant. Only two sisters and one brother survived to adulthood.
This paltry survival rate was a reflection of the abominable sanitary conditions that prevailed in the Old Town of Edinburgh
during the eighteenth century.

Intertwined along the traditional mile-long High Street,
which extended from Edinburgh Castle to Holyroodhouse (still
a Royal residence used by Queen Elizabeth II on her visits to
Edinburgh), grew the traditional "Old Town," which acquired

the unsavory reputation for density of living unsurpassed by any city in the British Isles. Bursting at the seams, the overcrowding was best exemplified by adding additional floors to existing tenements, which sometimes reached twelve stories in height where rich and poor lived cheek by jowl in slumlike conditions. The whole city had the appearance of a sinking ship, with the streets below dirty, rat infested, and deprived of the most basic elements of sanitation. As filth and excrement piled up in the narrow Wynds and Closes below, the humbler citizens bereft of air and water would warn the unwary above them not to empty the chamber pots over their heads. (A *close* is a Scottish term referring to an alleyway between two buildings, which was usually closed off at both ends by locked gates at night.) Whenever the bells of St. Giles Cathedral would toll on the hour, two quaint warnings often were heard: "gardy loo" *(gardez l'eau)* or "look out below for the water," as chamber pots were emptied into the streets below from on high. No wonder the city was plagued by endemic epidemics of typhus, dysentery, and the plague.

The Brodies came from an old Scottish family whose roots, according to legend, went all the way back to the ruler Macbeth immortalized in William Shakespeare's play of the same name. Through the centuries, the Brodies, whose estates lay close to Inverness, extended their sway over the lands of Moray, close to the river Spey in the northwest. It was only during the seventeenth century that a branch of the family, one of the sons of the laird, moved south to study law in Edinburgh. He became a successful barrister, making a lot of money at the end of a long career, and died at the age of one hundred. By that time, his son Francis, the father of our subject, had married the daughter of another affluent lawyer in the Old Town, who was a member of the merchant guild. Francis's brother was a distinguished and prominent surgeon at the Royal Infirmary, while Francis's own vocation was cabinetry. Francis was skilled in creating dining parlor tables, desks, cabinets,

Painting of the slums of Edinburgh, 18th century. (EDINBURGH CITY LIBRARY)

wardrobes, coffins, settees, wine coolers, exterior and interior doors, and window frames. Frequently his pieces were ordered for the completion of homes by well-known architects such as William Adams.

This vocation came at a propitious time, when the Old Town of Edinburgh was growing rapidly in numbers to some one hundred thousand people of wealth and culture—gentry, burgesses, and professional people—many of whom were building or expanding ancient homes and refurbishing fine apartments. A good instance is that of the Duke of Hamilton whose apartments at Holyroodhouse were extravagantly redecorated with many of Brodie's furnishings. One can well understand how Francis amassed a fortune estimated at ten thousand pounds at the time of his death. In addition, he owned a commodious mansion in the Lawnmarket section of Old Edinburgh, still standing intact as late as 1820. The mansion was built by a distinguished architect during the reign of England's King James II (1685–1688). It featured a chiseled outer door with brass decorations, arched windows, high ceilings, and exquisitely detailed workmanship in the various salons, as well as an elegant courtyard.

Though portions of Brodie's mansion can still be seen, most of the building was destroyed by fire, which consumed a great portion of the Old City in 1824. Much of this section of the city was later replaced by Victorian buildings on the street bearing the queen's name (Victoria Street). Besides the mansion, old Brodie owned various tenements at Canongate, at World's End Close, and also another near Parliament House. Like his father, Ludovick Brodie, Francis also became an author and member of the prestigious Signet Club, which included luminaries such as Alexander Runcinam, poet Robert Fergusson, painter Henry Raeburn, engineer James Watt of steam engine fame, and others who epitomized the brilliance of eighteenth-century Edinburgh. This represented the last great period of Scottish culture personified by such "greats" as Sir Walter Scott (1771–1822), Robert Burns (1759–1796), James Boswell (1740–1795), and others. With such assets, old Francis Brodie was fully admitted into the capital's select society and became part of the establishment. It is no wonder that members of his powerful guild of carpenters elected him Deacon of the Corporation (*wirich* in the Scottish dialect). In English usage of the time, the term *deacon* was devoid of the usual religious connotations with which it is associated in modern parlance. It simply meant "head of his craft or trade union," which was one of the largest and most powerful in the realm. As deacon of his craft, Francis could be henceforth referred to as Francis Deacon Brodie—as one would refer to a cardinal of the Catholic Church, say, as Francis Cardinal Spellman. The title was handed down to his son, William (thus known afterward as William Deacon Brodie), as a part of his name at the time of Francis's death.

This post of deacon carried with it many privileges. It gave the titleholder the right to collect money from various public works, such as the famous Tolbooth prison. It also ensured his election to the City Council (located next to St. Giles Cathedral, a formidable seat of power). He took a financial percentage from all city monopolies that included printing establishments, newspapers, chaise transportation to the Port of Leith, and the fisheries at the Forth, which contained the best oyster beds in Europe. Given these advantages one may well understand the famous description about men of his ilk: "omnipotent, corrupt, impenetrable, silent, submissive, mysterious, and irresponsible." Wealthy, prestigious, and the personification of respectability, Francis's health began to fail at about the age of forty.

We know very few specifics about young Brodie's early life and schooling, but we can make some guesses. It is all but certain that he attended elementary and secondary public schools focused on the teaching of classical literature. At the secondary level, classes would begin early in the morning, though the boys were allowed to return to their homes for an English-style breakfast. Back at school by ten o'clock, the boys were dismissed at three o'clock to dine at home, and then they returned for two final hours of schooling.

This left ample time for young Brodie and his mates to get acquainted with the many disreputable taverns along Cowgate, the Fleshmarket, the Grassmarket, Anchor's Close, and other places of ill repute, which may well have whetted the young man's appetite, as the publisher William Creech would have it, "in the life of folly and vice." We know enough of the young's man attitude in these early days of adulthood to be sure that he had no intention of following in his father's profitable career. In 1713 Great Britain was involved in American colonial projects in Newfoundland and Nova Scotia and later in conflicts with France—in particular, the French and Indian Wars in America (1743–1748). Even as a young boy, William's mind was filled with thoughts of heroic adventures across the ocean or at sea where fame and fortune could be achieved by, say, joining General James Wolfe in Quebec battling the Marquis de Montcalm or fighting the Spaniards or French at Quiberon Bay. With old Francis's connections with Westminster, it would not have been difficult for him to apply pressure on the Admiralty to find a midshipman's commission on any of His Majesty's Ships of the Line.

One can well imagine young William's disappointment in failing to persuade his father to use his influence in advancing the son's adventurous spirit on the high seas. Instead, and reluctantly, he took over his invalid father's profitable business, as well as the family mansion with the help of his sister, Mistress Jean, who kept house.

McKay caricature of Brodie with the tools of his trade (1788). (EDINBURGH CITY LIBRARY)

The most detailed description we have of Brodie's physical appearance is still that produced by the sheriff's clerk's office in 1788, when the latter was a fugitive from the law at the age of forty-eight. It also corresponds accurately with the few paintings we possess and McKay's caricatures of the man. He was of small stature (five feet four inches tall) and always looked younger than his age. He was broad at the shoulders and narrow hipped. He had dark brown eyes with large black eyebrows (the scar of a cut next to his nose later disfigured him somewhat). With a sallow complexion, he did not resemble his fair-haired Scottish ancestors but looked rather Asian. He had a speech defect "with his tongue doubling up at the roof of his mouth." Jet black hair twisted at the end or tied behind, coming far down upon his cheek, framed his face. His whiskers were very sandy at the end, high topped in the front, and frizzed at the side. He had a high smooth forehead.

Young William had a peculiar way of walking, taking long strides and striking the ground with his heel bending both feet inward. He usually would walk with a stick in one hand and moved in a proud swaggering style. His legs were small and thin though he had large feet. He usually was impeccably dressed like a dandy, wearing a blue suit and a striped duffel great coat with vest, breeches, and stockings along with silver shoe buckles. On the whole, the young man presented a most striking appearance. He was elected Deacon of Wrights in 1781, Trade Councilor in 1784, and Member of the City of Edinburgh's town council with all the privileges that this entailed.

Brodie might well have remained little known in the Edinburgh establishment had not the theater come to the city. There had been playhouses before, but they had been shut down by the severe Calvinist establishment, which regarded the theater as a place of sin—certainly reflecting the view of Brodie's father. Unexpectedly, a small theater was built on the slopes of Multersey's Hill at the far end of the partially completed North Bridge. This playhouse was called the Theater Royal. The London actor/manager of the West Digges Company gathered a few actors who began performing some classical plays, including Shakespeare, using English rather than the Lalland (Lowland) Scotch dialect, which was disappearing.

By far the greatest success was a play by John Gay, *The Beggar's Opera,* first performed in London and Edinburgh in 1728, in which the respectable and unrespectable worlds were turned upside down. The hero, a dashing erstwhile army officer turned highwayman called Captain Macheath, often short of money but never of charm, demonstrated that every man could be bought and sold for a price. Contemptuous of the consequences of his action, Macheath was convinced that any clever man was able to outwit authority. For Brodie, a romantic, Captain Macheath must have represented the perfect model and hero. The anarchy of Macheath's philosophy was particularly appealing. Whenever the West Digges Company performed the play in Edinburgh, Brodie was in attendance; he would not miss a single show. Gradually he learned the various tunes and verses by heart and began to sing or hum them, continuing to do so throughout his criminal career, even when facing death on the gallows in 1788. Macheath clearly was an influence on the development of Brodie's secret, second personality.

Another indication of Brodie's incipient revolt against respectability was his abandonment of the prestigious Signet Club, of which his father was a member, to join a burlesque group of young men with nonsensical rituals and modes of address called the Cape Club. Here Brodie's nickname became Sir Lluyd, while one of his friends was addressed as Sir Stark Naked. This social club became another means of escaping the dull and puritanical world of the Edinburgh establishment.

A bachelor who led a most respectable home life during the day attending to an ailing father, Brodie by night lived a life as extravagant as that of his hero, the captain from *The Beggar's Opera.* He succeeded in keeping two mistresses, Anne Grant, in whose name he kept a house at Cant's Close, and Jean Watt, who lived at Libertown Wynd. They were unaware of each other's existence although they lived at close distance from each other in the Old Town. Thus, with no more of a drug than a few beers or some wine imbibed in the taverns with which he had become familiar since his youth, or at the Cape Club, the deacon could unleash his other self, even while his father was still alive. Under cover of darkness and invariably wearing old black clothes for camouflage, Brodie began his double existence, subverting conventions and the order of society.

At first, apart from womanizing, two popular sports gained his attention: dicing and cockfighting. Excitement rather than winning was the principal attraction. Cockfighting was a sport of the greatest antiquity, and very popular in the British Isles, particularly in Scotland. Wealthy patrons would buy the birds, paying high prices for their fighting qualities. The cocks were carefully paired up before they fought and were placed in a ring two by two. Then large sums of money were staked on each bird, and the fight continued until one of the cocks died or gave up from exhaustion. Hidden from his father, Brodie kept his cocks in his wood yard off Brodie's Close, an alleyway near his mansion, until the day of the fight when Brodie's friend, Michael Henderson an eminent "cocker," placed them in the cockpit. Far from winning, the

View from inside Brodie's Close to High Street, Edinburgh. (RAYMOND T. MCNALLY)

Deacon is said to have lost large sums of money in the backing of his unsuccessful cocks. He was no luckier at dice or cards. He kept up appearances at Brodie's Close by entertaining lavishly during the day while increasing his expenses with the cost of two additional households, those of his mistresses and assorted illegitimate children. It should also be remembered that these expenses were incurred while his father was still alive and William had not as yet inherited his fortune.

Again the Deacon took his cue from his idol, the fictional Captain Macheath, who had experienced similar difficulties in *The Beggar's Opera* and assembled a collection of rogues the likes of "Matt o' the Mint," "Jenny Twitcher," or "Crooked Fingered Jack." Surely the Deacon could find the equivalent of these fictional, romanticized theives and scoundrels in the Edinburgh underworld with which he had become familiar during his nightly escapades.

The first meeting of Brodie and George Smith (note gamecock). Caricature by McKay, 1786. (EDINBURGH CITY LIBRARY)

William Deacon Brodie's transition from gambler to common thief probably occurred around the year 1786, when he met three shady characters with whom he became partners in a number of robberies that disconcerted and puzzled the honest, law-abiding and Church-oriented Calvinist, citizenry of Edinburgh. In July of that year, an Englishman named George Smith, a truant of sorts who at one time had been a hawker and at another a locksmith, appeared in town. He parked his belongings and his horse and buggy with Brodie's pub-keeping friend, Michael Henderson, who had an inn located at the Grassmarket. Falling ill, Smith sent for his wife who nursed him back to health. To pay his bills, Smith's wife opened a grocery store in Cowgate. Eventually, Smith came across two other have-nots while drinking at Henderson's Pub. One was Andrew Ainslie a one-time shoemaker in Edinburgh, and the other was John Brown (alias Humphrey Moore) who had rented a room at Barnet's Close. Brown was a former convict sentenced at the Old Bailey in London for life deportation, having been found guilty of murder and theft. No one seems to have known how he had escaped this punishment.

The three shady individuals—all of them in dire need of money—were introduced by Henderson to his friend Brodie, who soon recognized the value of these potential allies. The four-some established their nightly headquarters at Clarke's Tavern in the Fleshmarket Close and began to plot "how and where their kind of business could be conducted with success." The brain and captain of this group was quite obviously Brodie himself. It was, of course, essential for the Deacon to continue his normal activ-ities as a Wright and member of the City Council during the day when he must keep up appearances and converse with his social friends and peers.

Brodie explained to his associates that in Edinburgh, an honest city where burglaries were rare, it was a well-known fact that most of the merchants, shopkeepers, bankers, and ordinary householders kept the keys of their houses or warehouses hanging on a back door of their premises. It took very little imag-ination for Brodie, who knew and visited many of the merchants and businessmen in town, to arrange for one of the members of his gang, with wax lining his palm, to be ready to make an impression of the respective key for future use while Brodie talked to his potential victims on a social visit. Brodie himself kept several skeleton keys just in case they were needed. In this manner, from the fall of 1786 to 1788, the four men began an extraordinary series of well-planned thefts, all of them occurring at night with Brodie rarely participating in person.

The many thefts succeeded each other at alarming intervals, and their pattern was generally identical. On October 9, 1786, a goldsmith, Mr. James Wemyss, with a shop located near Parliament House, reported the loss of fifty gold and diamond rings, broaches, and earrings and diverse silver jewels during the night. Ten guineas were offered as a reward to anyone who could provide any information or had witnessed the theft. On November 6, hardware storeowner Mr. Davidson McKain was hit in a similar fashion in the dead of night with the loss of an unspecified number of articles stolen from his store. The Brodie gang used false keys and a small crowbar to gain entry. Smith entered the store, while Brodie stood watch outside. Three days later, Messrs. Johnson and Smith, private bankers on the Royal Exchange, reported the theft of 800 English pounds. On December 12, a tobacconist lost an unspecified amount of precious tobacco and snuff in what was, evidently, the coup of a connoisseur.

On Christmas Eve 1786, while most citizens were celebrating the birth of our Lord, another jeweler, Messrs. John and Andrew Bruce, lost a number of precious gold watches, rings, lockets, and other valuables. The depositions made by John and Andrew Bruce, later acknowledged in the course of the famous 1788 trial of Brodie by his accomplice George Smith, presented a good insight into that theft. Brodie told Smith that "the shop at the head of Bridgestreet, belonging to Messrs. Bruces, would be very proper for breaking into, as it contained valuable goods, and he knew the lock could be easily opened, as it was a plain lock." Smith asked Brodie to accompany him on the night of the theft, but Brodie declined, because he happened to be winning at cards in the house of James Clark, the vintner at the head of Flesh-market Close. So Smith went ahead and committed the robbery on his own. The Bruces petitioned the local sheriff to investigate the theft, which they said amounted to the value of 350 English pounds. From the stolen goods, Brodie took a gold seal, a gold watch-key set with garnet stones, and two gold rings. The robberies continued throughout 1787. One of the largest occurred in August that year—the forcible entry into a teahouse belonging to Mr. Andrew Carnegie, who lost pounds of precious China tea. Years later his descendant, Andrew Carnegie (1835–1919), emigrated to the United States, made his fortune in steel, and became a noted philanthropist.

Among the most daring raids in that crime-filled year was the loss in August of the three-hundred-year-old silver mace located in the Library of Edinburgh University. A shoe shop was burglarized in the same month, as well as a jeweler, Mr. John Tapp, who lost an undetermined amount of cash, some valuable paintings, and diverse pieces of jewelry. The *coup* of that year was a raid on well-known silk merchants Messrs. Inglis and Horner, whose shop was located at Cross Close off High Street. They lost valuable goods estimated at a worth of 300 to 400 pounds. This loss was sufficiently substantial for the owners to offer a 150-pound reward for the recovery of the property. They also petitioned Lord Sidney, secretary of state at the Home Office, to offer a royal pardon to anyone who could provide information leading to the arrest and conviction of the culprits.

By and large none of the merchants were ever able to recover the takings, as Deacon Brodie arranged for the stolen goods to be hastily exported from Scotland to England with different agents and sold at a discount in London. The cash was usually laundered by a certain Mr. John Tasker from Chesterfield, one of Brodie's principal middlemen.

On one occasion the Deacon was recognized by the well-to-do woman who owned the establishment, which happened to be one he frequented. She could hardly believe what she saw, nor would anyone have believed her.

In January 1788, Brodie and his cohorts were caught gambling and cheating with loaded dice at a tavern near Fleshmarket Close. He was playing with a certain James Hamilton, head of the guild of chimney sweeps, who lost a considerable amount of cash. Grabbing the dice Hamilton discovered that each was filled with lead in one corner. Furious, he demanded restitution from Brodie and his gang. The Deacon refused. According to some, Hamilton may have attacked the Deacon physically, the scar near his eye testifying to that assault. Mr. Hamilton filed formal charges against Brodie. Hamilton's petition stated that he had "accidentally" met Brodie and his friends at the tavern

Wall painting outside of Brodie's Tavern, Edinburgh showing William Deacon Brodie as a respectable citizen on the left and dressed as a burglar on the right. (CAROL MCNALLY)

near the top of Fleshmarket Close. Brodie defended himself by replying that while he and his associates were "innocently amusing themselves with a game of dice over a glass of punch," a certain Mr. Hamilton inserted himself into the group. Brodie claimed that he did not know the dice were loaded and "always considered all dices to be alike." Hamilton complained that "there are living instances of men, though born to independence and enjoying most ample fortune, can intermix with the very lowest class of the multitude." He chided that there are men like Brodie who "rather than associate with their equals, will descend to keep company with ostlers [meaning 'hotel owners'], peddlers, and stableboys." There were those, of course, who suspected that the Deacon, a protégé of the powerful Henry Dundas, Commissioner for Scotland, was guilty. Once again, however, Brodie was protected by the fact that he was a respectable conservative on the City Council.

By this time, however, one liberal Scotsman was already out to get Brodie. This man was Edinburgh's main bookseller, Mr. William Creech. He was a town magistrate, the son of a farmer from Fife, who was politically against Dundas conservatives, such as Brodie, and blamed the heightened numbers of crimes on the social degeneracy of the times. Creech rose above his humble beginnings by studying at the University of Edinburgh. As the Elder of St. Giles Cathedral, Creech was upset by the dramatic increase in the number of brothels, because he suspected that wanted criminals were being sheltered in them. He viewed Deacon Brodie as his chief adversary, and it was not long before Brodie played into Creech's hands.

At the beginning of 1788, Brodie and his gang planned the most daring caper of their lives, namely, the robbery of the General Excise Office of Scotland, where the taxes of all the citizenry were duly collected before being sent to Westminster in England. The Excise Office was thus an official branch of the British Civil Service. Scottish law was severe and direct about it: Burglary of any official establishment was automatically punishable by death.

The Deacon was familiar with the terrain of the targeted site, especially the old structure of the Excise Office then located in Chessel's Court, past Nether Bow, beyond an archway leading to its enclosure surrounded by palisades. One of Brodie's relatives worked there, and Brodie visited him often. In this way the Deacon became familiar with the movements of the watchmen on the premises. On the pretext of speaking with his kin, Brodie once took his minion Smith along with him. To their astonishment, they found that the keys to the outer gate were actually hanging behind it, much as in the case of the shops they had robbed in previous years. Thus, they were easily able to make an imprint of these keys, but this was not the case with the inner doors and vaults. Brodie knew that specialized tools would be needed to force those inner vault locks.

The clever Scotsman discovered that the Excise Office was left unguarded from 8 to 10 P.M. when a new set of watchmen took over their duties. By Tuesday, March 10, the conspirators had perfected their plan of attack at Smith's house in Cowgate. They assembled three masks, lanterns, pistols, braces, three whistles, and copies of the keys to the outer gates. Brodie wore a black slouch hat and black clothes.

Ever the showman, Brodie loved to sing songs from *The Beggar's Opera* as he completed his thieving endeavors. Just before the abortive March 1788 break-in at the Excise Office, Brodie was singing one of those tunes to his cohorts. During that snowy evening of Wednesday, March 8, 1788, Ainslie, the chief scout and watchman for Brodie's mob, kept watch outside the palisades to warn the others with three whistle blows should any major trouble occur. Meanwhile, Brodie, Smith, and Brown had the difficult task of entering the inner sanctum of the empty Excise Office and attacking the vaults by smashing the lock. Then, the unexpected happened. A Mr. Bonar, Deputy Solicitor of the Excise Office, had inadvertently forgotten legal papers in his office and had returned to retrieve them. The Deacon was in the office at the time but had not yet reached the targeted vault. Upon hearing the warning whistles, Brodie abandoned his position and fled, brushing past Mr. Bonar in the darkness, as Bonar left the office. Luckily Bonar did not recognize Brodie.

Meanwhile, the Deacon's minions (Smith and Brown) evidently oblivious to all but their task, proceeded with the intended theft. They broke into the cashier's desk and found a miserable sixteen pounds. Unfortunately for their scheme, they neglected to search farther into the secret vault beneath the cashier's desk where six hundred pounds lay hidden. Brown signaled Smith to cock his pistol and the two fled with their meager loot.

The Deacon regained his mansion quickly, abandoned his black suit, and, as an alibi, spent the early evening with his brother-in-law Matthew Sheriff in his fastidious new house in the New Town section of Edinburgh. Later in the evening, the Deacon joined one of his mistresses, Jean Watt, at Libberton Wynd so that she could provide an additional alibi. The next day Brodie met his partners at the tavern in Burnet's Close. He was in a jovial mood, but his buddies were glum and irate, due to their small take from the dangerous robbery, as well as the Deacon's cowardly course of action the night before. After much mutual recrimination, the partners in crime decided to meet at Smith's house in

Statue of Brodie outside Brodie's Close, Edinburgh. (RAYMOND T. MCNALLY)

Cowgate to split up the lack-luster spoils. Since the Deacon already owed his partners money, he received virtually nothing of the latest take. The disappointed cohorts parted in a somber mood. Smith and Ainslie crossed the bridge into New Town and left for New Castle by stagecoach heading south to England.

The Deacon thought he was home safe. The thoughts of his other accomplice, John Brown, however, wandered in a different direction. Brown was already a convicted felon and the prospect of a possible King's pardon, promised by the burglarized merchants Inglis and Horner, dangled before his eyes. Besides, the amount of money that he got for the break-in at the Excise Office was miniscule. It was time for him to take advantage of the Deacon.

CHAPTER TWO

The Deacon on the Run—
Trial and Conviction, 1788

Let us take to the road
Hark! I hear the sound of coaches
The hour of attack approaches,
To your arms, brave lads and load.

> —Favorite verses of William Deacon
> Brodie from John Gay's *The Beggar's*
> *Opera* (1728)

On Thursday March 9, 1788, all of Edinburgh was abuzz with the news of the bungled robbery at the Excise Office. Late on Friday night, the Irishman who called himself John Brown (aka Humphrey Moore) visited Mr. William Middleton of the sheriff's office. The offer of a pardon in exchange for evidence was enough for Brown to turn State's Evidence. A noted criminal, he knew that by English law a King's Pardon could cancel punishment for past and present offences. At first Brown planned to denounce only his companions Ainslie and Smith to the authorities; as for Brodie he hoped to blackmail him. The sheriff considered the accusations against Ainslie and Smith serious enough to send the sheriff to catch and imprison them at

Tolbooth, the main Edinburgh prison. When the news of the treachery of Brown and the arrests of Ainslie and Smith reached Brodie, he was at first petrified but then reflected that all the evidence against Ainslie and Smith was based only on the testimony of Brown, a common criminal. Brodie tried to gain access to the prisoners in order to bribe them into silence about his own criminal actions, but the authorities denied him such a visit. Up to this point, none of his companions in crime had denounced Brodie as a fellow conspirator, apparently becaue they all looked forward to being paid to keep quiet about his involvement. Brodie, however, panicked.

The forty-seven-year-old Deacon chose to flee Edinburgh. When the news reached Ainslie and Smith that Brodie had disappeared from the local scene, they decided not only to admit their own guilt, but also to implicate Brodie as the leader of their gang. Hence, only four days after the arrest of Ainslie and Smith, the Edinburgh's Sheriff's Office issued a warrant for the arrest of William Deacon Brodie on charges of breaking into the General Excise Office. A two-hundred-pound reward was offered for his arrest with fifty pounds added *if* Brodie was convicted. In a real sense, Brodie had brought his troubles upon himself by departing. Had he sat quietly in his mansion in Edinburgh, he might have gotten away with his audacious crime.

On Sunday, March 12, 1788, while the good Scottish Presbyterians were in church, Brodie fled in a carriage to London. Hence, the King's messenger for Scotland was given the difficult task of trying to apprehend Brodie before he could leave British Shores. The pursuit of Brodie in Scotland and in England lasted eighteen days, leading from Edinburgh to Dunbar in Scotland, and to Newcastle and York in England. The authorities, however, lost the scent in London, although the Deacon came close to being recognized on several occasions, as he himself later testified.

Brodie finally had reached London on March 23. He found refuge "with an old female friend." One of his cousins, a Brodie from Miltown, England, and his brother-in-law, Matthew Sherriff, an upholsterer who lived in New Town, provided some help but he needed funds. The Deacon was put in touch with an American attorney from Philadelphia who promised the finances for the fugitive to begin a fresh career in the New World.

The escape plan called for Brodie to avoid stopovers at English ports where he could be too easily picked up. No safe vessel, however, could be found immediately to take Brodie from London to New York. Brodie's associates finally managed to contact the owner of the *Endeavour,* a ship captained by John Dent. The vessel was supposed to sail from London to the port of Leith in Scotland, which would have been a dangerous stop for the Deacon. Secretly, orders were given to divert the vessel instead to Ostend, a Dutch port. The *Endeavour,* however, had already booked passage for a tobacco merchant and his wife, Mr. and Mrs. John Geddes, headed to the city of Leith. On the pretext that there was another passenger on board, a Dutchman by the name of John Dixon who had very

Amsterdam City Hall, 18th century. (ROYAL PALACE, AMSTERDAM)

suddenly become deathly ill, the Geddes were informed the ship had to be diverted from Leith to Ostend. The sick man was none other than William Deacon Brodie, who rarely left his cabin on board the ship.

The voyage proved to be a nightmare of misadventures for Brodie. The *Endeavour* ran aground at Tillbury, England, while sailing down the Thames, and the ship was forced to be tied up for two weeks. Bad weather on the English Channel crossing made any direct path to Ostend impossible. As such the Deacon had to disembark at Flushing and then set off for Ostend on a skiff, but as Brodie departed from the *Endeavour* he made another fatal mistake. Because the vessel was eventually proceeding on to Edinburgh with the Geddes couple on board, John Dixon (William Brodie's alias) gave John Geddes three letters: one was addressed to his good friend, the innkeeper and stabler, Michael Henderson at the Edinburgh Grassmarket; another to his brother-in-law Matthew Sherriff; and yet a third to Anne Grant of Cant Close, one of his mistresses.

When Geddes returned to Edinburgh he became suspicious about this so-called John Dixon who had given him the letters to deliver. Geddes read the many articles about the sensational robbery at the General Excise Office and about the Deacon who was on the run. The published physical descriptions of the fugitive's rather unusual appearance led Geddes to believe that there was little doubt that the self-proclaimed John Dixon was none other than the now notorious William Deacon Brodie. Added to this suspicion was the temptation of a handsome reward. John Geddes opened the letters, read them, and turned them over to the sheriff's office in anticipation of a financial windfall. In the crucial letters, however, Brodie never actually admitted to being the brains behind the innumerable burglaries that had plagued Edinburgh for more than two years. He apparently only alluded to his guilt in planning the robbery of the Excise Office, which, of course, was a fatal enough admission. The correspondence also contained useful information about the Deacon's flight from Edinburgh, his whereabouts, and his need to leave the British Isles for America as soon as possible.

Once informed of the fact that Brodie was in the Netherlands, the Scottish and English authorities reacted with haste. With the aid of British agents in Holland, they were able to retrace the Deacon's journey from Ostend to Amsterdam, where they presumed, correctly, that he was waiting to board the next available ship to take him to America. An Irishman named John Daly, who was in the employ of the British Consulate at Amsterdam, was given the task of finding and arresting Brodie.

Meanwhile, another of Brodie's accomplices in Edinburgh, George Smith, declared himself ready to confess everything and to implicate Brodie directly. The police searched Brodie's large mansion and found a pair of pistols wrapped in green cloth and a type of lantern usually used by housebreakers. At this point, however, it still seemed as if Brodie had gotten clean away.

While Brodie was hiding in Amsterdam, still under the pseudonym John Dixon, Daly, the British agent, had been informed by the captain of the *Endeavour* about Brodie's escape plans. There, two locals told Daly that they had encountered a shabbily dressed Scotsman carrying a black trunk. They pointed to an ale house where the fellow had taken refuge. Daly followed up the lead. He entered the establishment and called Brodie's name aloud. When no one answered him, Daly went upstairs and discovered the Deacon hiding in a cupboard. Daly arrested him and took him to the Amsterdam city hall for incarceration. The British consul and a Mr. Duncan from Edinburgh, who had agreed to identify Brodie, were already there. Later, Brodie, alias John Dixon, fought extradition from Holland to Scotland. He steadfastly held to his right of non self-incrimination and claimed protection under Dutch and English law. The local chief magistrate, however, cleverly tricked Brodie into admitting, somewhat obliquely, his real name. With that, the jig was up for Brodie.

Brodie was sent back to England for trial. On June 17, with his arms bound, Brodie was shipped from the port of Helvoet to Harwich with a sheriff-at-arms, Mr. Groves, in charge. He was taken to Bow Street in London where, on July 11, Brodie at last admitted his true identity. Nevertheless, while confined in the Bridewell jail, Brodie continued to be in good spirits and boasted about his Dutch adventure. It took less than fifty-four hours for a coach to take Brodie to Edinburgh from London. By July 17, 1788, he arrived back in Edinburgh and was held in custody in a cell at Tolbooth prison along with his three companions in crime, John Brown, George Smith, and Andrew Ainslie.

For William Deacon Brodie to be held in custody at the Tolbooth jail, awaiting trial, was truly humiliating and ironic as he, as a member of the city council, had collected revenues for the Tolbooth. Confined to a cell known as the "iron room," he was chained by one foot to an iron bar that extended the whole length of the cell—long enough to reach his bunk as well as a table where he could sit and write, play chess, or engage in other pursuits. The authorities denied him the privileges of having a knife and fork for meals.

Despite his dire situation, Brodie had not lost his spunk and sense of humor as evidenced when he complained in a note to a fellow town councilor who intended to visit him: "The nails of my fingers and toes are not quite as long as Nebuchadnezzars are said to have been, although long enough for a mandarin and much longer than I find convenient. . . . I'll be happy to see you. You will be sure to find me at home and all hours are equally convenient." Indeed he enjoyed prison visits by his friends, including members of his family. To the few visitors who still believed in his innocence, he challenged them to play chess, philosophized about his fate, and continued to hum tunes from his favorite, *The Beggar's Opera*.

The trial, which took place at the courthouse at Chessel Court adjoining the Tolbooth jail, could be ranked among the most famous trials in history both because of the nature of this unusual case, the oratorical flourish from a galaxy of legal luminaries, and the harshness of a sentence punishing a man for the theft of a relatively modest sum. Many famous jurists participated, and the most famous of them all, the Lord Chief Justice Braxfield, presided over the trial. "Old Braxie" later would serve as a model for one of Stevenson's most famous works, *The Weir of Hermiston* (unfinished at the time of the writer's death in 1894). Braxfield was a committed Scotsman who often spoke in his native language, while other Scottish barristers usually spoke a convoluted poor imitation of the King's English. (Braxfield was also noted for his sharp tongue and wit. Once, when over a bad dinner his wife complimented the cook for her piety, Braxfield bellowed, "I'd take a whure aff the streets gin she could lie a tattie," meaning "I'd take a whore from the streets if she could cook potatoes.")

A group of liberal lawyers led by the superb orator Henry Erskine, dean of the law faculty, who was the acknowledged leader of the Scottish Bar, defended Brodie. John Clerk was appointed defender of George Smith in his first important trial, and he opened with oratorical florid attacks on the Bench. These lawyers also used the trial as a means of attacking the Scottish establishment composed of conservative Tories and often controlled by the landowning Dundas family interests. Erskine vowed to break the Dundas's hold on Parliament and patronage. Harry Erskine's junior was Alexander Wight, who had been solicitor-general for five years under the Whig administration. The lord advocate was Ilay Campbell (pronounced "camel"), a conservative Dundas man. Local Whigs waggishly said that there were more camels in Scotland than in all the deserts of Arabia.

The jury was composed of Edinburgh notables including six bankers, four merchants, a number of professional people, and writers among whom was William Creech, who had long suspected the Deacon of being the brains behind the long list of thefts that had plagued Edinburgh during the preceding two years. On the appointed date, only two prisoners, William Deacon Brodie and George Smith, were paraded in a chaise post from the Tolbooth jail to the court house escorted by guards of the Seventh Scottish regiment on foot, picturesque in their red and black outfits. The Deacon was impeccably dressed as was his wont in a dark blue coat, a fancy velvet waistcoat, black satin breeches, white stockings, and shoes to match. Carrying a cocked hat by his side, his hair was fully dressed and powdered. He was the picture of respectability and defiance. In contrast, his cohort George Smith was poorly garbed and appeared broken and depressed. Ainslie was curiously missing from the dock. The secret reason for this was that the prosecution had decided behind closed doors that they could not rely wholly upon Brown's testimony, because he was a convicted felon and murderer sentenced to deportation. So the prosecution had crafted a deal with Ainslie, making it possible for him to turn state's evidence and corroborate Brown's testimony.

There are two major contemporary accounts of the trial of William Deacon Brodie and George Smith; one is by William Creech, and the other by Aeneas Morison who was a writer and a member of the Brodie defense team. The introductions and commentaries in each are very different. William Creech provides a lengthy moralistic preface with word-for-word accounts of the testimonies by witnesses, whereas Morison tends to summarize the testimony. William Creech, that "upright, pert, tart, tripping wight [meaning 'creature' in Scottish]," as the Scottish poet Robert Burns called him, was born on April 21, 1745, the son of Reverend William Creech, minister of Newbattle in Midlothian, Scotland. His father died four months after the birth of his son, and the boy was raised by his mother alone at Alkeith and Perth in Scotland. She later moved to Edinburgh with the idea of sending her son to the University there, but her friendship with the wife of His Majesty's Printer for Scotland, Alexander Kincaid, led to her son being offered a job in the bookselling part of the Kincaid business. When Kincaid retired from the business in 1773, Creech was left in charge of the publishing and bookselling business at the center of High Street in Edinburgh. He stayed as boss of the High Street business for forty-four years.

Creech was well known in Edinburgh as a particularly mean-spirited man. He became a member of the Edinburgh town council in 1780, a magistrate of Edinburgh in 1788, and, in 1811, Lord Provost. It was said that at Creech's supper parties the company was large, but the amount of food provided for them was small. Creech died unmarried on January 14, 1815. The following is a retelling of the trial based on an analysis of the biases of those involved and a fusion of the two presentations: We include here only the relevant parts of the trial transcript and not the legalistic arguments which would bore most readers. Creech's pompous introduction demonstrates his deep-seated hatred for Brodie:

It will readily be allowed, that few Trials more remarkable than the following have ever happened, if we consider the character and situation of the principle person tried, the nature of the crime, and the ingenuity and novelty of the means by which it was perpetrated.

An instance of a citizen, not only in a comfortable, but in a wealthy situation, and who frequently held respectable public stations in this metropolis, brought to trial for a crime of so dangerous and atrocious a nature, which only the lowest and most abject could have been supposed to commit, is not to be found in the criminal history of this country. The crime of the daring highwayman is venial, when compared with that of the insidious plunderer, under sanction of character. The crime of robbery, no doubt, is but too frequent; but is generally committed either by violence and force, where personal danger is incurred, or it is discernible by evident traces of fraudulent design and cunning.

It has, however, been reserved for present day to contrive a method of robbery that should evade all suspicion, and even baffle every possibility of detection, unless by the information of an accomplice. An individual unconnected, and possessed of art, might have remained in security without the smallest suspicion of guilt, for a long period.

Creech then went on to try to demonstrate the hypocrisy of Brodie who on February fourth and fifth of 1788, "sat as a Juryman to judge the crimes of others," specifically the trial of

Allan MacFarlane, officer of the Excise, and Richard Firmin, soldier in the 39th foot regiment. At that very time, Brodie and his gang were committing their robberies.

Finally Creech blamed Brodie's sink into depravity to his interest in gambling rather than good hard work:

What a serious and unlawful lesson does this Trial afford to the bulk of mankind, of humility, and circumspection in conduct! Where will they meet with a more striking example, *that the heart is deceitful and desperately wicked!* or a more powerful admonition to the self-examination of the motives of action! The neglect of early education, inattention to the acquirement of good principles and habits, and the associating with bad companions, often lead to fatal consequences, even with many whose situation and opportunities, if rightly improved, might have led to respectability to honor, and to opulence.

The first step to vice prepares the mind for further accessions of guilt. The restraints of conscience once overcome, give less resistance in every future breach of moral duty; and crime often succeeds crime, till the sword of justice falls on the guilty head.

Of all the vices of dissipated life, none, perhaps, is more fascinating, or more destructive to self-repose, to virtue, and to industry, than *gaming*.

The affluent, whose minds have not been trained to sober thinking, or habituated to useful exertion, naturally fly to this vice to escape the languor of inaction. But the temporary amusement, which it affords, by exciting hopes and fears in the listless mind, generally leads to an incapacity for any other employment; nay often to the most pungent distress; and not infrequently to self-destruction!

.

In Creech's description of the duality of human character, we see the core of the idea developed by Stevenson in *Jekyll and Hyde*.

Aeneas Morison, a writer appointed by the court to defend George Smith, was critical of Brodie's association with Edinburgh lowlife, but he was more sympathetic to both Brodie and Smith. Morison also provides an invaluable insight into the popularity of the trial: "During the whole time of this trial the Court was uncommonly crowded, notwithstanding that the fees of admission were raised as high as three, four, and five shillings. The heat was for a great part of the time intolerable; and the noise and tumult occasioned by orders given by the Court to clear certain parts of the house, frequently interrupted the business of the trial. But the audience who had paid for their places, were determined not to be turned out of them." The author also has a more complete version of the defense lawyer John Erskine's attempts to block the testimony of Andrew Ainslie than in the Creech account.

Erskine tried to demonstrate that the indictments by the public prosecutor were "too vague in his listing of the articles to be produced at the trial." To head off any suggestions that Brodie be sentenced to exile Erskine offered the following revealing example: In 1782 he had defended a certain Mr. Gordon, a sheep stealer, who was found guilty and sentenced to hang. Then, the king pardoned him on the condition that he be exiled for life. However, the man languished in prison, because the government could find no place to exile felons from Scotland "since the loss of America."

The British government had used parts of the American colonies, especially Georgia, as a penal colony. After the American Revolution of 1776, Britain had no readily available place left for prison exiles until Australia was later used for that purpose during the nineteenth century. During the late eighteenth century, there was a marked rise in the number of prisoners sent to the gallows in Great Britain, because the sentence of exile for life to the American colonies was no longer an option.

Erskine tried to discredit the testimony against Brodie by John Brown (aka Humphrey Moore) because he was a convicted felon who had been sentenced to exile in England. The clever defense lawyer then played upon Scottish national sentiments concerning the King's pardon given to Moore as "a foreign decree, to which we are not bound to pay any respect." Erskine challenged, "My Lords, I have heard it said that the King could make a *Peer,* but that he could not make a *Gentleman.* I am sure that he cannot make a rogue an honest man." The lord chief justice in charge, old Braxfield, however, rejected Erskine's objections to the testimony of Moore.

Brodie's main defense rested heavily on an alibi provided by one of his mistresses, Jean Watt, and Helen Alison, one of Watt's neighbors. Jean Watt identified herself as "not married." She declared, "The prisoner came to my house just at the time of eight o'clock and stayed there until a little before next morning." Watt's former servant Peggy Giles confirmed the testimony of Watts and added, "Mr. Brodie was used to sleeping frequently at my mistress's house." Everyone in court knew by that phrase that Watt was Brodie's mistress. Helen Alison, a neighbor of Jean Watt, who also resided in Libberton's Wynd, corroborated Jean Watt's and Peggy Giles' testimony.

Apart from Ainslie and Brown's testimony, the incriminating evidence of the circumstances leading to the numerous thefts and, particularly, the attack on the Excise Office were, to say the least, overwhelming. There were various witnesses to the actual break in: Mr. Bonar reentering his office brushed past a man (the Deacon) whom he could not really identify; a maid servant Janet Baxter who saw some shadows enter the building on that dark and snowy night, and so on. None of the victims, however, from previous thefts were able to pinpoint either Brodie or Smith as having broken into their homes or businesses.

More convincing was the material evidence that had been gathered by ransacking both Brodie's mansion and the cock pit and woodshed outside the mansion itself. Incriminating objects were found hidden behind a fireplace at the back of the shed: the black clothes into which Brodie had changed on his nightly escapades, the masks, whistles, lanterns, pistols, and other tools that had been used in the break-in. Brodie's letters surrendered by John Geddes, though containing only an inference concerning the break-in and nothing with reference to previous crimes, presented a clear indication that the councilman and the Deacon intended to leave Edinburgh for America, hence his need for money.

Brodie's sudden decision to escape, his change of names, his hiding in London, and his flight to the Low Countries at the very least indicated guilt as did the defendant's attempt to hide his real identity in Holland. Then too, the manner in which Brodie penetrated individual households by taking the imprint of keys on putty was carefully described by his two former associates, Ainslie and Brown.

It was because the prosecution knew that Brown's testimony could be shaken that they relied on Ainslie. In the end, he was the crucial witness, not only in relating the details of the break-in to the Excise Office, but in explaining the manner in which Brodie penetrated the homes, offices, and shops of Edinburgh during the previous two years. Apart from casting aspersions on the witnesses for the prosecution (Ainslie after all was a fellow thief), the defense devoted most of its broadsides to convincing the jury of the fact that Brodie could not have been present the infamous night and had various stories that seemed to place him elsewhere. (Apart from the account of the two tainted witnesses, there existed no convincing proof of the Deacon's participation in the thefts of the previous two years.)

In so far as the Excise Office was concerned, the defense relied mostly on the alibis provided by the culprit himself concerning the timing of his moves on the fatal snowy night of March 5, all of which were designed to prove conclusively that he could not have been present at Chessel Court during the break-in. The Deacon testified that he had spent that evening in the company of his loyal brother-in-law Matthew Sherriff, who confirmed that fact. Later, around 8 P.M., Brodie said he went to the home of his mistress Jean Watt, who resided close to his house at Libberton Wynd. Watt was a woman "with whom," stated John Clerk, "he had a peculiar connection." According to Clerk, he "remained in that house from said hour until about nine o'clock the next morning."

In the end, prosecutor Lord Advocate Campbell appealed to the jury saying Brodie was "educated as a gentleman, bred to a respectable business, and removed from suspicion, as well as from his supposed circumstances, as from the rank he held amongst his fellow citizens.... What excuse can be made for him? That he had frequented bad company; that he had abandoned himself to gambling, and every species of dissipation; that he has by these means run himself into difficulties, is surely no apology for him."

It was evident that his last words summarizing the case made an impact on the forty-five jurors: "Gentlemen, I shall only further add that if the prisoner William Brodie, a person who from the nature of his employment had frequent opportunities of being introduced in the houses of others, had been guilty of the crime laid to his charge and is allowed to escape punishment, the consequence to the inhabitants of this populous city may be of a most serious nature." While Campbell's statement was a severe judgment, few could quarrel with it.

Though willing to admit that Brodie in the past had trafficked with thieves, the defense made a final attempt to dissociate him from the conspiracy leading to the break-in at the Excise Office. Erskine brilliantly pleaded:

Gentlemen of the Jury, the present trial exhibits in the person of Mr. Brodie, in whose behalf I now address you, a singular phenomenon in the moral world: a man descended of an ancient and honorable family; left by a respectable father in opulent circumstances; educated in the manners and habits of a gentleman; bred to a reputable occupation, at the head of which he has frequently stood; and in virtue of that situation been a member of the town-council of this great city, standing at the bar of this high Court, accused of having leagued himself with the meanest and most abandoned of mankind, in the commission of a crime not less marked with moral depravity on the part of the perpetrators, than fraught with injury and danger to the public.

While admitting that Brodie had passed time with the lowlife of Edinburgh, Erskine asserted, "The folly of haunting, for any purposes whatsoever, the company of such men, is great indeed; but to subject the party guilt to the consequences of every enormity of which such associates may accuse him, on their bare testimony alone, would be a punishment far beyond offence [sic]; as such men would never fail to find some unhappy associate of better rank than themselves to substitute as a sacrifice to the public for crimes to which they had no accession . . . ." It was a nice try doomed to fail. Ainslie's previous testimony and Brodie's own attempt to flee proved to be decisive. The jury was convinced that the attempt of the robbery at the Excise Office had been planned by the Deacon over a long period of time.

The presiding Lord Chief Justice Braxfield then delivered his final instructions to the jury, which read as if he were instructing them to find Brodie and Smith guilty as charged. The judge mentioned, "Mr. Brodie's father, whom I knew, was a very respectable man." Then he went on to declaim, "That the son of such a man, himself too educated to a respectable profession, and who had long lived with reputation in it, should be arraigned at this bar for a crime so detestable, is what must affect us all, Gentlemen, with sensations of horror."

While the bells of the old Gothic tower of St. Giles Cathedral signaled noon, the jurors just emerging for a break were entitled to their midday refreshment—usually a glass of claret or Edinburgh ale brought to the courtroom—the vital vote was taken, and both George Smith and William Brodie were declared guilty of the crimes charged against them by the jury, which included Brodie's enemy William Creech.

Lord Braxfield read the stern sentence. He took the opportunity to declaim:

> To one of you it is altogether needless for me to offer any advice: You, William Brodie, from your education and habits of life, cannot but know everything suited to your present situation which I could suggest to you. It is much to be lamented that those vices which are gentlemanly vices are so favorably looked upon in the present age. They have been the source of your ruin; and, whatever may be thought of them, they are such as assuredly led to ruin. I hope you will improve the short time which you now have to live, by reflecting upon your past conduct, and endeavoring to procure by a sincere repentance, forgiveness of your many crimes. God always listens to those who seek Him with sincerity.

In the end Brodie and Smith were to be hanged, a decree that sadly epitomized the harshness of Scottish law in the late eighteenth century. In essence they were to be hanged for stealing a trifling amount of money from the Excise Office's vault. The court had rendered that verdict in an expeditious manner having been in session for only twenty-one hours. Returning to the Tolbooth prison, Smith looked utterly dejected. Brodie, however, took a Napoleonic pose, affecting coolness and determination. Attempting to cheer up his stricken condemned fellow in crime, he exclaimed, "What would you and I not give for six weeks longer. Six weeks would be an age for us." The date of the execution was set for October 1, 1788.

It is ironic that the two previously convicted criminals, Andrew Ainslie and John Brown, went unpunished for their crimes. Rather, the prosecution used their testimonies and confessions to implicate William Brodie and George Smith, two men with far cleaner records than Ainslie and Brown. The prosecution was so dedicated to convicting Brodie that they were willing to sacrifice two hardened criminals for it. It would not be the last time in the annals of law that justice was not served, only legality.

Back in jail, William Deacon Brodie's good cheer may have had a rational explanation. He was still hoping to cheat the hangman by asking his powerful friends in London and elsewhere to save him from the noose and, at the very least, face deportation where he could start a new life. He appealed to the few friends he had left in the city council, to his brother-in-law Matthew Sherriff, to the head of his clan, the Laird Brodie of Brodie of Inverness, the powerful Duchess of Buccleuch (pronounced Ba-*clue*), and the conservative Dundas faction at Westminster. He must still have been sanguine of obtaining a reprieve when he proposed marriage to Jean Watt and then had a secret wedding while in jail.

The influential friends, however, did not respond as the fateful day of October 1, 1788, approached, and Brodie seemed to prepare for the inevitable end. Though not a religious man, he was contacted by ministers of the Church and discussed with them the principles of "natural religion." Instead of praying, however, he preferred to sing tunes from his beloved *Beggar's Opera*.

The day of the execution finally came. The Deacon and Smith were allowed a last hearty beef dinner, which they washed down with copious glasses of port. A large crowd—forty thousand strong—had assembled outside the Tolbooth prison waiting impatiently for the two culprits to exit the jail and make their way to the small court at Luckenworth, located just outside the main entrance of St. Giles Cathedral where the platform, gibbet, and rope had been prepared. The prisoners soon appeared, surrounded by the prison guards in black and in formal robes.

The Deacon appeared, impeccably attired as always. Under the blue overcoat, he wore a black suit with a fancy silk vest to match, silk breeches and white stockings, and a cocked hat in hand, remarkably clean and neat. As he emerged from the jail, the Deacon played up to the crowd, bowing and addressing them. By way of contrast, Smith had a look of resignation in his ill-fitting clothes, evidently prepared for his grim fate. Viewing the huge crowd from the gallows, however, Brodie seemed to wish to say a few words but, in the end, all he could utter was, "this is *awful.*" Funeral orations followed by members of the attending clergy. Regaining his *sangfroid* Brodie turned to Smith and said, "Go up Georgie, you are the first" to mount the gibbet. There may have been a reason for this unusual request, a final attempt to cheat death and continue his war against the world of authority. This hope might help explain the Deacon's good humor and bravado during the last moment before execution. Brodie was still convinced that there was a means of escaping the hangman's noose.

During the last days spent at the Tolbooth jail, Brodie had made what seemed a reasonable request: "Since none of my relatives can bear to be with me in my last moments it would be some consolation at my last hour if my body could be handed over to some friends." The request was readily granted by the lord provost.

The plan was to save Brodie from instant death caused by the breaking of his neck when the noose tightened. The man entrusted with the complicated task of saving Brodie from "the wuddie" was a French physician, Pierre de Gravers, who was a

Professor of Anatomy and Physiology at the Medical School of the University of Paris. It seemed that he had proven his arts in a number of instances where culprits condemned to be hanged succeeded in surviving their death sentence. First, the gibbet had to be altered quickly by one of the conspirators, and the rope had to be cut short to cushion the fall. The Deacon himself had designed the alterations while in jail. De Gravers had also rigged Brodie with a special steel collar that was to be hidden under his vest or waistcoat. For additional safety a small tube was inserted inside his throat to avoid suffocation. Wires were also carried down both sides of his body from throat to foot to counteract the jerk of a fall and blunt the blow of a gallows drop. Thus, following Smith's execution the hasty changes were made giving Brodie time to mount the platform, which he did with great agility. As the hangman was about to bind his arms, which could have stymied the projected *coup,* Brodie, in a gesture of courage and defiance, asked that his hands be left free, which was agreed to. He then untied his cravat, buttoned up his coat and waistcoat high enough to hide the steel collar, and then helped the hangman adjust the noose (to avoid the latter's fingering him around the neck). He then placed his left hand down his waistcoat—presumably to control the whiting that was in place—put the unusual white cap over his head as custom enjoyed, and threw his handkerchief to the crowd.

To the consternation of all present, the gibbet did not work. The Deacon's friends had cut the rope too short. In fact, the so-called execution failed twice. Keeping up appearances, Brodie denounced the hangman as a "bungling fellow who did not know his trade." It was only following a third try that the gibbet worked and, for those assembled, justice finally prevailed. Believing it was all over, the town councilor, magistrates, and clergy threw the traditional party, called "the daid check," at Cleriheugh's Tavern at the city's expense.

As soon as they dispersed, Brodie's friends, as had been pre-arranged, cut down the so-called corpse, placed it in a cart, and sped at breakneck speed down the slopes at Nether Bow to the Deacon's mansion where de Gravers was waiting with a lancet to bleed Brodie in an attempt to revive him. Apparently, his efforts were of no avail. In spite of all the precautions taken, Brodie's neck had been fatally broken. Thus provisions for a Christian burial were made. In fact, Brodie himself had made such prepara-tions just in case the attempt to save his life failed. He also had made a will in jest, knowing full well that his considerable fortune (his mansion, tenements, bonds, cash, his considerable assets in furniture, and so forth) would either be seized by the government or sold by auction.

Just before he was executed, Brodie had written a letter to the Duchess of Buccleuch, the wife of a prominent member of Edin-burgh society, requesting that his remains be laid to rest in the cemetery attached to the Church of St. Cuthbert, the Buccleuch parish churchyard. Lady Buccleuch graciously granted the dying man's request but only on the condition that the grave be unmarked. Brodie's unmarked burial site was placed between that of Dr. Alexander Adam, a former rector of the local high school, and that of David Herd designated as grave twenty-one and twenty-three respectively. Therefore, Brodie's resting place became grave number twenty-two placed in the middle of the other two. Given the scandalous double life the notorious Brodie had led, plus his trial and conviction, one can well understand why his relatives, his two sisters, brother-in-law, and head of the clan Lord Brodie conspired to block any mention of the Deacon's existence on his tomb. Brodie's name is also absent from the family Bible, which has survived and serves as a kind of genealogical guide in Scotland. In fact, the city council, the Church, the magistrature, and the leading Edinburgh newspapers were equally intent upon wiping away all memories of the Deacon's wrongdoings. Some persons even called for the banning of *The Beggar's Opera,* which had inspired Brodie in his lifetime and which they feared might lead others to crime.

The first to exploit the Brodie name was actually his sworn enemy William Creech, the moralist, publisher, and author. He published his *The Trial of William Brodie and George Smith* in 1788, which became an immediate bestseller and was followed by a second edition within a week. Somehow, the story of this double-faced, good-and-evil, lighthearted, forty-seven-year-old boy, who never grew up and died for stealing four pounds, struck a cord with the public. The author, Henry McKensie, perhaps summarized Brodie's career best when he observed, "There was a strange profligate sort of pleasure in villainy for its own sake."

Was the Deacon really executed in 1788? His grave was opened years later to accommodate repair work that was being done in the churchyard, but they didn't find a skeleton, not even a single bone. This discovery gave some credence to the

Brodie's tomb at Buccleugh Graveyard, Edinburgh. (CAROL MCNALLY)

numerous legends that maintained that Deacon Brodie had cheated the hangman at the time of his alleged death. Some Scots traveling to America reported seeing the "executed" man walking the streets of New York or Philadelphia; others purported to have recognized his inimitable self strolling the streets of Paris in the post–French revolutionary period. Still others saw him on some island in the West Indies and elsewhere. Thus, partly because of the empty tomb (like that of the historical Dracula), the legend of Brodie and his survival lived on in spite of the attempts to wipe away all traces of his existence.

Meanwhile, the new Scottish establishment (merchants, bankers, writers, lawyers, and professional people) began to leave the quaint, narrow, overcrowded, and unhealthy Closes and Wynds of the Old Town for the elegant and respectable Georgian City, which was emerging on the hills to the west. Among the first to construct a house in New Town was Matthew Sherriff, Brodie's brother-in-law, who built a home on Bunker Hill Street, named in memory of the famous battle leading to American independence fought on June 17, 1775.

CHAPTER THREE

The Double Life of
Robert Louis Stevenson, 1850–1884

*The idea of sin attached to particular actions
absolutely, far from repelling, soon exerts an attraction on young minds. I can never again take so
much interest in anything, as I took, in childhood,
in the doing for its own sake what I believed to be
sinful. And generally, the principal effect of this false
common doctrine of sin is to put a point in lust.*

—From *The Letters of Robert Louis Stevenson*

On November 13, 1850, sixty-two years after the execution of Deacon Brodie, there was born in the New Town of Edinburgh, Scotland, to Thomas Stevenson and his wife Maggie Balfour, a sickly little boy named Robert Louis Stevenson who could not sleep at night. Facing his bed was a finely chiseled cabinet (still in existence today) bought by his father at an auction. It had been made by a certain William Brodie. Young Stevenson's nurse, Allison Cunningham, tried to relieve the boy's suffering during the endless nights by relaying stories to him, among them the double life of the builder of the cabinet. Germinating in the child's imaginative mind, in due course, was the Deacon's double life.

The family first lived at 8 Howard Place in Edinburgh on the banks of the river Leith near the Botanical Gardens. It was a year before the opening of the Great Exhibition at the Crystal Palace in London, which marked the dawn of a new machine age in the British Isles. Robert remained the only child of Thomas and Margaret Isabella Balfour Stevenson. Seeking a less humid air for their sickly boy, the family moved at first to 1 Inverleigh Terrace and then in January 1857, with the child barely seven years old, to fashionable 17 Heriot Row, an elegant street in the new Georgian town with houses in neo-Greek styling. This section was essentially built for wealthy merchants, businessmen, and professionals though a few famous literary figures such as the poet Percy Bysshe Shelley (1792–1828) and Arthur Conan Doyle (1859–1930), the creator of

Number 8 Howard Place, Edinburgh, RLS's birthplace and home between 1850 and 1852. (RAYMOND T. MCNALLY)

Sherlock Holmes, also at one time or another had houses there.

This new town presented a stark contrast to Brodie's over-built Old Town described in previous chapters. New Edinburgh lay opposite the fetid valley of Nor'Loch across a bridge on land acquired by the city. A talented architect named Robert Reed designed each section as a geometrician might: three parallel streets ending with a close. This was in vivid contrast to the sinuous and narrow divides between the built-up insalubrious tenements of the Old Town. No wonder the wealthy left the slums to the have-nots, to disintegrate further. By the time King George IV had formally opened New Town in 1822, the city of Edinburgh had assumed a new distinctive double personality and reaffirmed the dividing line between rich and poor. Describing his native city in an early work, Stevenson made mention of this double identity: "Half capital and half country town the whole city leads a double existence." Later, as a student, when he was able to personally experience the "lowlife of Jamaica street" in the Old Town, Louis harps on the same theme from a different perspective: "To look over Southbridge and see the Cowgate below full of crying hawkers is to view one's rank in society from another in the twin-kling of an eye." These two aspects of Edinburgh inexorably impacted Stevenson's worldview and colored his double existence.

Another view of Stevenson's birthplace and home. (CAROL MCNALLY)

Young Louis was immeasurably proud of both of his parents' families. His mother's upper-middle-class ancestors, the Balfours, were, for some three centuries, judges, lawyers, ministers of the Kirk, and, most important, Covenanters who rebelled and fought against the intolerance of the official English Church. He could also boast that the Balfours were related to two of the greatest poets of Scotland, Sir Walter Scott and Robert Burns. Proud as he was of his Balfour pedigree, Robert Louis was even prouder of the accomplishments of his father's family. When daydreaming about early Scottish ancestry, Louis, at various times, toyed with the idea of writing a family history. According to one genealogist, the Stevensons were of Scandinavian origin migrating to Scotland as barber-surgeons in the service of Cardinal Beaton, archbishop of Glasgow, who crowned Mary Queen of Scots at Stirling in 1543. More precise is the information concerning the accomplishments of his three generations of lighthouse engineers who achieved international fame working for the Board of Northern Lights. Young Stevenson could legitimately boast that there was not a single lighthouse on the High Seas "from the Island of Mann northwards up to Berwick which had not been built by one of our blood . . . and when these lighthouses light up at dusk along the Scottish coast I am proud to think that they were due to the genius of my father."

The relationship between Louis and his father was particularly close during early boyhood. On those frequent nights when young Louis could not sleep because of illness, his father would stay up with the boy and read to him. Tragically, when the father realized later in life that Louis had no thought of following in his professional footsteps and had rejected his religious beliefs, the sentiments turned into a love/hate relationship and brought much suffering to both father and son. Nonetheless, these early bonds were never severed completely. Louis spent most of his early life in his room, the victim of bouts of fever, sleeplessness, and repeated nightmares.

In the absence of his mother, a nurse, Allison Cunningham, also known as Cummy, took her place

RLS as a child with his father, Thomas Stevenson. (THE WRITERS' MUSEUM, EDINBURGH)

as Louis's second mother. A rigid Calvinist, she made the youngster aware that only the "elect" would be saved from damnation, that any levity or mirth was evil. Theater was forbidden, of course. Cummy also told him how his mother's ancestors, the Covenanters, were brutally persecuted in Edinburgh's Grassmarket by English "dragons." Louis's long and uncomfortable nights were softened by her tenderness. She

Allison Cunningham, "Cummy," RLS's nanny. (THE WRITERS' MUSEUM, EDINBURGH)

displayed the patience of an angel and consoled him during his coughing crises. "I remember distinctly," states Stevenson in an autobiographical note, "the way in which she lifted me from bed and enveloped me in a blanket. She took me to the window where I could plunge my sight into the darkness of the star-filled night and with the help of the streetlights I could see other sick beds so long as the gas continued to burn across the windows. It was a period of fever and melancholy." Such night impressions anchored in the young boy's subconscious as he saw the city tinged in a brownish hue in his land of the counterpane and his windowpane.

We have lost the essay that Stevenson, as a child, wrote on Deacon Brodie, but later as a young man Louis became deeply conscious of the many stories associated with Brodie's name. Influenced by Cummy's puritan preaching, the precocious child stayed on the side of good to preserve himself from hellfire. Thus, he dictated essays to his mother, such as "The History of Moses" and the "Book of Joseph," much to his father's liking. But it was

Cummy who called Stevenson "her boy" and "Little Lew"; even as an adult she called him "her little son." His family and friends called him Lou or Louis, not Robert because there were always so many other relatives called Robert.

At an early age Louis was enrolled at Cannonmills on Rodney Street in 1856. Later, in 1857, he went to a private prep school on East India Street owned by a Mr. Henderson, which lasted intermittently until 1861.

The tall awkward boy became an easy butt of his classmates' jokes. Thanks to this badgering, he thought of himself as having an ugly spidery body, lanky arms, and a chicken breast. Because of his ungainly appearance Louis was called a "smout" by his parents, a nickname against which he protested. Louis was then shortened to Lou, but in the end, the French version of *Louis* seemed the most acceptable. Most of his biographers and admirers refer to him simply as RLS.

Louis's desultory, oft-interrupted primary school education was compensated by summer vacations at the Presbytery of Colinton a few miles southwest of Edinburgh on the river Leith. This was the retreat of his maternal grandfather Pastor Louis Balfour, the husband of his beloved aunt Maggie. The rustic rural cottage located near the church and cemetery was, in Louis's mind, transformed into a magic and often frightening fairyland. Judging by his "Reminiscences of Colinton Manse," an essay written in 1870 (and published in 1901), these vacations represented the happiest days of his youth. Accompanied by his favorite cousin, Bob—Robert Alan Mowbray Stevenson born October 7, 1856, son of Alan Stevenson and brother of Katharine (the future Katharine de Mattos) who eventually went insane—he was particularly drawn to the cemetery and the gloomy passages leading to it. As Stevenson wrote in his *Reminiscences*: "Often after nightfall I scrutinized the darkness of the night from the windows of the Presbytery in the hope of seeing 'spunkies' [ghosts] playing around and cavorting in the middle of the Tombs." He would then dictate ghost stories to his cousin, though religious themes still prevail (a new version of the "Book of Joseph"). The death of his grandfather in 1860 brought these idyllic summer days to an end.

RLS as a student. (THE WRITERS' MUSEUM, EDINBURGH)

Other schools followed for Stevenson: the Edinburgh Academy in 1861, a private boarding school at Loring Grove in Perthshire, Scotland, yet another on Frederick Street in Edinburgh where Louis showed interest only in editing a school magazine. It gave him an opportunity to write about imaginary travels to the South Seas or stories about adventures with pirates, legendary Scottish heroes, and natives in various exotic places. Evidently his parents had been most unsuccessful in cultivating Louis's mind to loftier thoughts. Knowing of his fondness for Colinton, his father rented a summer cottage in the Pentland Hills, not far from Edinburgh, in the village of Swanston, where Louis and his cousins Bob and Katharine could relive the idyll of Colinton.

Because of his parents' ill health—the father was spitting blood while his mother's lungs were affected by the cold winds of the New Town—Louis's education was interrupted by travel to England and the Continent. This was a period when physicians

Margaret Stevenson, RLS's mother.

thought that a warm climate and famous spas were instrumental in improving health. The family undertook a trip to southern England, and then to the elegant spas in Germany frequented by European aristocracy. Afterward came Italy, the French Riviera (the first of many tours and one of Louis's favorite retreats), and, of course, Paris, the city of light. It delighted Louis to roam across the countryside, to be immersed in sunny climes and escape from the foggy winters, nasty winds, and dark cell of his homestead at Heriot Row in Scotland.

Unwittingly, his parents had opened a door to a new life, infinitely more fascinating than preparing for the inevitable engineering school or visiting lighthouses along the Scottish coasts, a career for which he had been predestined since birth. The first inkling of open rebellion occurred in 1867. Louis, aged seventeen, was to enroll at Edinburgh University to study science and technology, essential for a lighthouse engineer. During the summer he was to inspect lighthouse-building sites. Louis did his best in terms of passive resistance: The eccentricity of his appearance, his long hair, his overall Bohemian aspect did not endear him to faculty and other engineering students. In the end he simply refused to attend his engineering courses.

As a young adult, Stevenson continued to be burdened by his father's career expectations and his puritan restrictions, only rebelling against them in the confines of his imagination. As his health slowly improved, however, Louis was finally able to act on what he previously only fantasized about as a child, and he began to give into these temptations. His preoccupation with the darker side of society continued to build, and he became independent enough to act out his dual life.

He was living in a city of extreme social contrasts that offered Stevenson a stage on which to enact his fantasies. He stated that the "loiterers" of the dark inner city alleys are the "... true character of the scene" in Edinburgh. These people lived in the Old Town and the Stevensons lived in the New Town. The dual nature of the City of Edinburgh fed Stevenson's desire for a more liberated lifestyle. The vivid contrasting characteristics of the Calvinist countryside in the New Town and the seedy alleys in the Old Town split the city of Edinburgh, just as it began to split the personality of Robert Louis Stevenson himself.

During his late teens and early twenties, Stevenson eventually surrendered to the temptations of the Old Town as he grew further and further separated from his family and the New Town. During these years Stevenson's life began to resemble in some aspects that of Deacon Brodie's. Louis began to socialize in the taverns and bars of High Street. Some of Brodie's favorite taverns were still open and serving wine, beer, whiskey, or laudanum—the popular Victorian aspirin favored by the upper class. Occasionally Louis would try

RLS as a young Bohemian student.
(THE STEVENSON HOUSE COLLECTION, MONTEREY STATE HISTORIC PARK)

a tincture of opium with traces of morphine, which could induce mood swings or personality shifts. "I love the night in the city, lighted streets and the swinging gait of harlots." He was fascinated with the companionship of vagabonds, sailors, and smugglers. Louis was turned off by the monotonous lives of the establishment who were complacent in their religion. Stevenson describes such people as "altogether out of key . . ." saying they live life with ". . . a grand human indifference." Louis was attracted to the Old Townies whose stories and lifestyles filled his suppressed desires for mischief.

Then too, Louis was particularly fond of and preoccupied with prostitutes whom he found, in a sense, more honest than the average Scottish women in that they sold their wares openly to the highest bidder. In turn, they took to him affectionately. In fact, Louis felt so emotionally drawn to these women of ill repute that he may have secretly married one. In the midst of his revolt he stated, "I . . . want women about me and I want pleasure. . . ." From his many nights in the taverns, Stevenson developed an emotional bond with the bottle as well, and this remained with him for his entire life. In a letter to his friend Charles Baxter in 1872, the writer stated, "Happiness is a matter of bottled stout . . ." By way of protest, Louis chose this student period to openly rebel and defy the moral values that had been ingrained within him by Cummy and his parents.

Eve Blantyre Simpson, who was friendly with young Stevenson and later wrote a book about him, noted that when Stevenson visited her family during the 1870s, "He would pace up and down, flourishing his hands, stepping carefully with his head poked forward and nodding 'till we nicknamed him the Guinea-fowl, and expatiate on the double-life, speaking again and again of the Deacon. He would wonder what burglary some esteemed citizen of his own day was guilty of." Eve Simpson also recalled that, "One evening he broke out into a species of Jekyll and Hyde plot. Deacon Brodie, the hypocritical villain, who appeared as a pillar of the church, and an able craftsman before his fellow townsmen, and was really a gambler and a burglar." She further testified that he, Stevenson, was intrigued by the two-sidedness of human nature, "Commingled out of good and evil, the smug front to the world, the villain behind the mask."

Meanwhile, a new circle of friends joined Louis and encouraged him to pursue a literary career. James Walter Ferrier and his wife Anne proposed that he send articles to a new student periodical *Edinburgh University,* and that he write plays because they headed a small theater group. Another member of this inner circle was Charles Baxter, a law student at the time, with whom Louis maintained a correspondence in the darkest day of revolt against his father. Yet another was Walter Simpson, a literary critic who got Louis elected to the prestigious Saville Club in London.

One very meaningful encounter that took place later in 1875 was with William Ernest Henley (1849–1903), a crippled poet as thoroughly Bohemian as was Louis. Sporting a reddish beard with hair the same tinge, Henley was incurably ill as one of his legs was affected by bone tuberculosis—a factor that may have tightened the link with Louis. These two men who, superficially speaking, did not resemble each other became inseparable friends because of their similar physical suffering and their common desire to make money out of writing plays for the theater. All these influences gave Louis the opportunity of exploiting what these people alone deemed his very unique literary talents. This consisted mostly in writing articles, essays, and studies on a great diversity of subjects—a journalism of sorts—travelogues, history, adventure stories, plays, poems, and some philosophical notes in varied periodicals and magazines, which hardly drew much public interest. Nor did this writing earn much money for Louis, who continued to be almost entirely dependent on his father's generosity. One might look upon that early period of Louis's writings as an attempt to try his talent mostly on his friends, who grew into kind of a mutual admiration society. They created a myth around their friend that served him later in his more serious literary pursuits. If he was not as yet *RLS,* the initials that stuck to his name when he became famous, Louis Stevenson was at least a name the *literati* could talk about, though very few read him or knew exactly what he had written to date.

Indeed, Stevenson was woefully aware of his limited talents as a writer and complained on more than one occasion that he was not talented enough to write great literature. He may have long known this to be ruefully true when he wrote, "I am read by journalists, by my fellow novelists and by boys."

In modern parlance we might say that Louis enjoyed good public relations owing to his personal charm and to his literary friends. Financially, it was years before he could make a penny from his avocation. Among the capital sins of Louis and his friends in the eyes of his father was that of inventing a new language called "jink" and, worse still, making public profession of his agnosticism in the avant-garde Speculative Society of which he was a member.

Louis's parents finally became aware of their son's sinful conduct in the bars and his close relations with prostitutes. They thought of him as a walking scandal. The son of a member of the Royal Arts Society had become a disgrace to his family. Initially, in an attempt to save his puritan reputation and theirs as well, the Stevensons made up myths about what Louis did at night. They spread these lies telling neighbors, relatives, and friends that their son went to bars only occasionally after class and that he was timid and delicate with women. They insisted to all that their offspring was innocent of all evil. They tried, in short, to keep him from what he had desired for so long.

Arguments with Louis followed concerning his rejection of his father's religion and prim way of life. Thomas told him that it was unthinkable that his only son should not follow the tradition of several generations of lighthouse builders that had brought fame to the family name. Taking his courage into both his hands, Louis told his father emphatically that he would never be an engineer but wished to devote himself to literature.

After a long argument, Thomas at least obtained Louis's consent that he would enroll in the law faculty at the University of Edinburgh in October 1871, hopefully leading at least to an honorable career as a jurist. Louis promised that he would abide by his father's wish, though in his heart he knew he would become neither a lawyer nor a judge.

Initially, Louis pretended to enroll in some university courses though he rarely took notes and gradually did not bother to attend many classes. The arrival of his cousin Bob Stevenson soon provided the distraction he needed. Brilliant, elegant, romantic, and pleasing to the ladies, the good-looking youth soon thwarted whatever good intentions Louis may have had. Instead, it was back to women, taverns, practical jokes, and laughter. "Laughter," states Louis at that period, "was our principal activity . . . laughter and a deep anger against the life we discovered all around us."

What was not a joke, but infinitely more meaningful as far as Louis was concerned, was the theme of doubles—his own double existence (e.g., Stevenson still led a respectable life at Heriot Row

Heriot Row as it looked in the 1930s. (THE WRITERS' MUSEUM, EDINBURGH)

but he continued his wild lifestlye when he was away from home) and double ideology, even as it pertains to politics. RLS admired the Duke of Wellington, who was victorious over Napoleon Bonaparte in 1815, a hero in his mind about whom he wished to write a book. For this project, paradoxically enough, Stevenson consulted the writings of William E. Gladstone (1808–1898) the Liberal Statesman whom he despised for abandoning the ideals of the British Empire. Louis's beloved General Charles Gordon (1833–1885), nicknamed Chinese Gordon, a martyr to the Mahdi rebellion in the Sudan in 1885, was in a sense a victim of Gladstone's pacifism. Yet, in turn, Louis was outraged at the Conservative government's persecution of the Fenians, an Irish-American Group aiming at establishing an Irish Republic. (Lord Salisbury, as head of the Conservative party, succeeded the liberal Gladstone as England's prime minister in 1885.) At one point, even Stevenson threatened to settle in Ireland to fight for Irish home rule.

Pro-imperialist and pro-Irish nationalist, there was little consistency in Louis's double thinking. Together with his cousin Bob he joined the Conservative party but shortly thereafter declared himself a Socialist and founded a secret society, the first article of which was the abolishment of the House of Lords. Because of these equivocations and turnabouts, the tension with his father continued. The atmosphere at 17 Heriot Row became unbearable and may have contributed to the illness and, ultimately, to the death of his father and the deterioration of Louis's own health.

Deeply unhappy, Stevenson sank into a deep depression as he confronted his double existence. It was in 1873 that the lightening finally struck! The crisis point in the relationship of the father and son was reached when Louis returned from a brief vacation in Malvern. During his absence, Thomas had discovered a letter that suggested that Louis was an agnostic. There were shouts, tears, and condemnations. Both his mother and father became desperate. In self-defense Louis espoused a kind of rational agnosticism. He stated that he accepted the moral ideals of Christianity but rejected the Church and the behavior of most people who called themselves Christian but were, in actuality, hypocrites. Furthermore, Louis could find no proof for the existence of God. In the end his father never really recovered from the double blow of his only son having abandoned both his religion and the career for which he had been predestined. In spite of many attempts to repair the damage between father and son, even with Louis's marriage, a permanent rift had been created between them. The wound never really healed. When the elder Stevenson died in 1887, the two were unreconciled.

Number 17 Heriot Row, Edinburgh, RLS's main home from 1857–1880. (CAROL MCNALLY)

Thus, in 1872 began years of crisis that were to lead both Louis and his father to the edge of despair, and even folly. It was in order to distract himself that

Louis turned to women. This time, not to the young prostitutes in the Old Town with whom he once had flirted, but to older women who could fulfill the role that his mother never could because of her cold temperament and ill health.

Louis clearly needed another Cummy to console him or give him motherly affection and understanding. As the crisis with his father was brewing, he escaped to the English countryside where he sought the kind of solace he had found in Colinton and later at Swanston in the company of a Balfour cousin named Maud who was married to the Reverend Babington. He ended his journey in the quaint English village of Cockfield in Suffolk, East Anglia, in very picturesque surroundings. On one of his walks on July 26, 1873, Louis noticed a beautiful woman named Mrs. Frances Sitwell, a well-educated Irish lady, thirty-four years of age. She was recently separated from her clergyman husband and had come to stay with Louis's cousins. Louis enjoyed long conversations with his "Fanny," which was her nickname. Through her he became friends with Professor Sidney Colvin, Professor of Art at Cambridge University, who was also infatuated with Fanny. Louis wrote countless love letters to Fanny, but she was actually in love with Colvin, whom she eventually wed after her husband passed away in 1903. However, Fanny and Louis remained good friends for a number of years and kept up a lengthy correspondence.

Swanston Village outside Edinburgh, where RLS spent several summer vacations. (THE WRITERS' MUSEUM, EDINBURGH)

IN SEARCH OF DR. JEKYLL AND MR. HYDE

In the archives of the Edinburgh Library are the originals of the letters that were written by Louis and Fanny. Colvin had severely censured them when they were published as a part of Stevenson's works. In a letter (numbered fifty-one) to Mrs. Sitwell, and dated autumn 1874 from Edinburgh, Stevenson addressed her as his Madonna and gushed, "O my dear, if you knew how I desired your presence." Another Christmas letter, dated 1874, read, ". . . this letter shall be to you as a son's Christmas kiss. And I think, Madonna, that you love me . . . you must be happy: I will not have a sad deity in my chapel . . . [signed] faithful friend and son and priest." In a letter dated December 29, in Edinburgh, Stevenson called her "my mother" in French; "il me manque rien, sinon ta présence, ma mère. I have never been happier in the thought of you than now." Yet in another letter, dated January 1874 from Edinburgh, Stevenson identified with Edgar Allan Poe's famous beloved, "those whom the angels named Lenore," as Stevenson wrote, "Dearest Mother. This is E. A. Poe: because I feel that, in the heavens above the angels, whispering to one another, I can find, among their terms of burning love, none so devotional as that of my mother."

Louis had succumbed to Fanny's Irish charm and fallen passionately in love with her—he was twenty-two while she was thirty-four. Judging from their correspondence, Louis would have liked to have an affair with "his mother" Madonna. Even at the outset, however, the letters never suggest that Fanny was genuinely in love with her suitor, though initially she must have reacted positively to his advances. With time Fanny became frightened at the overwhelmingly passionate tone of Louis's letters, which continued for quite a time, particularly when she began developing strong feelings for Colvin. The tone of the correspondence

RLS as a barrister, a counsel admitted to plead in British superior courts of law.
(THE WRITERS' MUSEUM, EDINBURGH)

finally changed when Louis realized that there was no future in their relationship, though Fanny continued to show an interest in Louis's life and career judging from his correspondence with her in her later years. As was his wont, the writer had clearly accepted the double relationship with Fanny and Colvin, his literary counselor.

In the meantime, Thomas Stevenson continued the cold war against his son. Blaming the boy's cousin for Louis's behavior, he was banned from the family home on Heriot Row. The situation was ameliorated in a surprising way. To placate his father, Louis took his bar examination after three months of preparation to catch up on the three years of schooling he had missed. To the amazement of all, he passed. This achievement gave his father a false hope that he would at least pursue a legal career. Louis actually became a member of the bar in 1875 in London without the least intention of practicing law.

Louis's double life was clearly wrecking his health and he resorted to Cummy to comfort him while Fanny was with Colvin in London. Stevenson's health was deteriorating so seriously that he was now vomiting blood. For the first time the great London lung specialist Dr. Andrew Clark was deeply concerned and made a fateful diagnosis. Tuberculosis was for the first time mentioned. The remedy was to leave the poor Scottish climate and the deathly winds there to recover in the sunny south of

France. When Louis reached the Riviera in the fall of 1873, he was close to total collapse. A five-month long cure in Menton under a blue sky, orange groves, and olive trees soon restored his health and gave him a new lease on life as did the attention provided by an attractive Russian lady at the Hotel Mirabeau where they were staying. She was a Russian princess, Sophia Garshine, Louis's senior by ten years and mother of a little girl.

Echoes of Louis's suspected life of debauchery with Fanny Sitwell and the amoral tone of his writings, in particular the offensiveness of his critique of the very institution of marriage in *Virginibus Puerisque* (begun in the 1870s and published in 1881) became, finally, in the eyes of his father, truly unpardonable sins. Louis himself was banned from the family home at Heriot Row, chased away from the paternal homestead just as his cousin Bob had been. Cut off from all financial help, Louis was compelled now to live with his Bohemian friends, particularly Bob.

With the end of Louis's tryst with Fanny Sitwell, his "Madonna," circumstances were ripe for yet another mother. During the fall of 1875, Bob had enrolled in an art school in Paris. In 1876 Louis accompanied his cousin to his summer school at the village of Grez-sur-Loing near Pontoise, a few miles out of Paris in the beautiful forest of Fontainebleau.

There Stevenson became acquaintanted with a liberated American woman, Mrs. Frances

RLS at age twenty-five in 1876, shortly after he fell in love with Fanny Osbourne. (THE WRITERS' MUSEUM, EDINBURGH)

Mathilda Vandegrift Osbourne. She was ten years his senior and separated from her husband, a philanderer named Sam Osbourne. (Louis had briefly noticed her on a previous journey to the school.) Born in Indianapolis in March 1840, she was, by an odd coincidence, also nicknamed Fanny. She lived with her two children, Isobel (usually called Belle), eighteen years old and studying art, and Lloyd, a younger son. Fanny was just then recovering from the tragic death of yet another son, Harvey. Louis was immediately smitten by this proud, savage woman who boasted extraordinarily seductive eyes.

At the end of the summer of 1876, Louis followed Fanny to Paris and settled in Montmartre. Their affair may have begun at the time, even though she was not yet divorced from her husband who still supported her. Though called to order by his disapproving parents, this time Fanny's appeal was irresistible. Louis spent the Christmas of 1876 with her.

From 1877 onward, Louis no longer had a home in Edinburgh. His family subsidies were cut, and, like a gypsy, he settled with whosoever would receive him: William Ernest Henley, Edmund Gosse, or Sidney Colvin in London. Stevenson, however, preferred Paris where he bought a shoddy barge called the "Eleven Thousand Virgins of Cologne." The umbilical cord with Heriot Row was finally cut when Louis attempted to eke out a living by writing articles and a variety of play reviews.

In April 1877 a thunderbolt appeared out of the clear blue sky: Fanny's husband decided to come to France and, in spite of his numerous infidelities, wanted his wife back. She refused to return to him. Louis definitely became her suitor in the summer of 1877, while leading a miserable existence between his barge on the Seine and her quarters at 5 Rue Ravignan. Subsidies from friends and the small sums Louis retained from his journalism no longer sufficed, particularly now as Fanny had lost her husband's stipend.

Meanwhile, Louis's general health deteriorated once again. This time, more seriously, as did his eyesight, because he had contracted purulent conjunctivitis. Both Fanny's husband and Louis's father were obdurate in refusing any help, which left the two lovers penniless in Paris. Thomas Stevenson hoped that sooner or later "the American" would disappear from Louis's life as had the first Fanny. For Fanny and her two children the only possible solution was to return to America in August 1878 and obtain a divorce. As Louis saw her off, they did not know if they would ever see each other again. During the months that were to follow, Louis experienced a dreadful loneliness. To console himself that fall, he undertook a journey of eleven days to the Cévennes in central France on a donkey called Modestine, walking some 120 miles. This trip was to result in the best of his early travelogues, *Travels with a Donkey in the Cévennes* (1878), and had special appeal to young readers. (It became a companion volume to Stevenson's *Inland Voyage,* an account of a canoe trip in Belgium and France that was also published in 1878.)

But his heart was with Fanny in California. Against the advice of all his friends, who were beginning to have doubts about his mental stability, and virtually penniless, Louis embarked on August 7, 1879, on the S. S. *Devonia* sailing from Greenock, a Scottish port near Glasgow, to New York. He took second class tickets that afforded him a table where he could write, because the cheapest passage—steerage—did not provide such amenities. It was a very sick traveler who disembarked alone and lonely in New York on August 17. The further three thousand miles across the American continent with a convoy of emigrants in horse and wagon was even more of a nightmare, and Stevenson came very close to death in the mountains of California. In Monterey on the California coast midway between San Francisco and Los Angeles, he put up at a hotel managed by a French lady, Madame Girardin. Virtually destitute and desperate for money, he decided to write various accounts of his American misadventures. He even tried his hand at writing a Western. He also appealed to his friends for money, but the bridges with the Old World were cut irretrievably.

In the meantime Fanny had relocated to Oakland to hasten divorce proceedings, while Stevenson moved to San Francisco in mid-December 1879 to be closer to her. He settled in at the Irish Inn at 608 Bush Street. Stevenson made it a point of honor to help Fanny, who was left without resources of her own. Nevertheless, he himself felt helpless as his health was further weakened by an attack of malaria in 1880. His hemorrhaging was more violent than ever before, and the diagnosis of the American local doctor Bamford was even more alarming than that of the English doctors. Stevenson's was a case of advanced tuberculosis. Defying convention, Fanny, his new "mother," took him into her home in Oakland where Louis struggled for six weeks between life and death. Even so he continued to write for hours each day. He began writing an autobiography and wrote the first draft of his most famous poem, *Requiem*.

With the divorce finalized, Fanny and Louis were free to marry on May 19, 1880, in San Francisco. Stevenson and Fanny Osbourne were formally wed in the home of Reverend William A. Scott, a Presbyterian minister. On the wedding certificate, Fanny identified herself as "a widow," not as a divorcée, probably out of a false sense of respectability; in fact, her husband was still alive, so she was not a widow. The end of the nightmare seemed at hand when Baxter, with whom Louis corresponded, warned his parents of the couple's financial plight and Louis's precarious health. Unexpectedly a missive from his father arrived which stated that he was finally willing to send his son an allowance of two hundred pounds per year.

The newlyweds spent the next six months in a one-room apartment in San Francisco and had a honeymoon of sorts in the mountains of California in a mining ghost town called Silverado, two thousand feet high in the Napa Valley. There they stayed until Louis could regain sufficient health for them to travel back to Europe. Much as Louis admired America, he longed to return to his native Scotland. "The happiest lot on earth," Louis wrote, "is to be born a Scotsman." This statement illustrates yet another of the paradoxes in his many lives. Now husband and wife, together with Belle and Lloyd (her children), returned in the comfort of first class from New York to Liverpool sailing on the steamship *City of Chester* on August 17, 1880.

Difficult as it was for his parents to accept the marriage, they were present to greet the new family when they disembarked at Liverpool. Fanny was introduced at Heriot Row and was duly impressed by upper-class living conditions in Edinburgh. A journey to Louis's beloved Highlands turned out disastrous for his health, however. It became clear that he was so consumptive that it would be impossible for him ever to become attuned to the harsh climate of this native land he loved so much.

The prescription of his physician uncle, Dr. George Balfour, and the famed Sir Andrew Clark was for the Stevensons to move to Davos a village high up in the Swiss Alps peopled by tubercular patients. Davos, where life slowed down and the smell of death was all around, proved to be a miserable experience for Louis who spent his time playing war games with his stepson Lloyd. Stevenson also began writing depressive essays about the miserable life of his fellow patients, thus exhibiting one more discordant note in his personality. Finally, tired of his Swiss prison, Stevenson decided to leave Davos on the advice of his Swiss doctor, Ruedli. The latter recommended the more congenial climate of southern France. Following diverse peregrinations in October of 1883, Louis and Fanny finally settled in Hyères where they rented a tiny chalet surrounded by an olive garden near an ancient ruin on a hill dominating the town.

Louis and Fanny spent sixteen months in Hyères, which Louis deemed "the happiest in his life," a phrase he often repeated. From Hyères in southern France in the late autumn of 1883, Stevenson wrote to his former lover Fanny Sitwell, showing his fears about his newly won mental stability and his sense of humor: "It is impossible for me to be serious as for a camel to go through the eye of a commercial traveler. Something gave way within me, like a trap falling; and ever since I have not ceased to laugh. Heaven grant that I be not fey! Do you know what fey is! A certain careless mirth and high spirit is supposed in Scotland to be the forerunner of destiny. The Greeks thought so too; and from ought I know, the Mesopotamians . . ." [signed] "R. L. McIdiot Stevenson of Bedlam." (The reference to "Bedlam" is to the infamous London insane asylum, which had its institutional counterpart in Edinburgh.) There is still a plaque on the chalet at Hyères called "La Solitude," which has survived:

> Here
> During 1883–4
> Lived the English author

Robert Louis Stevenson
He declared "I was
Only happy once
That was at Hyères."

His health partially restored, Louis was additionally buoyed by the attention given him by a young and attractive Swiss French maid that they engaged, Valentine Roch, who was to look after him during the next ten years (1881–1891). In the absence of Fanny, she would often share the room with Louis, which have led some critics to speculate that she had an affair with him, as it is well known that some tubercular patients often have intense sexual urges. Valentine's presence certainly complicated Louis's tense relationship with Fanny (who finally dismissed the maid later in Honolulu). Having regained his strength, Louis once again plunged back into serious writing. Encouraged by the favorable review of his *New Arabian Nights* (1882) he soon completed *A Child's Garden of Verses* (1885) and dedicated this collection of poems for children to Cummy. Meanwhile, his *New Arabian Nights* represented his first popular book for the general public. It contained, among many episodes, a fascinating story called "The Suicide Club," the members of which wished to die but couldn't quite do it by themselves.

Returning from Hyères, Louis's health collapsed once again. At one point his doctors almost give up hope of saving his life. His bleeding problems became so grave that his right hand had to be immobilized in a sling attached to his body and he was limited in his speaking. Reading became impossible for him due to conjunctivitis in his eyes. Altogether, Louis was struggling to stay alive. His old companions, Charles Baxter, William Henley, and his cousin Bob, took him in hand in January 1884, and he returned to the French Riviera briefly without Fanny. His friends began to think that Fanny was not suited to be his nurse as word of her eccentricities spread. They began to suggest to Louis that she was mad. Upon hearing these rumors, Fanny never truly forgave them.

Toward the end of the summer of 1884, Louis left the southern coast of France, which he loved so much, for the last time. This period had proved to be another broken link in the Bohemian stage of his life, and marked some of his happiest days. Louis was never to return to France.

Things were not, however, as hopeless as they seemed. Imperceptibly, a basic change was going to take place in his life. Thus far Stevenson's writings were largely inconsequential—journalism of sorts—articles written for both obscure and prestigious periodicals, that were read mostly by his friends in a mutual admiration society. Stevenson's name was well known in part because of his charm, his eccentricities, and his letters. The public knew him by name more than they knew what he had written, and none of his writings or plays had brought him any money. But *Treasure Island,* begun in September 1881 in the Scottish Highlands and continued at Davos as an attempt to amuse Fanny's son Lloyd, was to change all of that. It is still considered a masterpiece by most critics. At Stevenson's death it had brought him 75,000 pounds while *The Black Arrow,* a fifteenth-century tale set during the English War of the Roses that was begun in 1883 and finally published in 1888, was, at first, even more successful than *Treasure Island.* In the fall of 1883, the Philadelphia publisher Lippincott was sufficiently impressed to offer to pay Louis 450 pounds for an account of a journey through the Greek Aegean Islands. Hence, by 1884 RLS's thoughts centered on making money as an author living from his works independent of his coterie of friends who had helped create "the Stevenson legend" on the basis of fairly meager pickings.

Another change in Stevenson's life was the apparent reconciliation with his parents and their reluctant acceptance of his marriage to the *wild* American who used her every charm to win them over. Above all, though, this period marked the ascendancy of his wife Fanny to become. henceforth, the dictator of his household, his over-caring nurse, literary counselor, and collaborator of sorts. She became the ultimate guardian at the gate, deciding who would or would not be admitted into Louis's presence—a testimony to her strength of character. In terms of his health, there followed three nightmarish years, which Louis later remembers having hated. Paradoxically enough, they proved to be the most productive years in his life, finally giving birth to the work for which Louis, arguably, is best remembered, the *Strange Case of Dr. Jekyll and Mr. Hyde.*

As a child Louis had escaped the moral restrictions of his upbringing by acting out the lives of exciting villains or saints, as well as fabricating new modes of crime and punishment in his imagination. Later he dealt with the problem in some of his verse. In a poem called "Stormy Nights" written some seven years before *Dr. Jekyll and Mr. Hyde,* Louis had tried to describe his own dual nature and temptations fighting the conservatism of his puritanical cage and upbringing:

> And how my spirit beat
> The cage of its compulsive purity;
> How—my eyes fixed,
> My shot lip tremulous between my fingers

I fashioned for myself new modes of crime,
Created for myself with pain and labor.

Using a different venue, he tackled the same problem in other ways. For example, in 1875 he wrote about Francois Villon, a French poet he much admired, who was both a student of the art of poetry and also a housebreaker and thief. In *The Lantern Bearers* (1887) written for *Scribner's Magazine,* he depicted thieves in the shape of tonsured clerks or even priests and monks. In Louis's novel *Kidnapped,* published in 1886, he described the cruelty of David Balfour's Uncle Ebenezer plotting to deprive his nephew of his rightful inheritance but, at the same time, making note of the good side of the uncle's nature.

In 1883 Louis had already confessed to his life-long interest in the two aspects of man's nature exemplified by the experiences of his own life. "I had long been trying to write a story on the subject, to find a body, a vehicle for that strong sense of a man's double identity which must at times come in upon and overwhelm the mind of every thinking creature." To support a major contention of this book that Robert Louis Stevenson continued to be fascinated by the Brodie double-life case during much of his lifetime, Stevenson was still struggling from time to time to complete his own final revised version of a play, *William Brodie, or the Double Life.*

Stevenson's play had had a long torturous history. As early as 1869, when Stevenson was only about nineteen years of age, he had presented an early draft of his proposed Brodie play to the writer William Ernst Henley, and Henley liked the idea. (It is interesting to note that the crippled Henley may have been a model for the Long John Silver character in Stevenson's famous novel *Treasure Island.*) The two authors went on to rewrite the play many times.

As a twenty-eight-year-old student, Stevenson returned to the project of writing the Brodie play, again enlisting the help of his friend William Henley. An initial draft of the play was written between October 1878 and January 1879 by the co-authors under the title *Deacon Brodie or The Double Life: A Melodrama Founded on Facts in Four Acts and Ten Tableau,* and had at first been printed privately. After several revisions it was offered to the great Victorian actor Henry Irving, but it soon became clear that the latter was not interested in acting on stage the double life of Deacon Brodie. Henley revised the play on his own. Henley then offered the play to the manager of the Princess Theater in London, Walter Gooch. Like Irving, however, Gooch turned down the offer. A third attempt was made through Sidney Colvin to interest the actor John Clayton, but he also disliked the play.

Discouraged, Henley had to wait until December 28, 1882, to get it produced for the first time by Haldane Critchon's Company at Pullan's Theater of Varieties in Bradford, England. Later it was staged at Her Majesty's Theater in Aberdeen in April 1883 and the Prince's Theater in London in July 1884. "But after a desperate campaign," wrote Stevenson in 1887, "we turned out the original drama of Deacon Brodie as performed in London and recently, I believe, successfully in this city [New York]. We were both young men when we did that and I think we had an idea that bad-heartedness was strength. Now the piece has been overhauled, and although I have no idea whether the piece will please an audience, I don't think Mr. Henley or I are ashamed of it" (*New York Herald*, September 8, 1887).

At the outset of the published melodrama, Brodie enters, closes, locks, and double-bolts both doors and says, "Now for one of the Deacon's headaches!" He goes to the clothes press in his room and proceeds to change his coat saying, "On with the new coat and into the new life! Down with the Deacon and up with the robber!" He then changes his neckband and ruffles and mutters, "Eh God! How still the house is! There's something in hypocrisy after all. If we were as good as we seem, what would the world be? Trysts are keeping, bottles cracking, knives are stripping; and here is Deacon Brodie flaming forth the man of men he is!—How still it is! . . . My father and Mary—Well! The day for them, the night for me; the grimy cynical night that makes all cats gray, and all honesties of one complexion. Shall a man not have *half* a life of his own?—not eight hours out of twenty-four? . . . Only the stars to see me!" Brodie then goes out the window.

In the Brodie play, Stevenson dwelt on the good and respectable side of the Deacon's personality "A great man in his day, well seen in society, crafty with his hand as a cabinet maker . . . who could sing a song with taste"—a clear reference to the Deacon's hero, Macheath of *The Beggar's Opera*. "Many a citizen was proud to welcome the Deacon to supper."

Brodie's philosophy is that all men are evil deep inside themselves; everything else is merely a disguise or a mask. In his Deacon Brodie melodrama, Stevenson plays upon this notion of masking and unmasking. To become another person one must don the disguise of one's other self. Taking off the usual daily cover, one discovers his inner self, as Brodie did within the play. When Brodie leaves his bedroom at night he declares, "Lie there, Deacon! Sleep and be well tomorrow. As for me, I'm a man once more 'til morning." That last sentence was a favorite one, which Stevenson often used about himself. In the play Brodie presages notions in Jekyll and Hyde, "On with the new coat and into the new life! If we were as good as we seem, what would the world be? The city has its vizard on, and we—at night we are our naked selves."

When Brodie finds out that his uncle, the fiscal procurator, had been smuggling in brandy, he delighted in declaiming, "Rogues all! Rogues all! 'Tis the last word of my philosophy, and it will soon be yours." He considered that there was no real distinction between his thieving ways and the practices of Scottish businessmen. "Every man for himself, and the devil for all," he stated, "they call that cynicism in France, but here we call it business instinct."

The Brodie play was set in High Street of Edinburgh, the main street of the Old Town and the closes that run into it. One of the main settings was Brodie's own workshop in Brodie's Close, as it is still called today. The area is located in the Lawnmarket end of High Street in Edinburgh, near Edinburgh Castle. Farther down behind the Royal Mile were the slums such as Libberton's Wynd, where Brodie's mistress Jean Watt once lived with their two children. Anne Grant, his other mistress, resided on Cant's Close, which was below Niddry Street in the same seedy part of town. Across the street is Fleshmarket Close, where the Deacon's favorite tavern, Clarke's, once stood. Those authentic historical settings are in the drama, and Brodie himself is specifically identified as "William Brodie, Deacon of the Wrights, Housebreaker and Master Carpenter." The *Deacon Brodie or the Double Life* also includes portrayals of Brodie's accomplice John Brown, as well as Ainslie the thief.

What separates Stevenson's Brodie from other so-called "virtuous men," is his courage and ability to free himself from his over-righteousness. In the play, when confronted by his uncle

William Lawson, the fiscal procurator, Brodie admits to his life-long addiction to leading a double life as a criminal: "Don't weep, my good friend; I was lost long since; don't think of me; don't pity me; don't shame me with your pity! I began this when I was a boy. I bound the millstone round my neck; it is irrevocable now. . . . And all for what? By what? Because I had an open hand, because I was a selfish dog . . ."

When apprehended at the end of the play by the Bow Street runner named Hunt, Brodie says his last words, "One moment, officer: I have a word to say before witnesses ere I go. In all this there is but one man guilty; and that man is I. None else has sinned; none else must err. . . . Mr. Procurator-Fiscal, that is my dying confession." Brodie then snatches his dagger from the table and rushes upon Hunt, who parries and runs him through. Brodie reels across the stage and cries, "The new life . . . the new life!" He dies as the curtain comes down. Much of the spirit of the Brodie drama of the double life was incorporated into Stevenson's *Jekyll and Hyde* story and later in *The Master of Ballantrae* (printed in 1889) in which two estranged brothers, James and Henry, act as doubles very much in the manner of Jekyll and Hyde.

The Birth of Jekyll and Hyde at Bournemouth

I am pouring forth a penny dreadful; it is damn dreadful . . . they call it Dr. Jekyll, but they also call it Mr. Hyde . . . but for all my tale is silly, it shall not be very long.

—Robert Louis Stevenson writing to
Sidney Colvin in the fall of 1885

At the end of June 1884, Louis left his beloved French Riviera for England, allegedly because of a cholera epidemic, but, in actual fact, because his health had further deteriorated, instead of improving. The usual consultations with his doctors took place with Dr. George Balfour and Dr. Thomas Brinton in London and with Dr. Mennell in Richmond. The symptoms varied, as did the diagnoses and the advice of his doctors: intermittent cough, liver and gastric ailments, and, above all, constant hemorrhaging. Send the patient back to Davos? Try the Riviera again? Or any one of the numerous resort spas of Europe? In his letters of this period Louis poked fun at his tormentors' questions and mimicked the late English King

George III (1738–1820), who was ridiculed for his habits of questioning specialists of the period as he suffered from the disease porphyria and ultimately went mad. "In the words of his Sacred Majesty George III: What? What? Why? Why? Why?" And RLS signed himself "an Invalid from Davos, Torquay, Menton, Nice, Cannes, Hyères, and Bournemouth."

Indeed, Dr. Mennell of Richmond prescribed a particular watering place and winter health resort in Hampshire located on the south coast of England facing the Isle of Wight. Because of its good air and sheltered position surrounded by pine woods, it was a favorite spot for persons suffering from pulmonary conditions. Like Davos, Bournemouth had been essentially a huge sanatorium for tubercular patients since 1835. Another reason for going there was the fact that Fanny's son Lloyd had just been moved from Edinburgh to a private school in the area. Finally, it was a good meeting place for Louis's convalescent father to recover from the wintry and foggy climate of Edinburgh. It would also help seal the ongoing reconciliation with Louis and Fanny. Waiting for his father whom he hoped would be able to visit, Louis often spent the latter part of the winter of 1884 wandering from one rooming house to another, not too distant from the beach. By November he and Fanny had rented a furnished house called Bonalie Towers in fashionable Bransome Park, a healthful location surrounded by pine trees, on West Cliff overlooking the sea.

The couple's surprise must have been great when Louis's father offered to buy a small but handsome villa called Seaview on the cliff nearby as a wedding present for Fanny who had made every effort to win over the old man. This was to be their home (though Thomas Stevenson most likely thought that he had equal title to it) during the next three years, from May 1885 until the summer of 1887. Stevenson paid tribute to his father by renaming the villa Skerryvore, the name of one of the "noblest of all extant deep sea lighthouses, Dhy Hearach" built on the Scottish coast by Allen Stevenson, his uncle.

Skerryvore, Bournemouth in the 1930s. (THE WRITERS' MUSEUM, EDINBURGH)

Later Louis built a miniature model of that famous lighthouse, which greeted visitors at the gate of the garden. Fanny, who had never owned a house in her life, was delighted to have finally advanced to the status of a "bourgeois lady" after years of Bohemian existence.

Louis was also prepared to give it a try, though perhaps he was never more aware of the hypocrisy and playacting involved in camouflaging his inner self—pretending to be what he was not while secretly yearning for his former Bohemian life. Indeed for Louis the three years at Bournemouth were probably the most miserable in his life and yet by far the most productive—another contradiction. "I have a house now," he exclaimed on October 22, 1885, to his friend William Lowe, "and a fine one too though it is small and is damn comely. I am now a beastly householder." The villa was well located on the cliff with a beautiful view of the sea on the brink of a hill called Alum Chine. Two stories high, yellow stuccoed on the outside, and covered with ivy, the little house, ambitiously called a villa, had a blue shingled slate roof. It was hopelessly commonplace. The jutting extravagant entrance hall gave the visitor a glimpse of the stairways leading upstairs to

RLS from a photo taken by his stepson, Lloyd Osbourne, Bournemouth at Skerryvore in 1885. (THE WRITERS' MUSEUM, EDINBURGH)

the bedrooms on one side and to the two entertaining rooms and kitchen on the ground floor. One salon was painted blue while the dining room was red in hue.

Among the many paintings decorating the walls of the blue drawing room where Stevenson habitually received his guests was John Singer Sargent's portrait of a contorted Louis "large eyed and chicken boned," walking in his oriental dining room in a velveteen jacket and twisting his moustache. At one corner one catches a glimpse of his wife in a wild Indian dress looking like a ghost. She was seated on a chair that had belonged to Louis's grandfather and was later dubbed the "Henry James Chair," for Louis's favorite American novelist liked to sit there. Sargent was never pleased with this particular painting, nor, for that matter, was Louis. Fanny considered it a jewel and kept it to the end of her life. A "Magic Mirror," which reflected the other side of the room, given him by his new found American friend, was immortalized by the latter's verse: "The mirror speaks." The other painting and knickknacks decorating the walls of the salon completed the impression of Victorian decor, as did the furnishings of the red dining room, the furniture being chosen by Louis's father and Fanny on a shopping spree in London. It included a piano that Louis often used when he could not write, exercising his hands on the clavier and dreaming of composing and playing in his bed, though he had little talent.

Louis was probably fondest of the little garden—his only avenue of escape from the house that he considered a prison—which had more character than the villa. William Archer describes the demesne, or, as Fanny liked to refer to it, the court, extending over the edge and almost to the bottom of the Chine hill. Here among laurels and rhododendrons, broom, and gorse the garden merged into a network of paths and stairways with tempting seats and unexpected arbors at every turn. Fanny liked to grow tomatoes, little cultivated in England at the time, and she also introduced Indian corn, as well as a kitchen garden with raspberries, apples, and pears for the family's use. Louis played at gardening, but he destroyed more plants than he saved. The writer delighted in sitting on the porch behind the house feeding the pigeons, while viewing the distant sea framed by the multicolored flowers carefully kept by his gardener. The household had three other servants; the French maid Valentine Roch; a housekeeper named Mary Anne Watts; her daughter, Anne; Beaucox the gardener; a private doctor named Thomas B. Scott; a Skye terrier called Bogue, soon to be killed in a dog fight in 1886; and a cat called Ginger, bought in a London exhibit. This was Victorian living at its best. Louis had often dismissed the great liberal politician William E. Gladstone as representing bourgeois respectability, as had his father. In the end, however, Louis had to admit that he too led a bourgeois existence patronized by Fanny and entertained by new proper social acquaintances, all of whom were carefully screened by his wife.

Among them was their neighbor Adelaide A. Boodle who dubbed herself the game keeper. She became a lifelong friend and revealed a very intimate account of life at Skerryvore in her book *RLS and His Sine Qua Non* (1926). Louis the freethinker felt obliged to entertain the Vicar of St. Andrew's Church, the Reverend Beclair. Sir Percy Florence Shelley, now a rich young man who had inherited his grandfather's estate and title and, more recently, the royalties of his mother's bestseller *Frankenstein,* was an occasional visitor at Skerryvore. A graduate of establishment schools, he had reneged on all the liberal good causes of his father the poet. His wife, Lady Shelley, occasionally made note of the physical resemblance that existed between her father-in-law and Stevenson, which made Louis feel uncomfortable. Thomas and Maggie visited their son often, sometimes giving the impression that Skerryvore was less a gift than a bridge to Heriot Row, which the young couple had abandoned. Among the genuine friends of whom Louis was fond was the American writer Henry James, though, perhaps the initial contact was made to ingratiate himself with Fanny, a fellow American. There were occasional escapades from Skerryvore with former friends, such as with Henley, who, in Fanny's eyes, was increasingly *persona non grata,* to Paris to meet the sculptor Auguste Rodin. However, these excursions were generally few and far between. In the meantime, perhaps due to his overwhelming effort to be untrue to his inner self and play this "double part," Louis's health seriously deteriorated at Skerryvore. Yet, the blood on his handkerchief and the medicine bottle on the mantlepiece would not color his view on life, nor lead him to despair.

Regardless, Louis described himself as the wooden-faced invalid and a hunchback with a white face, a prisoner of his own house and garden obliged to carry his arm in a sling as he had done on the French Riviera. He was even afraid of taking long walks on the West Cliff of Bournemouth, which was not too far distant. The writer made a point of using his persistent ill health as an argument for cutting himself off from the outside world, except for the few friends who Fanny tolerated. Apart from describing his symptoms, no one, not even Dr. Scott the local physician, had any idea for a precise diagnosis. Louis described himself as "bouilli (boiled) out of a pot of fever" while the doctors discussed the symptoms and their analyses in whispers: subacute rheumatism, congested kidney, recalcitrant liver, constipated gall bladder duct, headaches, pleurisy, dyspepsia, hemorrhaging, tenia, influenza, fevers, and persistent colds. Fanny would not allow Louis to shake hands with anyone who showed the slightest signs of ill health. Reading Louis's letters of this period, one gets the impression that they were health bulletins destined to explain away his inactivity. To his father he confessed, "I have been nearly six months in a strange condition of collapse when it was impossible to do any work and difficult to write the merest note. I am now better but not yet my own man in the way of brains and in health." To William Archer Louis, he complains of his periods of depression and that he is no longer able to take long walks near the sea . . . that he stripped himself of all the pleasures of life . . . even impotence was slowly closing in upon him. Louis, however, never totally lost hope.

His consolations, he confessed, were few: writing letters to his parents and to his few remaining friends, dabbling at the piano, drinking the good burgundy that was always available for their few friends—though he was never drunk—and, in spite of all his ills, he still enjoyed a good meal.

As Louis's health deteriorated, Fanny assumed an increasingly authoritarian role as a nurse and, more accurately, a policeman or perhaps a warden at the gate blocking Louis's access to the outside world. Visitors, particularly those she disliked such as Henley, were denied access under a variety of pretexts mostly on the ground that Louis's frail health would not allow him to be exposed to germs—even a cold could be dangerous. She even rationed exposure to those she liked, such as the painter Sargent and James and William Archer. As a self-appointed nurse, she knew how to lift Louis onto the bed in a variety of positions comfortable to him, usually in a kneeling position with his face to the pillow holding him up in the air, while he drew out his feet, which could have snapped his brittle bones, with the aim of stopping the bleeding. With the same end in view, powders were used, such as Calomel or Ergotin, which affect the brain, and laudanum, an opiate. Other forms of intimidations followed and were exploited by Fanny. She demanded to oversee and to be consulted with on Louis's manuscripts in the rare moments when Louis was well enough to write.

Fanny Osbourne, RLS's wife. (THE WRITERS' MUSEUM, EDINBURGH)

Occasionally, she would insist on co-authorship, although she had little evident talent.

Fanny persuaded Louis to give up certain literary genres such as poetry and plays, which brought little to no money, in order to make her expensive Victorian household more solvent and be able to pay the butcher and the baker. This was one point where Louis was in agreement with her, that when poverty comes in, love usually flies out of the window. Judging from Louis's letters, one may gather the impression that Louis himself was occasionally ready to chuck himself out of the window—but, in essence, Louis never really thought of suicide. Secretly Stevenson was resentful and unhappy during the Bournemouth stage, which in a sense reminded him of his imprisonment at 17 Heriot Row. Now a prisoner in his own house, it seemed far worse. In Edinburgh as in Bournemouth, his inner self dreamed of adventures, journeys to out of the way places, seeking more exotic climates than the so-called English Riviera.

What was his reaction to Fanny as his nurse and jailer? Writing to his parents after several years of marriage, but before Bournemouth, Louis paid a glowing tribute to his wife: "I love her more than ever and I admire her more. I cannot think what I have done to deserve so good a gift. My marriage has been the most successful in the world. She is everything to me. Wife, brother, sister, daughter and dear companion and I would not change to get a goddess and a saint." He should have added the word *mother* to the tribute.

Inevitably there was friction between husband and wife. Louis at first expressed it by use of irony to his intimate friends and parents. When Fanny returned from Hyères in May 1885 to pack some of their belongings, Louis wrote to his parents, "There came here a lean brown bloodshot woman claiming to be Fanny. I have taken her in provisionally. She had stolen much finery and her head ached." And again when Fanny returned from London on October 25, 1885, he noted, "The wife arrived with her pulse at 102." To his close friend William Henry, Louis admitted (January 1887) of his rocky relationship with Fanny. "My wife is peepie and dowsie" (two Scottish expressions meaning fretful, whining, and dismal, and languid and weak, respectively). To Henry James on December 23, 1881, "She is a woman not without art, the art of extracting the gloom of the eclipse from the sunshine. We fell out my wife and I the other night; she tackled me savagely for being a canary bird; I replied politely that there was no use in turning life into *King Lear*, presently it was discovered that there were two dead combatants upon the field each slain by the arrow of the truth and we tenderly carried off each others' corpses. . . . Fanny was in a fit of black gloom."

At other times he compared his wife to the "Simoon," a wild witch who blew wild weather, a nickname concocted by Henley. Louis tries to explain his wife's temper tantrums "by various inexplicable attacks, now in the pleasant morn now at the noon of night" whereas he at least "was a regular invalid."

Louis was perfectly aware of his wife's mood swings, hypochondria, and other imperfections, which were to increase after the Bournemouth phase and cause increasing unhappiness to both of them. In fairness to Fanny, it should be added that, given Louis's temperamental outbursts coupled with his ill health, he was not exactly the easiest man to live with on a variety of counts. On the whole he continued to be deeply dependent on Fanny to the end of his life. Adelaide Boodle, always in awe of both celebrities, laid emphasis on Fanny's extraordinary devotion to Louis adding, "I doubt if she ever allowed him to know what agony she lived through. She guarded him from every risk."

Because of Stevenson's own ill health, Fanny's policy of isolation, and his father's illness, Louis was in a self-deprecating mood during the spring of 1885 on the eve of the famous nightmare. All the more so as he thought that he had bridged an important step from journalism to becoming a writer of genius among that minority able to live from their writings alone.

He had been highly paid for his first adventure story, *Treasure Island,* the success of which aroused the jealousy of Henley and the admiration of no less a personality than the great statesman William Gladstone himself. "It appears," wrote Stevenson "that Gladstone talks all the time of *Treasure Island;* he would do better to attend the Imperial affairs of England."

Generally Louis's writing had greatly improved even prior to his stay at Skerryvore, which was exemplified by such plays as *Admiral Guinea* and *Beau Austin,* both written during the summer of 1884. The novels (*Macaire* and *Markheim*), which followed during the autumn of 1884 and completed later, were generally well received as was *The Dynamiter* begun with Fanny in Hyères in April 1885 and finished at Skerryvore. Stevenson had a way of starting many works, abandoning them for a time, and finishing them later, such as *Markheim,* finally finished in 1887, and some, like *The Great North Road,* not at all. *The Dynamiter* was dedicated to two police constables, William Cole and Thomas Cox, both of them severely injured in diffusing a bomb supposed to blow up the Westminster Parliament.

Despite his productivity, however, Stevenson's mood was somber. He continued to feel that he did not have the genius of a Byron or Shelley, whom he admired. Overreacting along this line in one of his letters, he stated that he considered himself "no better than a fool." He often wrote silly letters that could barely be understood by his friends. When Fanny purchased her famous cat Ginger in October 1885 he exclaimed: "When a cat comes in the door literature flies out the window ... not that there is much to fly from here." He also called himself "an imbecile" and an "impure writer." Yet he was offended at criticism. For instance, when William Archer found fault with some of the chapters in

Inland Voyage and *Travels on a Donkey,* Louis objected on the grounds that his friend did not notice "his change of style."

Louis loved Celtic music. He played the tin whistle and the flageolet, a small flute that he enjoyed playing in bed. He also became fascinated with Russian writers, in particular Tolstoy. He was upset by the brutal evictions of the Irish from their farms by the British. Louis developed a weird "Tolstoyan" solution, according to his stepson Lloyd, "We were all to go to Ireland, rent one of those farms, and be murdered in due course." As RLS expressed it with oratorical flourish: "The murder of a distinguished English literary man and his family, thus engaged in the assertion of human rights, will arrest the horror of the whole civilized world, and bring down its odium on these miscreants." Fortunately for Stevenson and family, the wild scheme never happened.

To his parents he wrote in January 1886, "We writers are whores, some of us pretty whores, some of us not, but all whores of the mind, selling the public the amusements of our friends as the whore sells the pleasure of the bed. . . . I am a pretty sick whore anyway."

In spite of this self-deprecatory mood the reviews of most of his recently published works were good and they sold well, particularly in America. The New York publishing house of Charles Scribner's and Sons was ready to offer handsome royalties for *A Child's Garden of Verses,* published in March 1885. As "a literary whore," Stevenson wished above all to be solvent and able to pay the high costs of Skerryvore. Such was the ambiance and his frame of mind as we reach that famous September 1885, the month of the nightmare that simulated Louis to work out the *Strange Case of Dr. Jekyll and Mr. Hyde.*

Stevenson was on the verge of a nervous breakdown, possibly a manic depression, taking copious doses of laudanum or any of the other drugs in his pharmacy when Fanny heard him crying in his sleep. She woke him. He was infuriated and screamed at her, "I was dreaming a fine bogey tale."

We know that dreams and nightmares were very much part of Stevenson's existence and he could drift into sleep quite effortlessly, because it brought him respite from the pain. Unlike most of us, however, he tended to remember quite vividly his dreams, the unconscious source of many of his stories. In an essay on dreams that appeared in *Scribner's Magazine,* he characterized his "brownies" as he called them, as the "little people" who play like children upon the stage in the "small theater of the brain kept brightly lighted all night . . . after the jets are down and darkness and sleep reign undisturbed in the remainder of the body."

The morning after, he began jotting down his memories of the nightmare. His stepson, Lloyd Osbourne, recalls the events that followed. "Louis came down to luncheon in a very preoccupied state of mind, hurried though his meal—an unheard of thing for him to do—and on leaving said he was working with extraordinary success on a new story that had come to him in a dream and that he was not to be interrupted or disturbed even if the house caught fire . . . at the end of three days the mysterious task was finished, and he read aloud to my mother and myself the first draft of the *Strange Case of Dr. Jekyll and Mr. Hyde.* I listened to it spell bound *[sic].* Stevenson, who had a voice the great actors might have envied, read it with an intensity that made shivers run up and down my spine."

Louis was radiant and thought it was the best thing that he had even written. While they all waited for Fanny's approval, "Her praise was constrained; the words seemed to come with difficulty;

and then all at once she broke out with criticism . . . he had missed the point she said, had missed the allegory; had made it merely a story—a magnificent bit of sensationalism—when it should have been a masterpiece. Stevenson was beside himself with anger. He trembled; his hand shook on the manuscript; he was intolerably chagrined. His voice bitter and challenging, overrode my mother's in a fury of resentment. Never had I seen him so impassioned, so outraged and the scene became so painful that I went away unable to bear it any longer."

Stevenson retreated to his sickbed for a long time. According to Lloyd when he himself returned, he found his mother pale and desolate seated alone by the fireplace and staring at it. Louis supposedly descended the stairs, admitted that Fanny was right and threw some papers into the fire.

According to another version, however, it was Fanny who stormed out of the room. When she returned her husband pointed to some papers burning in the fireplace. He led her to believe that he had burned the manuscript, and he confessed that he had to destroy it because it was "all wrong" as he put it. (Stevenson had burned manuscripts in the past.) "In trying to save some of it I should have got hopelessly off the track. The only way was to put temptation beyond my reach." But what was the specific temptation? Did he really burn all that work for which he so desperately needed money? The mystery remains. We do know that Fanny was often worried about the "unacceptable" content of much of her husband's work.

The closet homosexual and noted writer John Addington Symonds wrote about *Dr. Jekyll and Mr. Hyde,* "Viewed as an allegory, it touches upon one too closely. Most of us at some epoch in our lives have been upon the verge of developing a Mr. Hyde."

In any case, Stevenson set to writing at a furious pace. According to his stepson Lloyd, he wrote 64,000 words in six days, or more than 10,000 words per day. (Actually, the published story numbers only about 25,000 words, some 103 pages or so in print, and hence is technically called a novella rather than a novel in its formal sense.) Still, Stevenson must have written an average of more than 4,000 words per day. As a point of comparison, most fiction writers in his day averaged about 1,000 words a day. Amazingly, Stevenson corrected the novel, wrote, and rewrote it within a mere ten weeks. It was a stupendous achievement. He seemed refreshed and revitalized, going about with a happy air. He appeared uplifted as though he had come into a fortune, and looked better than he had in months.

By the late 1880s, mass literacy and the mass literary market had come into being, over the objection of many critics such as B. C. John, who complained about the literature of the street in the *Edinburgh Review* in 1887. He declared these writings to be a disgrace to civilization and warned, "The garbage of the Penny Dreadfuls was poisonous to the masses." Undoubtedly pleased with the success of his book and the royalties that came in, Stevenson continued to be ambivalent and even unduly modest about his talents and described his work in derogatory terms. The words *Gothic pygmy* and *Penny Dreadful* continued in his correspondence. "There must be something wrong in me," he wrote, "or I would not be popular." He occasionally signed himself, "with the hand of Jekyll and not Hyde," as if ashamed of the latter.

The Strange Case of Dr. Jekyll and Mr. Hyde, printed in time for the generally booming Christmas market of 1885, at first met with indifference on the part of bookstore owners. In fact, many booksellers generally refused to stock it, because their stores were already well filled with other books for the Christmas rush. Louis was depressed by all this.

Upon the appearance of Stevenson's the *Strange Case of Dr. Jekyll and Mr. Hyde,* an unsigned book review of it appeared in the American magazine, *Saturday Review,* dated January 9, 1886. (We know now that the review was written by the noted literary critic Andrew Lang.) Lang called it an "excellent and horrific and captivating romance," and praised Stevenson for his original approach to the idea of the double. Hyde is "all unlike that in William Wilson" [Poe's story of a double by that name]. Hyde exhibits an "unlikeness" to Jekyll and his "hideous appearance, and appalling vitality, and terrible power of growth and increase, is, to our thinking, a notion as novel as it is terrific." The critic proclaimed, "We would welcome a specter, a ghoul, or even a vampire gladly, rather than meet Mr. Edward Hyde," and warned, "every Jekyll among us is haunted by his own Hyde." James Ashcroft Noble in his review that came out on January 23, 1886, in the journal *Academy* declared, "It is, indeed, many years since English fiction has been enriched by any work at once so weirdly imaginative in conception and so faultlessly ingenious in construction as this little tale. . . ." Then the critic compared the Stevenson story favorably to Nathaniel Hawthorne's *The Scarlet Letter.* He added, "In spite of the cover and the popular price, Mr. Stevenson's story distances so unmistakably its three-volume and one-volume competitors, that its only fitting place is the place of honor."

However, it was a basically positive, unsigned book review of the *Strange Case of Dr. Jekyll and Mr. Hyde,* printed in *The Times* (London) on January 25, 1886, that finally made booksellers take notice. *The Times* termed it a "finished study in the art of the fantastic," and added,

> Nothing Mr. Stevenson has written as yet so strongly impressed us with the versatility of his very original genius in this sparsely-printed little shilling volume." As the reviewer continued, "Slight as is the story, and supremely sensational, we remember nothing better since George Eliot's *Romola* than this delineation of a feeble but kindly nature steadily and inevitably succumbing to the sinister influences of besetting weaknesses." In referring to Stevenson, the reviewer claimed, "Never for a moment in the most startling situations, has he lost his grasp of the grand ground-facts of a wonderful and supernatural problem. . . . Each apparently incredible or insignificant detail has been thoughtfully subordinated to his purpose." In comparing the story with "the somber masterpieces of Poe" the critic found that "we may say at once that Mr. Stevenson has gone far deeper," because "Mr. Stevenson evolves the ideas of his story from the world that is unseen, enveloping everything in weird mystery, till at last it pleases him to give us the password."

Within six months, from January to June of the year 1886, Stevenson's book blossomed into a bestseller with some forty thousand copies sold in England alone and two million in American sales, often pirated, where the story was extremely popular. Overnight Stevenson became a rich man who could finally afford a comfortable lifestyle on his own. He became one of the first self-sustaining writers capable of living solely on the income from his book royalties.

To John Addington Symonds, Stevenson was more explicit. He wrote in March 1886: "*Jekyll* is a dreadful thing, I own it; but the only thing I feel dreadful about is the dreadful thing of the war between the members." The literary critic concurred, "At last I have read *Jekyll and Hyde*. . . . It is indeed a dreadful book because of a certain moral callousness and want of sympathy a shutting out of hope . . . it has left such a painful impression on my heart that I do not know how I am ever to turn to it again." At the same time, Symonds admitted, "As a piece of literary work it was the best that Stevenson had done."

Bathing in the success of his novella, it was clear the Skerryvore phase in Stevenson's life was rapidly drawing to a close. Its passing was linked to the rapidly deteriorating health of Louis's father who had always looked upon the lavish gift he had made to Fanny as his own retirement home. During the spring of 1887, Thomas's mental and physical health, increasingly a source of worry to Louis, had taken a drastic turn for the worse, and both Louis and Fanny were urgently called to come to Edinburgh at the beginning of May. When Stevenson finally arrived at 17 Heriot Row it was too late, his father did not even recognize his son. He died on May 8, 1887. His father's passing came as a terrible blow and drained Louis of his remaining strength. He caught a chill and, on his doctor's advice,

Thomas Stevenson, RLS's father. (THE WRITERS' MUSEUM, EDINBURGH)

was unable to attend the elaborate funeral. During the next few weeks, while confined to his bed, Louis had time to dwell on the difficult father/son relationship that had profoundly affected his whole life and became the theme of two other masterpieces: *The Master of Ballantrae* and the unfinished novel *The Weir of Hermiston,* perhaps his greatest single literary work. With his father's death, the Skerryvore stage of Louis's life had ended. The proceeds of his father's will, coupled with the royalties from *Jekyll and Hyde,* gave Louis the financial independence to escape from his Bournemouth prison. Free at last!

Louis bade farewell to his friends, many of them for the last time. In saying good-bye to such close associates as Edmund Gosse, Stevenson conveyed sadness, nostalgia, and, even, a sense of crisis. He then left the keys to the house in the hands of his good neighbor Mrs. Boodle. Eventually, the house was let but Louis was never to see Mrs. Boodle, nor, for that matter, Bournemouth or his beloved Scotland again—though his furniture eventually followed him to the South Seas.

He did not know it at the time, but he was leaving Europe for good. In spite of Fanny's protest and that of many of his friends on August 21, together with his mother, Maggie, Fanny, Lloyd, and Valentine Roch, he left for Le Havre to embark on the *Ludgate Hill,* a tramp steamer, for New York. His doctors had advised restoring his failing health in the fresh air of the Rocky Mountains in Colorado.

In his pocket Louis had an invitation from a wealthy admirer, Mr. Charles Fairchild, who had commissioned Sargent to paint Louis at Skerryvore, to visit him at his mansion in Newport, Rhode Island. Arriving in New York on September 7, 1887, the author of *Jekyll and Hyde* was greeted as a celebrity by hordes of journalists. William Lowe immediately recognized "the tall and distinguished gentleman wearing a velvet jacket and a peculiar hat" as he disembarked with his party at dockside. Not used to popular fame and somewhat taken aback, Louis, together with Valentine Roch, took refuge with the Fairchilds at their summer resort in Newport while Fanny and Maggie stayed in New York. All sorts of literary offers followed his arrival. Among them the editors of *Scribner's Magazine* offered Louis $3,500 for an article during the next three months. Other attractive offers came from the *Herald* and other newspapers and periodicals.

Abandoning the idea of the Rockies, at least for the time being, Louis preferred to keep close to New York and rented a cottage in the Adirondack Mountains in upstate New York on the banks of Saranac Lake, about seventy miles south of the Canadian border. It was a healthful climate and a way of recapturing the spirit of Silverado, and, above all, reliving Scotland on American soil "in the eye of many winds the dear hue of peat in spite of the lack of heather." This retreat, "The Little Switzerland of the Adirondacks," was in essence an attempt to rekindle the spirit of Scotland in America as he began writing *The Master of Ballantrae*, another tale of doubles. Eventually, however, the harsh winters of the Adirondacks were destined to drive Stevenson elsewhere.

In the meantime, while attempting to recover his health during the summer in the Adirondacks in 1888, Stevenson began negotiating with the Boston playwright Thomas Russell Sullivan (1849–1916) to write a theatrical version of his *Jekyll and Hyde* novella. Encouraged by the young actor Richard Mansfield (1854–1908), Sullivan had initially approached Stevenson in June 1886 and then visited him personally at Saranac in 1888. Louis signed a contract to sanction Sullivan's dramatization of his *Jekyll and Hyde* novella in return for an unspecified amount of money. The play had already opened at the Madison Theater in New York City with the then relatively unknown Richard Mansfield playing the dual role of Jekyll and Hyde. Fanny and Maggie had stayed in New York at the Hotel St. Stephen's in order to attend the initial production on December 12, 1887; Louis was too ill to be there. However, the play went on to become a success in America and to carry Jekyll and Hyde beyond literature into pop culture, though Stevenson did not make much profit from the play performances, largely due to the duplicity of Mansfield.

CHAPTER FIVE

The Story Line of the Strange Case

Did I request thee, Maker, from my clay
To mould me man? Did I solicit thee
From darkness to promote me?

—Adam's words from Book X of Milton's
Paradise Lost (1608–1697), used as an
epigraph by Mary Shelley in *Frankenstein*

When one reads Stevenson's tale, the full impact of the narrative can best be felt if one tries to forget, at least temporarily, that Jekyll and Hyde are in fact two persons in one person, because the reader does not discover this fact until later on in the novella. It is similar to the case of Count Dracula in Bram Stoker's classic tale in which one only gradually becomes aware that he is the vampire. In addition, as the Russian writer and critic Vladimir Nabokov (1899–1977) has suggested, the present-day reader might also try to forget all the movie versions. In the real world, however, most readers are not capable of forgetting such matters. The moment Dr. Jekyll appears, we know he is also Mr. Hyde, just as we know when Count Dracula appears that he is the vampire. In addition, Dr. Jekyll is not a medical doctor as he is usually presented in the movies, but a chemical researcher. He uses the laboratory at the back of his house to perform chemical experiments. He is not an active member of society but lives the life of a neurotic reclusive bachelor. He has no fiancée. The movie plots overwhelm us, however, which is a good reason for analyzing the original story:

The style is epistolary; the account is told through a series of direct reports and narratives, as in the novels of Wilkie Collins and Bram Stoker. The note at the preface to Bram Stoker's *Dracula* could well stand as the preface to Stevenson's *Dr. Jekyll and Mr. Hyde:*

> How these papers have been placed in sequence will be made manifest in the reading of them. All needless matters have been eliminated, so that a history almost at variance with the possibilities of later-day belief may stand forth as simple fact. There is throughout no statement of past things wherein memory may err, for all the records chosen are exactly contemporary, given from the standpoints and within the range of knowledge of those who made them.

Hyde, though the central figure, never speaks to us directly. He is almost never directly observed. Again and again we are told about the reactions Hyde provokes; rarely about Hyde himself.

In the novella, Gabriel Utterson functions as the first main narrator. He and his male friend and distant relative, Richard Enfield, go for regular Sunday "rambles," which they both count as "the chief jewel of each week." Though the two men are opposites, they enjoy each other's company. So, at the outset we are confronted with the common notion that opposites attract. Near a "certain sinister block of building," the two ramblers come across a strange back door to Jekyll's house, which Enfield names as "Blackmail House" on "Queer Street." Utterson doesn't wish to admit to his friend

Spencer Tracy as Hyde on the run. (BETTMANN/CORBIS)

that he truly knows that the strange door is the back entrance to Dr. Jekyll's house, but the fact is that he does, as the reader later finds out. So, at the outset we see Utterson not acknowledging what he prefers to keep hidden—another recurrent *motif* in the novella.

Enfield then describes his previous personal encounter there with "some damned Juggernaut" who trampled a small girl of maybe eight or ten and "left her screaming on the ground." At the time Enfield insisted that the scoundrel make restitution to the child's parents. So, the despicable fellow walks up to the strange door, opens it with a key, and returns with "another man's cheque for close upon a hundred pound." When Utterson asks what the name of that man was, Enfield replies, "It was a man of the name of Hyde." Because the others suspect that the check may not be valid, Hyde waits around with them until morning when the banks open.

Utterson is so fascinated by Enfield's story that he is determined to go in search of Mr. Hyde. After obviously knowing, though not admitting, who occupies the building in front of that strange back door, Utterson goes home to his bachelor apartment and reads the last will and testament of Henry Jekyll, which the doctor has had him prepare. Jekyll's will states that in the event of his death all of his possessions are to pass into the hands of his "friend and benefactor Edward Hyde." Utterson fears that Hyde is blackmailing Jekyll and that he is "paying for the capers of his youth."

Utterson then visits Dr. Hastie Lanyon, who had once been a close friend of Dr. Jekyll until Jekyll ventured into what Lanyon considered his morally reprehensible and "wrong" theories. Hastie Lanyon is a bigoted, narrowminded Scottish medical doctor. When Utterson asks him if he knows Hyde, Lanyon is quick to declare that he knows nothing of this Mr. Hyde. Utterson's interest has been piqued, however, and he resolves to solve the mystery. He lies in wait at "Blackmail House" on "Queer Street" at the rear entrance to Dr. Jekyll's house and laboratory. Eventually Utterson encounters a small, plainly dressed figure approaching the strange back door and queries, "Mr. Hyde, I think?" The snarling Mr. Hyde, seemingly secretive, hides his face at first. Then "as if upon some sudden reflection" he confronts Utterson directly, who appears not to recognize Jekyll but to see a kind of distorted image of himself in the face of Hyde, as if in a mirror. It is as if he does not wish to acknowledge that his friend could turn into such a creature.

Utterson finds that "Mr. Hyde was pale and dwarfish, he gave an impression of deformity without any namable malformation, he had a displeasing smile." Robert Louis Stevenson thought of himself as physically ugly like his literary creation Mr. Hyde. Stevenson's boyhood friend and writer H. B. Baildon, in his book *Robert Louis Stevenson: A Life Study in Criticism* (1901), felt that Stevenson's face compensated for his "spidery" body, because "The whole face had a tendency to an oval Madonna-like type.

But about the mouth and in the mirthful mocking light of the eyes there lingered a ready Autolycus roguery that rather suggested slyly Hermes masquerading as a mortal . . . about the mouth there was something a little tricksy and mocking." The careful reader of the novella the *Strange Case of Dr. Jekyll and Mr. Hyde* may recall that Dr. Jekyll's own overtly suspicious appearance had "something of a slyish cast" about it. In describing Hyde, Enfield insists, "He must be deformed somewhere; he gives a strong feeling of deformity."

Hyde, whose physical appearance is never precisely described in the novel, seems often to be a dark, eschewed mirror image of Jekyll, both similar to Jekyll and yet somehow strangely different. The Hyde image in the mirror is like counterpoint in a Bach fugue or in Escher's *Convex and Concave,* namely, both repetitive and contrasting.

Utterson next quizzes Jekyll's butler Poole who notes "something queer about Hyde." When Utterson learns that Jekyll has issued orders that Hyde must be obeyed, however, Utterson asks whether Poole has ever met Hyde, and Poole responds with the assertion, "He never *dines* here." He thereby asserts the social distance between Dr. Jekyll and Mr. Hyde, since Jekyll would never invite an obviously lowlife person such as Hyde to dinner in his own home.

Later at his dinner party held for his old male cronies, Jekyll appears to be "quite at ease" as he confidently informs Utterson that he can be rid of Hyde any time he wishes. Jekyll begs Utterson to be patient and help Hyde, though, especially when Jekyll is no longer evidently present.

Nearly a year later in the story, Utterson is shocked to learn about the brutal murder of Sir Danvers Carew, a prominent member of Parliament. A maidservant from the Jekyll household, who witnessed the murder, identifies the killer as "a certain Mr. Hyde who had once visited her master." Hyde evidently bludgeoned the old white patriarchal figure in a gratuitous act of anger. Utterson is asked to identify the body of Sir Danvers, who had been one of Utterson's clients. A broken cane is discovered in the nearby gutter, and Utterson recognizes it as one he had given to Jekyll several years ago. Utterson goes with Inspector Newcomen to Hyde's apartment in Soho, where they find the other part of the broken cane, but Hyde remains missing.

Utterson visits Jekyll in his study, which Stevenson terms Jekyll's *cabinet* in the French or German usage of that word as a "small room" or "study." (This archaic usage of "cabinet," however, may be Stevenson's sly oblique reference to an actual cabinet, the piece of furniture made by Deacon Brodie, which was in Stevenson's nursery.) Utterson accuses Jekyll of harboring Hyde, but the good doctor retorts that he "will never set eyes on him again." And, referring to Hyde, Jekyll asserts, "I am quite done with him." Jekyll is trying to convince himself and Utterson that he is in control of his Hyde.

Even though the police search and offer substantial rewards for the capture of the murderer of Sir Danvers Carew, Hyde is never found. The case of Dr. Carew's death remains unsolved. Meanwhile Jekyll renews his interest in charity work and joins society again. (There is no suggestion in the novella that Dr. Jekyll runs a clinic for poor people, as is shown in many of the movies, especially in the 1935 version with Fredric March.) Two months later, however, Poole, Jekyll's trusted butler, informs Utterson that Jekyll has become a recluse again and will see no one.

Utterson visits Dr. Lanyon who declares that Jekyll is "a doomed man." When Utterson notes that Jekyll is sick, Lanyon, holding up a trembling hand, loudly states, "I wish to see and hear no more of Doctor Jekyll. . . . I am quite done with that person; and I beg that you will spare me any allusion to one whom I regard as dead." Lanyon's disavowal of Jekyll echoes Jekyll's earlier disavowal of Hyde. Lanyon declares that he has been so shocked that he cannot bear speaking about it. We later learn that the actual sight of two persons in one has been too much for Lanyon.

Within a week Lanyon becomes ill and suddenly dies only two weeks later. Utterson then examines a sealed envelope with an enclosure marked, "Not to be opened till the death or disappearance of Dr. Henry Jekyll." However, out of feelings of professionalism and loyalty to his deceased friend Lanyon, Utterson places the unread document in his private safe. Then Utterson goes to Jekyll's house but prefers to talk with the butler, Poole, on the doorstep in the open air rather than enter into "that house of voluntary bondage," as he calls it.

On the subsequent Sunday, Utterson and his friend Enfield are taking their usual rambling walk through the city streets. There follows an incident based on Stevenson's nightmare, according to Stevenson's own words, "I dreamed the scene at the window." Utterson and Enfield catch a glimpse of Dr. Jekyll through a half-open window, and he looks ghastly with "an expression of such abject terror and despair." As a result, the two men become very worried about the sad state of Jekyll's health.

A few days later, on "a wild, cold, seasonable night of March," Poole visits Utterson with the renewed conviction that Dr. Jekyll has fallen prey to "foul play." Jekyll has locked himself in his laboratory. Poole considers the "thing inside" not to be his master but a dwarf. Poole tells Utterson that "him or it, whatever it is" in Jekyll's laboratory has been sending him notes requesting a specific drug to be purchased from London chemists, and then the thing began "weeping like a woman or a lost soul," because of some assumed impurities in the drug purchased.

Even though the voice of Hyde inside his laboratory door begs them not to do so, Utterson and Poole are determined to force their way into Jekyll's laboratory. Upon breaking down the door of the laboratory, Poole and Utterson find the body of what they think is Edward Hyde "sorely contorted and still twitching." They are still incapable of recognizing that Jekyll is Hyde. Poole and Utterson assume that Hyde has killed Jekyll. The dead Edward Hyde is discovered "dressed in clothes too large for him, clothes of the doctor's bigness." He is accompanied by the stench of the cyanide capsule, which he had evidently smashed between his teeth to cause death. Evidently Hyde has found it impossible to change back into Jekyll, so he has lost his cover. So, because Hyde can no longer hide inside Jekyll, he must face the gallows and ingests the cyanide instead.

Poole and Utterson find a cheval glass, which is a large mirror in which one can see one's full figure, and they find it strange that Jekyll had the cheval glass brought into his study where it did not belong. Jekyll must have obviously used it to observe his full figure transformations into Hyde. Poole whispers to Utterson, "This glass has seen some strange things, sir."

(Mirror images and illusions are an important part of the *Jekyll and Hyde* story. Mirrors distort our image and turn it around on us. The mirror life is so mysterious that in many cultures the mirror is feared. Cocteau used this image in his cult movie *Orpheus* in which one moves into the strange life inside the mirror. Many fables, such as the story of Snow White, contain references to the magic and fear of mirrors. In a short note, Jekyll confesses to being in a "nameless situation," referring to his strange relationship with Hyde, and he advises Utterson to read Dr. Lanyon's narrative.)

The Lanyon document reveals that, in early January, Lanyon had received a message from Jekyll asking for "some powders, a phial, and a paper book" from Jekyll's own laboratory to hand over to a messenger. At midnight the messenger, who is Hyde, arrives, mixes the chemicals in a glass, and asks to leave. Lanyon, however, demands that Hyde stay and even brandishes a pistol to detain him. Issuing a dire warning, Hyde drinks the potion and gradually turns into Henry Jekyll. Lanyon concludes, "The creature who crept into my house that night was, upon Jekyll's own confession, known by the name of Hyde and hunted for in every corner of the land as the murderer of Carew."

At the end of the novella is "Henry Jekyll's full statement of the case." Utterson reads Jekyll's own story of the main events, which appears as if it could have come from the pen of Deacon Brodie. For example, Jekyll confesses that he was born into a rich family and was "inclined by nature to industry, fond of the respect of the wise and good among my fellow-men, and thus, as might have been supposed, with every guarantee of an honourable and distinguished future."

In addition, Jekyll claims, "The worst of my faults was a certain impatient gaiety of disposition." The terms *gaiety* and *gay* were clearly used in the nineteenth century to indicate "addicted to social pleasures and dissipations." Jekyll admits that he "found it hard to reconcile" his self-professed gaiety of disposition "with my impervious desire to carry my head high, and wear a more commonly grave countenance before the public." Brodie led a similar life. Both hid their pursuits of pleasure under the mask of outward respectability of dress and demeanor. Both tried to deceive the public, as well as their families and close associates.

Jekyll's own research has led him to try to fathom what Stevenson called, "the perennial war among my members," meaning the conflicting feelings he sensed within himself. Jekyll concludes his final statement with the tragic words, "I bring the life of that unhappy Henry Jekyll to an end."

CHAPTER SIX

Hyde, the Beast Within Us

The wild beast, which lives in man and does not dare show itself until the barriers of law and custom have been removed, was now set free.

—Ivo Andric, *The Bridge on the Drina*
(1977)

Who is Hyde? One main appeal of the novella is that it is so ambiguous that no single interpretation entirely explains the tale. It lives up to its title as a "strange case." For example, Stevenson wanted his tale to expose hypocrisy: Jekyll appears to be a hypocrite, however, in his own "final statement of the case" he asserts, "I was in no sense a hypocrite." Is he telling the truth, or is he lying? No one can tell. But we all do know that it is typical for hypocrites to deny that they are. Hence, one cannot take such statements at their face value. Much of what is said and described is shrouded in mystery, denial, and secrecy. Stevenson himself, consciously or unconsciously, seems to have imbedded a number of clues in the story, which suggest ways to interpret the story and the true nature of Mr. Hyde. Indeed, the form of the story, told by several narrators, suggests that he means for us to interpret Hyde in several ways simultaneously. The *Jekyll and Hyde* story clearly touches upon the following central themes: the need to acknowledge and accommodate the base instincts within all humans, drug addiction, and the fear of the double.

Clues

According to Stevenson's own words quoted in an interview with New York reporters in 1887 and one in 1888 with San Francisco reporters, the name *Jekyll* should be pronounced with an initial long *e* hence "Geekill" not "Dzeckle" or "Jeckel" the way one often hears it. Stevenson knew French, so this suggests that the surname might signify "*Je* kill" meaning "*I* kill" and hence the title of the novel could be read simply as "I Kill and Hide." Mr. Hyde is obviously one who hides. *Hide* in Scottish refers to "an animal's skin, or is applied with pejorative force to female domestic animals and to women," according to the *Scottish National Dictionary.* Lest this investigation into Stevenson's choice of words be thought pointless, the fact that Stevenson enjoyed playing on words is clear from the novel when he has Gabriel Utterson say, "If he be Mr. Hyde, . . . I shall be Mr. Seek." So Utterson's search for Hyde is like the hide-and-seek children's game. Hyde has hidden, and Utterson is determined to find him, "ready or not"!

In the novella Dr. Lanyon's first name is "Hastie" meaning "rash." He is the one who impetuously wants to witness Jekyll's transformation into Hyde with subsequent disastrous consequences. The character Enfield is Utterson's "distant kinsman" and a "man about town" meaning a kind of social butterfly. The walks of the two men are called "rambles," which, according to Samuel Johnson's 1755 dictionary, meant, "to wander loosely in lust." The typical "man about town," Enfield strangely returns from "some place at the end of the world" in the city at three o'clock in the morning! The reader is left to guess what Enfield himself has been up to before that. The last name of the primary narrator, Gabriel Utterson, may mean only that he is the one who speaks (and thereby breaks the silence being kept by several of the characters). His first name is that of the archangel who is God's messenger.

Stevenson dedicated his *Jekyll and Hyde* story to his closest and most gifted female relative, his cousin, Katharine de Mattos née Stevenson. As a youngster he had played happily with his dearest cousin Katharine, when they raced ponies during summer holidays at Peebles and North Berwick along the Scottish coast. Katharine visited Skerryvore often, while Stevenson was writing his *Strange Case of Dr. Jekyll and Mr. Hyde*. He sent her a presentation copy of his *Strange Case of Dr. Jekyll and Mr. Hyde* on January 1, 1886. The dedication was a modified version of the second stanza of his poem "Ave." The words of the dedication are important, because they reveal clues to some of the essential meanings hidden in the story:

> It's ill to loose the bands that God decreed to bind
> Still will we be the children of the heather and the wind
> Far away from home, O it's still for you and me
> That the broom is blowing bonnie in the north countrie.

The first line of the poem echoes in the Scottish idiom the timing of the biblical phrase, "What God has joined together, let no man put asunder," or "It's evil to try to separate what God ordained to be united in one." Humans thus learn to live with the often contradictory selves within them, as ordained by God. Hence, Dr. Jekyll is wrong in trying to disengage his lower self, Hyde, from himself. In the subsequent lines, Stevenson reminds his cousin of their common Scottish heritage from which they cannot escape. They must remain "children of the heather and the wind," and the "broom," a wildflower of the Scottish countryside, "the north country," continues to lure them back home no matter how far away they go.

Hyde and the Unconscious

The tale predates Freud's work but supplies the classic Freudian case of a person caught between seemingly irreconcilable tendencies—the demands of the unconscious self and the desires of the ego. Jekyll is trapped by "the lower elements in his soul" and the demands of polite society. In *Civilization and Its Discontents,* Freud felt that in the modern world the price of the social progress of civilization is paid for by individual sexual repression and unhappiness. These pent-up sexual desires generally erupt in acts of violence. The more Jekyll tries to suppress the Hyde within him, the more his Hyde side comes to dominate. Even Jekyll's initial ambivalence toward Hyde can be seen as typical of schizophrenic patients.

Jekyll confesses that Hyde "was knit to him closer than a wife." Because Jekyll and Hyde are two persons in one, however, one could argue that Jekyll is essentially in love with himself, like Narcissus. When speaking of Hyde, Jekyll avers, "This, too, was myself." Hence, it is not the typical Calvinist dualism of soul versus body; the story is about good and evil within all men. In his 1927 book on Stevenson the Anglo-Catholic writer G. K. Chesterton brilliantly noted, "The real stab of the story is not the discovery that one man is two men; but in the discovery that the two men are one man." So, it is not Jekyll or Hyde, but Jekyll and Hyde together.

Operating on his premise that there is a primitive duality in all men, Jekyll, who is drawn both to good and ill, erroneously intended to try to separate the good and the bad for the benefit of humanity, because he assumed that, once freed of the bad side, the good side of man could soar to incredible heights. Through the use of a potion, however, Jekyll releases the Hyde within him, and Jekyll gradually realizes that his evil side is no longer under his control. It is psychologically significant that the repressed Hyde comes to the surface usually when Jekyll is relaxing, because it indicates that when Jekyll has his rational guard down, his sensual side (Hyde) emerges. (Freud's theories of id, ego, and superego are based on observation of unguarded, vulnerable moments in the lives of his clients.) For example, the second transformation into Hyde occurs when Jekyll is resting in the park and later, after Jekyll has fallen asleep, he awakens as Hyde. But the moral balances of the story are more complicated than Jekyll suggests. Unlike what one sees in the many film adaptations of the story, Dr. Jekyll is *not* a virtuous man. The patently evil Jekyll uses his doctor status as a mask for his secret pursuit of vice as Hyde.

In Stevenson's first draft of the story, Jekyll's main intention apparently was to create Hyde in order to carry out his own evil desires. After Fanny expressed her disgust with the sensationalism of the story, Stevenson apparently added the moralistic motives such as Jekyll wanting to be a benefactor of mankind and his feelings of guilt as expressed in his last "statement of the case." He vaguely claimed that the new Jekyll "had always been known for his charities."

Hyde may be evil, ugly, and bestial, but to Jekyll, he is desirable. Jekyll likes turning into Hyde, whereas, after committing a crime, Hyde wants to turn into Jekyll only in order to avoid the gallows. Jekyll is guilty of "moral insanity." Jekyll represents upper-middle-class society with its emphasis on "appearances." He is "a large, well-made, smooth-faced man of fifty, with something of a slyish cast perhaps, but every mark of capacity and kindness." So, Jekyll is a hefty man, whereas Hyde is smaller in stature. This fact presents problems in the novel, because when Jekyll turns into Hyde, the clothes are obviously too big for Hyde. Hyde is Jekyll's mask. Jekyll's valet, Poole, tells Utterson about Hyde, "Sir, if that was my master, why had he a mask upon his face?"

Hyde is also out to overturn the traditional values of Victorian society. He is a young social upstart like the historical Napoleon. It is not by chance that Stendahl's Julien Sorel in *The Red and the Black* (1830) is an admirer of Napoleon, as is Raskolnikov in Dostoevsky's *Crime and Punishment,* which Stevenson was reading in French exactly while he was composing his *Jekyll and Hyde* story. In fact, Stevenson declared that *Crime and Punishment* was easily the greatest book he had read in a decade. Jekyll finds that Hyde represents "my lust for evil gratified and stimulated, my love of life screwed to the topmost peg." Thus, Jekyll also experiences "a cold thrill of terror" arising from worries that his double life might be uncovered. It should be remembered that Stevenson's model, Deacon Brodie, also committed his crimes not for money but for the thrill of getting away with them and worried intensely about being discovered.

Hyde could also be the son whom Jekyll never had. The other males are afraid of showing their emotions, but Hyde is not. The character of Hyde may mask several other identities: Hyde could be a caricature of Douglas Hyde, the Irish rebel, and of the fighting Irish hooligan generally. Irish were often portrayed as childish, emotionally unstable, apelike, and violent. The threat of Fenianism and the Irish home rule controversy split the British Liberal Party in 1886. The Carew murder in the novel echoes the brutal murder of Lord Frederick Cavendish, secretary for Ireland, and Mr. Burke, the undersecretary, in Dublin in 1882, known as the Phoenix Park Murders. The Invincibles, a radical offshoot of the Fenians, purchased special Sheffield knives abroad and used them to carve up their two victims. It was front-page news in British newspapers and remained a political thorn in the side of the Irish Nationalist leader and politician Charles Stewart Parnell (who favored Irish home rule and peace with England) as late as 1890.

Hyde and Addiction

The powders taken by Jekyll, which represent such an important element of the story of the transformation into Hyde, should more properly be attributed to the drug laudanum, or any of many other drugs in Louis's pharmacy chest that he used to ease his pain or stop the hemorrhaging. Jekyll's drug or potion may be seen only as a convenient vehicle for him to release his dormant evil tendencies. It is not the potion alone that turns Jekyll into Hyde. Jekyll was leading a double life long before he took the potion, as is evidenced by his own statements in the novella. The story is not purely scientific, but rather a blend of science and non-science. Hence the tale is often properly characterized as science fiction, like Mary Shelley's *Frankenstein*.

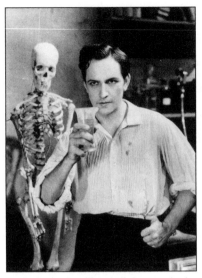

Frederic March as Dr. Jekyll about to drink the potion. (BETTMANN/CORBIS)

Like a bad habit, over time, Jekyll inadvertently, and without the use of the drug, succumbs more and more to Hyde. Jekyll worries about this and confesses, "At all hours of the day or night, I would be taken with the premonitory shudder, above all, if I slept, or even dozed for a moment in my chair, it was always as Hyde that I awakened. . . . I became . . . solely occupied by one thought: the horror of my other self. . . . The powers of Hyde seemed to have grown with the sickliness of Jekyll. And certainly the hate that now divided them was equal on each side." As Jekyll puts it in the novel, "Yes, I had gone to bed Henry Jekyll, I had awakened Edward Hyde."

Double doses of that second concoction of the drug are needed to turn Hyde back into Jekyll, because Jekyll is becoming an addict. As in the case of much drug addiction, Jekyll experiences the unheralded "return trips," which he comes to fear, because he has lost control of the Hyde within him. Stevenson wanted to make the involuntary change from Jekyll into Hyde an essential part of the story.

There is some alchohol drinking and drug addiction in the novel. Utterson likes an occasional gin and old mellow wine, whereas Jekyll prefers his own brews. Jekyll also calls his drug a "potion," a "draught," and a "mixture." Upper-crust Victorian society was drug-ridden. One was accustomed to taking regular doses of laudanum, a type of red-colored tincture akin to opium, the way one consumes aspirin today for common headaches. When Jekyll first transforms into Hyde, he compares the experience to the pleasure of drinking wine, "I felt younger, lighter, and happier in body; within I was conscious of a heady recklessness . . . sold a slave to my original evil; and the thought, in that moment, braced and delighted me like wine."

Like most of the male characters in his *Jekyll and Hyde* tale, Louis enjoyed good wine, whiskey, and pleasant conversation with male friends. He also experimented with drugs—a common practice among the British upper class, many of whom were unaware of actually being addicts. Stevenson frequently ingested an alcoholic tincture of opium, which usually contained a trace of morphine. The *Jekyll and Hyde* addiction was familiar to him in real life. Hyde, when confronting Lanyon, speaks like a typical drug addict. He impatiently demands, "Have you got it? Have you got it?" Once Lanyon has turned the drug over to Hyde, Hyde challenges, "And now, you who have so long been bound to the most narrow and material views, you who have denied the virtue of transcendental medicine, you who have derided your superiors—behold!" Before Lanyon's eyes Hyde takes the drug and becomes Jekyll.

One of the moral messages in the novel is that like Richard Wagner's late 1850s opera *Tristan und Isolde,* the *Strange Case of Dr. Jekyll and Mr. Hyde* is also about taboo love. In Wagner's opera (as in the legend upon which the work is based), Tristan has been sent by his lord of Cornwall to pick up and deliver Isolde, but the two fall in love and instruct the maidservant Brangane to administer a death potion to both. Brangane gets the love potion mixed up with the death potion and inadvertently gives the love potion to Tristan and Isolde. This drug releases them from their restraints and allows them to consummate their forbidden love. The potion, however, is not the cause of their consummation, merely a condition, just as the sail of a sailboat is not the cause but the condition for sailing, and the wind is the cause. In the case of Tristan and Isolde, their love is the cause.

Jekyll is an addict. His main tragedy is that he cannot accept the fact that he has a complex, sometimes even contradictory, personality. Jekyll erroneously thinks that he can stay in control of Hyde and that he can get rid of Hyde whenever he wishes. But he cannot. Even though Jekyll protests in the end that Hyde is "another than myself," Jekyll is Hyde. In Oscar Wilde's novel *The Portrait of Dorian Gray,* Dorian Gray, like Jekyll, also confesses his interest in transforming drugs, because he "had always been enthralled by the methods of natural science, but the ordinary subject-matter of that science had seemed to him trivial and of no import. And so he had begun by vivisecting himself, as he had ended by vivisecting others." Like Jekyll, Dorian Gray intends to go beyond the mundane science of his day and move into the realm of the transcendental, into the realm of what we today call science fiction.

Hyde and Sexuality

There is a great deal of sexuality in the novel, but it is ambiguous. References are made to *queer* and *gay,* but their specific meaning in the context is not always clear, even though several scholars have noted that at least by 1900 the homosexual meaning of the word *queer* had already entered English slang. But the vagueness appears to be a deliberate ploy on the part of the author to tantalize the reader. One cannot confirm exactly what these references mean, but one cannot deny them either. The homosexual interpretation is not the *only* interpretation, but it is a possible one, as supported by some textual evidence. All of the main characters in the novel are middle-aged bachelors. Their only relationship to women is that of lord to servant. All of the males are seemingly celibate, which might partially account for their pent-up emotions. Jekyll's only attachment is not to any woman, but to his old male friends, Utterson and Lanyon, and especially to young Edward Hyde. The narrative is grounded in the atmosphere of English men's clubs, where women were always excluded.

In his notebook now preserved in the Beinecke Collection at Yale University Library, Stevenson has Jekyll admit, "I became in secret the slave of disgraceful pleasures" that led on to "a mire of vices," which were "criminal in the sight of the law and abhorrent in themselves." The line "my life was double" are crossed out in the manuscript. The main criminal vice on the minds of most readers at the time was "gross indecency with a male person," which had been discussed in great detail in Parliament in 1885 and had led to the Henry Labouchère amendment making "gross indecency" between males a criminal act. It can only be assumed that Stevenson was fully cognizant of the parliamentary debate.

During the nineteenth century, manliness was considered to be the opposite of childishness, not of womanliness. A young male was expected to grow up and develop from being an irresponsible child to becoming a responsible "real" man. A boy might have some homosexual relations in public schools (which were private), but he was expected to grow out of that. His elders warned him "to pull himself together." It was unspeakable that any male should be womanly. On the opposite side of the sexual spectrum

Queen Victoria, could not even conceive of any woman actually being a lesbian. So, for the queen, lesbianism simply did not exist, and, therefore, there was no reason to ban it. Male homosexuality, however, was taboo and outlawed.

It is not by chance that Wilde (1854–1900) greatly admired Stevenson and referred to him as "that delicate artist in language" (letter to Oswald Sickert, dated May 1892). In his essay "The Decay of Lying," Wilde called Stevenson specifically "that delightful master of delicate and fanciful prose" (*The Complete Works of Oscar Wilde,* Vol. V, p. 15).

Living a double life was especially typical for Victorian homosexuals. In Oscar Wilde's 1899 satirical play *The Importance of Being Earnest,* living the double life is called "Bunburying." Wilde, like Stevenson, loved doubles. In *The Importance of Being Earnest,* Wilde treated doubling, or "Bunburying," comically, but had treated it seriously in *The Portrait of Dorian Gray* (1891). In that book Lord Henry Wotton often sounds like the cynical Brodie of Stevenson's early play. The main character, Dorian Gray, resembles Jekyll and Hyde: He lives by day in a respectable mansion in the upper-class part of London, but he also maintains living quarters in the seedy part of the city. Dorian Gray is able to give full vent to his evil desires, because he wears a special kind of mask. His portrait bears the evidence of his evil deeds. In the end of Wilde's story, Dorian stabs the portrait and dies, as Jekyll dies at the end of Stevenson's novella.

A constant battle is going on among the parts of a divided self in the story. As for the seemly strange union of Jekyll and Hyde, as Stevenson wrote, "It was the curse of mankind that these incongruous faggots were thus bound together." Such a tormented life of double identities in one man must of necessity, end in suicide, in Stevenson's view.

There is a lot of play on naming things and not naming them in Stevenson's story. For example, Jekyll writes to Utterson, "I have brought on myself a punishment and a danger that I cannot name. If I am chief of sinners, I am chief of sufferers also. I could not think that this earth contained a place for sufferings and terrors so unmanning." Jekyll's mention of "a danger that I cannot name" has the uncanny ring of "the love that dared not say its name," that is, male homosexuality. In addition, all of the main characters find Hyde disgusting, because there was something "unspeakable" about him; "unspeakable" was already a code name for a Victorian homosexual. Jekyll warns his lawyer Utterson, "I am painfully situated, Utterson; my position is a very strange—a very strange one. It is one of those affairs that cannot be mended by talking." Jekyll further confesses, "I have really a great interest in poor Hyde. I know you have seen him; he told me so; and I fear he was rude. But I do sincerely take a great, a very great interest in that young man." Utterson is so upset that he needs to confront Hyde, so that, "He might see a reason for his friend's strange preference or bondage (call it what you please)."

Two of Stevenson's friends, Edmund Gosse and John Addington Symonds, were homosexuals. The latter objected to *Dr. Jekyll and Mr. Hyde* and wrote to Stevenson, "I doubt whether anyone has a right to scrutinize the abysmal depths of personality. . . . At least I think he ought to bring more of the distinct belief in the resources of human nature, more faith, more sympathy with our frailty. . . . I seem to have lost you so utterly that I can afford to fling truth of the crudest in your face. And yet I love you and think of you daily."

For their creations, most writers draw upon those persons whom they have met in life, but, generally, no character in a novel is an exact representation of a historical personage. Most personages in literature are composites. Concerning the character of Gabriel Utterson, George Balfour asserts that the Stevenson family legal adviser Mr. Mowbray, "a grim, dry, warm-hearted old bachelor was, I have always fancied, the original of Mr. Utterson." For example, like Utterson, Mowbray was a tolerant fellow. He put up with young Stevenson's eccentricities, including Stevenson's avowed atheism and rebellion against his father.

Stevenson's favorite male cousin Robert A. M. Stevenson, whom Louis fondly called Bob, introduced Louis to some fellow painters including one big, yellow-bearded, good-looking woman-izer named Enfield, who turns up as Stevenson's "man about town" and Utterson's friend in the *Strange Case of Dr. Jekyll and Mr. Hyde*.

Long before Jekyll releases the Hyde within him, he has been leading a double life of outward respectability but actual lowlife behind closed doors, much like Deacon Brodie did in real life. Stevenson declared that Hyde "was not good-looking . . . and not, great gods, a mere voluptuary. There is no harm in a voluptuary; and none, with my hand on my heart and in the sight of God, none—no harm whatever—in what prurient fools call 'immor-tality'. The harm was in Jekyll, because he was a hypocrite—not because he was fond of women; he says so himself; but people are so filled of folly and inverted lust, that they can think of nothing but sexuality." Stevenson did not wish Hyde to be seen as sexually active. "Hyde," Stevenson claims, "is no more sensual than another." In fact, Hyde is only like a "sedulous ape," that is, a hard-working animal, the very same epithet that Stevenson gave to himself.

Hyde is also a kind of man-beast, a sort of werewolf. Hyde is evil not simply because of some sexual proclivities, but due to "the essence of cruelty and malice, and selfishness and cowardice, and these are the diabolic in man." Hyde is "drinking pleasure with bestial avidity from any degree of torture to another." He is also "relentless like a man of stone." Hyde is superhuman "like Satan." The fear of a reversion in the evolutionary process troubled Victorian society. Hyde is a throwback, an example of atavism. Because humans came from animals, why not a possible reversion to beast-like behavior? He is the Darwinian "missing link" between ape and *homo sapien.*

Hyde is wild like a child. Utterson fears that "poor Henry Jekyll" is in deep trouble, due to the fact that "He was wild when he was young." A young British male was expected to "sow his wild oats" as a young man, but then grow up to become a responsible adult, but Hyde had remained a child. Just as Jekyll is neither completely good or bad, nor is Hyde completely bad or good. He only kills one man, Sir Danvers Carew; Hyde, however, eventually develops into a kind of sadist who loves to see others suffer. Nonetheless, Jekyll says about Hyde, "But his love of life is wonderful; I go further: I, who sicken and freeze at the mere thought of him, when I recall the abjection and passion of this attachment, and when I know how he fears my power to cut him off by suicide, I find in my heart to pity him." Hyde, however, knows Jekyll's moods better than Jekyll knows those of Hyde.

Stevenson's fiction also reveals a life-long personal preoccupation with the relations of father to son. Jekyll specifically refers to Hyde as his "son." Stevenson's own father was a domineering patriarch, whom Stevenson evidently both hated and admired. In the novel Hyde attacks fatherly authority not only by burning the letters of Jekyll's father but also by destroying the portrait of Jekyll's father, which all appear to be part of a secret wish of Stevenson himself.

Though young Stevenson formally forsook his father and family and turned his back on his past, he turned out to resemble his father especially toward the end of his life. In his last novel, *The Weir of Hermiston*—still unfinished at the time of his death in 1894—the focus of the narrative is upon the difficult relationship between an authoritarian father and his son who is seeking an identity.

The great Russian critic Vladimir Nabokov, famous author of *Lolita,* the tale of a middle-aged man lusting after a nubile female teenager, wanted readers to forget about classifying Stevenson's story as a detective story. In the opinion of the present authors, however, the tale can be read as a detective story. There is a puzzle to be solved concerning the facts of a strange case. The plot revolves around the need to solve the puzzle. There is the intrepid investigator in the person of the lawyer Gabriel Utterson who goes in search of Hyde, like a Sherlock Holmes.

The Double

The German writer Jean Paul Richter coined the word *Doppelt-gänger* in 1796, which is defined as "one who sees himself" (later the *t* was dropped from the middle of the word). When one sees another person exactly like oneself, one is doomed to die.

In his essay "The Uncanny," Sigmund Freud explores the notion of the *heimlich,* meaning "homey," as contrasted with *unheimlich,* signifying "unhomey" or "uncanny." It is the recognition of that which should have remained hidden. The alter ego is essentially an evil omen. The double is at first a yearning for impossible immortality and then becomes the fear of death itself.

Fyodor Dostoevsky (1821–1881), often dubbed "the father of the psychological novel" was, like Stevenson, intrigued by the notion of the double. In 1865 he presented his revised story entitled *The Double. A Petersburg Poem*. The subject germinated in the Russian author's mind for a long time. Dostoevsky was under the influence of "The Nose," one of the most original and disturbing stories in literature written by his predecessor Nikolai Gogol (1809–1852). It is a tale of a man "split in two." In "The Nose" a man wakes up one morning, and his nose is gone. He looks under the bed to see if it rolled off during the night, but he cannot find it. He is embarrassed. What can he tell his friends when they see only skin where his nose used to be and they ask, "What happened to you?" In desperation the hero goes to the lost-and-found section of the police to report his missing nose, but the local bureaucrat berates him as a suspicious revolutionary or madman. While walking along the Nevsky Prospect, the main avenue in Petersburg, he sees his nose all dressed up in a major's uniform. The nose is his double. The dressed-up nose goes into a local chapel to have a rendezvous with a lovely woman. So the nose is not only on a higher level than he in society, but his nose is also more successful with women. How humiliating! The double is frighteningly better than the hero himself.

Originally Dostoevsky called his own doubles' tale "The Adventures of Mr. Golyadkin." Like Stevenson's *Jekyll and Hyde,* Dostoevsky's tale is one of gradual mental derangement. Mr. Golyadkin, who admits that he has "no strength of character" and is repressed, engenders Mr. Golyadkin Jr., just as Jekyll gave birth to Hyde whom he called his "son." The young Golyadkin is, like Hyde, "the personification of baseness." Golyadkin senior's double allows him to release his suppressed desires, just as Jekyll's transformation into Hyde permits Jekyll to vent his basic emotions. And, just as Hyde threatens to dominate Jekyll, so the young

Golyadkin is a threat to the very existence of Golyadkin senior. Like most doubles, he is the herald of death.

In his short story entitled "Markheim," which Stevenson wrote about the same time as his *Jekyll and Hyde* tale, a disturbed intellectual kills a greedy antique dealer, much in the way Dostoevsky's Raskolnikov kills the stingy old woman in *Crime and Punishment*. In fact, the Stevenson story can be seen as a transformation of the Dostoevsky tale to a Calvinist English setting. Markheim feels that God, who knows all things, will forgive him. Like Raskolnikov he accepts responsibility for his crime. Even when Markheim is offered a chance to escape by a person who may be the devil or his own double, Markheim prefers to confess his crime. He has a way out of his dilemma, namely suicide, as in the case of *Jekyll and Hyde*. Markheim says, "If I be condemned to evil acts, there is still one door of freedom open—I can cease from action. If my life be an ill thing, I can lay it down."

The character of Shakespeare's Crookback, King Richard III, also influenced Stevenson's portrayal of Hyde. Concerning the monstrously evil hunchback Stevenson wrote, "He is a fellow whose hellish energy has always fixed my attention" (letter to Sidney Colvin, October 1883, in the Tusitala edition.) Both Freudians and Jungians hold that it is dangerous for any human to try to repress that "hellish energy" which is Hyde and is within each of us. Jekyll attempts to do so and goes mad, but the character from Shakespeare Hyde most resembles is Caliban from the *Tempest,* a savage, monstrous, lyrical, "mooncalf" who acts from pure unrestrained impulse.

One of Stevenson's contemporaries, Christina Rosetti (1830–1894), a great poet, had a similarly terrifying vision of a double: While she was in her great room at All Saints Hospital in Eastbourne, England, on the "paperless bare wall" she noticed a spider frightened by his double: "That spider saw, without recognizing, his black double, and was mad to disengage himself from the horrible pursuing presence . . . To me that self-haunted spider appears as a figure of each obstinate impenitent sinner, who, having outlived enjoyment, remains isolated irretrievably with his own loathsome self." Joseph Conrad's *The Secret Sharer: An Episode from the Coast* (1910) is another tale about a double, similar to Stevenson's story. The main character is identified simply as the captain of a ship, which is unfamiliar to him, and where there is "no sign of human habitation as far as the eye could reach." He feels uneasy and alienated from himself, his ship, and his environment. There is no wind. No sound. He feels like a stranger. Out of nowhere appears a swimmer named Leggatt who comes aboard and turns out to be the captain's doppelgänger. The captain calls him his "secret self" or "second self," his "double" or "the secret sharer of [his] life." He shields and protects his double, similar to the ways in which Jekyll at first protects Hyde. The captain, however, knows that he must let his double go eventually. So, he helps Leggatt swim away from the ship in violation of the law. The captain then tosses his hat in the sea, as if "it was saving the ship, by serving me for a mark to help out the ignorance of my strangeness."

In his final statement of the case Jekyll declares, "Man is not truly one, but truly two." To which a wag might counter, "What! Only two?" However, Stevenson has Jekyll become prophetic when he claims that he is scientifically ahead of his times with his research and that one day the individual will be seen as "a mere polity of multifarious, incongruous, and independent denizens." It is no wonder then that Stevenson's popularization of the fascinating psychological notion of multiple personalities persists today.

Advertisement for the Jekyll and Hyde Pub, Hanover Street, Edinburgh. (RAYMOND T. MCNALLY)

The *Jekyll and Hyde* theme echoes throughout history, because most humans often sense the presence of a double inside themselves. So the *Strange Case of Dr. Jekyll and Mr. Hyde* applies not just to politicians and writers but to most of us, saints and sinners. Some of us succeed in suppressing inner evil tendencies (often with problematic psychological results), while others sometimes fail. But we all recognize the importance of the human struggle between good and evil. Most of us fight the battle on a daily basis with our innermost selves. That is part of the reason why Stevenson's *Jekyll and Hyde* tale continues to appeal to generation after generation. Reading about Jekyll and his Hyde and the presence of the double in us allows most of us to experience both pity and fear vicariously, so that the real Hyde within us does not need to emerge and walk down our city streets or countryside in broad daylight.

CHAPTER SEVEN

Sunset in the South Seas, 1888–1894

Here he lies where he longed to be,
Home is the sailor, home from the sea,
And the hunter, home from the hill.

> —Last three lines of the poem *Requiem*
> (1879), on Stevenson's gravestone at
> Vailima in Samoa

In the late mid-1800s Sam McClure, the editor of the *New York Sun,* asked Stevenson to write a series of voyage letters from the exotic South Seas in the Pacific. He would pay the author $15,000. Fanny immediately seized upon this opportunity.

She rented a magnificent ninety-four-foot schooner named the *Casco* with luxury appointments and embarked with Louis, Maggie, Lloyd, and the inescapable Valentine Roch on June 28, 1888, with six sailors on board. For Louis it was to be a voyage during which he confronted every possible danger. The ship set sail from San Francisco to the Marquise Islands, the Fakarava Lagoon, Tahiti (reached at the beginning of October), Papeete, the Sandwich Islands, and, finally, Hawaii by January 1889, where Valentine and Maggie disembarked to return to Scotland. The rest of the party continued the journey on the Schooner *Equator,* leaving the Honolulu Islands for Butaritari, Apemana, and, finally, the capital of Upola, Apia, in the Samoa archipelago. There Louis bought a 314-acre jungle estate called Vailima. The island's only link to civilization was a boat that stopped once a month at Apia on its journey from San Francisco to Sydney, Australia. It was on this isolated island that Louis finally regained some of his health and a new productive lease on life. Every time he left the Island for Australia or elsewhere, he relapsed into his habitual spells which had so affected him at Bournemouth. In essence he had become a prisoner of this island, doomed to spend the rest of his life among the natives until his death in 1894, three years before Stoker published his book *Dracula.* At first Louis was content building a small cottage, but eventually he constructed the largest and most luxurious house on the island with bathrooms and running water. The project soon swallowed up his substantial resources.

RLS and his family in Honolulu 1888. (THE WRITERS' MUSEUM, EDINBURGH)

As they heard of Louis's decision to stay at Vailima, surrounded by natives and involved in local politics (the Island was under a triple German, British, and American protectorate), his friends thought that Louis had lost his mind. In fact, it was Fanny who became the problem, both physically and emotionally, in that she gradually drifted toward insanity. In contrast, Louis experienced one of the most productive and enriching periods of his literary career, a bit comparable with the Bournemouth phase.

However, it is interesting to note that in spite of his immersion in local politics and fondness for his new home, which his friends could not understand, Louis

RLS at Vailima. The last photograph taken of him. (THE WRITERS' MUSEUM, EDINBURGH)

remained an exile from his beloved Scotland at heart. Writing to Baxter, who had become his agent he stated, "You are still—as I first saw you in the venerable city which I must always think as my home . . . the sights and thoughts of my youth pursue me and I see like a vision the youth of my father and of his father and the whole stream of lives flowing down there far in the north with the wound of laughter and tears come to cast me to it in the end on this ultimate island and I bow my head before the romance of destiny." As he gazed upon the vast expanse of the blue Pacific Ocean, Cummy's baby did not forget his old nurse and liked to reminisce about the past. "Do you remember when you used to take me out of bed in the early morning to show me the hills of Fife even though the dawn of morning may have seemed brown." He told Colvin, "The sound of rain beating on the roof" of his Vailima house was sweet to him because it was "all smells of the good wet earth with a kind of Highland touch." In Apemana Louis wrote some very nostalgic verses:

The tropics vanish and me seems that I

From Halkerside, from topmost Alemuir

Or steep Caerketton, dreaming gaze again

Far set in fields and woods the town I see

Spring gallant from the shallows of her smoke

Cragged spired and turreted, her virgin for

Beflagged

To Baxter again he reminisced about the Edinburgh of his early years:

You remember—can we e'er forget

How in the soiled perplexities of youth

In our wild climate, in our scowling town

We gloomed and shivered, sorrowed, sobbed and feared

The rare and welcome silence of the snows

The laggard morn, the haggard day and night

The grimy spell of the nocturnal town

Do you remember and could one forget?

Even in books inspired by the South Seas, such as *The Wrecker*—serialized in 1891 and 1892—completed at Apia in collaboration with Lloyd, Louis inserted sections on Paris and memories of an artist's life at Fontainebleau and Barbizon.

Stevenson's nostalgia for Scotland is best expressed in his works on Scottish themes on the island, even though he would have liked to write on many more such as his family history—real or imagined—linking his forebears to Scottish heroes of the past such as the MacGregors and the Robroys. He was interested in all the legends exploited by Sir Walter Scott in spite of his friend's assertions that one could not write about Scotland on a Pacific island. If *St. Ives,* written in collaboration with Lloyd, was left unfinished, and *Castronia* (1892) titled *David Balfour* in the American edition, was finally completed "intent only on race and place." Louis wrote *The Weir of Hermiston,* a magnificent but unfinished piece and dedicated it to his wife. *The Weir of Hermiston,* which was published posthumously in 1896, was closely modeled on Lord Braxfield, Brodie's hanging judge.

Concerning Stevenson's *Ballads,* the literary critic Sir Edmund Gosse (1845–1928) was perhaps unfairly critical of such efforts. "I confess we are all disappointed. The effort to become a 'Polynesian' after Scott is a little too obvious, the inspiration too mechanical . . . it is very nice to live in Samoa but not healthy to write there." Both Louis and Fanny were deeply hurt by reactions of this kind—particularly Fanny who was suspected of having staged and planned Louis's exile to the South Seas.

Nor was Skerryvore, the birthplace of *Jekyll and Hyde,* ever far from his thoughts and correspondence. Initially Stevenson planned to establish a trading company with his stepson Lloyd called "Jekyll and Hyde and Company." By a quirk of fate, he was involved in attacking a certain Reverend C. M. Hyde who had questioned the personal ethics of a Catholic missionary called Father Damian. Bringing his furniture from Skerryvore to fill his far more grandiose mansion at Vailima—a most expensive undertaking—stretched his finances to the limit. Louis undoubtedly wished to establish a tangible link with the location that had produced his most famous book *Jekyll and Hyde.* Indeed he often thought of Skerryvore, the rhododendron garden, the West Cliff, and the blackbirds in the Chine Hill. (Skerryvore was later destroyed by Nazi bombs during World War II.)

He also paid a final tribute to his father's family by hanging in the living room a large picture of the famous lighthouse that had given its name to the Bournemouth house. Agnostic since the age of seventeen, Stevenson further evoked memories of family life at Heriot Row by reciting regular prayers together with his mother, Maggie, and the rest of his extended family. This image may well epitomize the last Samoan version of Louis's double existence. He had assumed the role of *pater familias* much like his father.

Stevenson may have had a premonition when he wrote to Baxter, "I shall never see Auld Reekie, I shall never set my foot again upon the heather, Here I am until I die and here I will be buried." On Monday, December 6, 1894, toward sunset at Vailima, his estate in Samoa, Stevenson went down into his cellar to get a bottle of his favorite Burgundy wine. According to one version, after uncorking the bottle in the kitchen, he suddenly screamed to his wife, "What's the matter with me? What's this strangeness? Has my face changed?" Why was he afraid that his face had changed? Was he worried that in the end, like a Jekyll, he himself had turned into a Hyde? He left us with yet another enigma. All that we know for certain is that a blood vessel had burst in his brain and that he died a few hours later from a cerebral hemorrhage at 8:10 P.M. He was a young man, only forty years of age.

All his life Stevenson fantasized about becoming a sailor or a hunter, but his weak health would not allow him to become either. Stevenson, like Mozart, remained emotionally and physically a child in need of nursing all of his life. However, he enriched our lives as a great storyteller; at his gravesite on top of neighboring Mount Vaea an aged native chief turned toward the grave and intoned, "Tofa tusitala, tofa tusitala" meaning "Sleep, O teller of tales, sleep, O teller of tales" in Samoan, a language that Stevenson had learned. On his gravestone are the revealing verses of his famous poem *Requiem,* from which the lines at the beginning of the chapter are taken:

> Under the wide and starry sky,
> Dig the grave and let me lie.
> Glad did I live and gladly die,
> And I laid me down with a will.
> This be the verse you grave for me:
> Here he lies where he longed to be,
> Home is the sailor, home from the sea,
> And the hunter, home from the hill.

There is more to the story. *Jekyll and Hyde* remained an extremely profitable book. Its success underwrote the further adventures of Fanny Osbourne, who had been so closely connected with its creation. Stevenson who had vanquished tuberculosis at Vailima in the end had died partially of stress brought on by the physical and emotional problems of Fanny, whose mind in the end veered close to insanity. But following Louis's death Fanny miraculously recovered from her various ailments. She then spent the rest of her life fighting to perpetuate his memory and sometimes deform it after his death, in order to highlight her own role in the creation of *Jekyll and Hyde.* This, in essence, is how yet another legend surrounding Stevenson was born after his death.

From 1894 to 1897, Fanny continued to hold court at Vailima—mentally deranged a good deal of the time—initially with Louis's mother, Maggie, who soon returned to Scotland. Quite suddenly Fanny decided that she must perpetuate Stevenson's reputation closer to home. She left the island in 1897 (the year that Stoker wrote *Dracula* and, coincidentally, the same

Bas relief of RLS by the American artist Auguste St. Gauden, inside St. Giles' Cathedral, Edinburgh. He was originally portrayed with a cigarette in his right hand but it has been replaced with a quill pen. (CAROL MCNALLY)

year that Maggie died in Edinburgh). Fanny sold the Vailima property for a pittance and settled initially in Scotland, later moving to France and elsewhere. In 1903 she returned to America where her life with Stevenson had begun after her divorce. She bought a vast house located (note the coincidence) at the corner of Hyde and Lombard street overlooking the Bay of San Francisco with space enough to contain all of Louis's treasures, souvenirs, and furniture from Samoa. There she discovered a new lease on life with the help of the spirit of Tusitala. The house was sturdy enough, because it survived the fire and earthquake of 1906, which destroyed a good portion of the city. Today it is a Carmelite monastery.

At the age of fifty-eight, Fanny finally regained some semblance of her sanity and, like Hyde, sensed a new kind of youth. Always attractive, now in her middle age she became beautiful in a deeper sense, gregarious, and developed an amazing power of seducing young men. The first was a young artist-designer, Geletter Burgess, who bore a distinctive resemblance to Stevenson and had made it his objective to mimic Stevenson's mannerisms. He was only thirty years old, thus eighteen years her junior. There can be little doubt that in the course of time Fanny and Geletter became lovers—the third and probably last one—though not the last man in Fanny's life.

Geletter, however, committed the blunder of exploiting her love by selling articles Fanny had written without asking her permission. The gaffe cost him her favor. As a result, he was suddenly asked to move out of the house.

A few years later, Fanny's daughter Belle, who, after divorcing her husband Austin Strong (Stevenson's secretary in Samoa), met a good-looking young journalist at Doxeys, a San Francisco bookstore where she was working. The heir of a wealthy California family, Edward Salisbury Field was the son of the founder of an Indiana-based publishing house, Bobbs Merrill. At that time Edward—he was called "Ned"—caught the extraordinary eyes and exotic countenance of a lady visiting her daughter's bookstore. The lady was Fanny, and it was a fateful meeting. Upon being asked who this exotic lady was, Belle introduced her mother, adding, "Her name is Fanny; she is the widow of Robert Louis Stevenson the author and perhaps second mother of *Jekyll and Hyde*." At first glance Ned became infatuated and smitten with Fanny. He was younger than Geletter, her former lover, being only twenty-three years old to her sixty-three. In other words, the same mother/son relationship was repeating itself for the third time. They became inseparable.

Together they went on the grand tour of Europe similar to that taken by Stevenson and Fanny previously: first to Skerryvore at Bournemouth in England, then on to Paris, Grez, and Fontainebleau where she had first met Louis. They then journeyed to Montmartre in Paris and followed the trek of Stevenson's donkey, Modestine through the Cévennes, the villa in Hyères, and other places dear to Louis and Fanny on the French Riviera and Switzerland where they had sojourned thirty years before. All of this journey had Ned at the wheel of a new Ford automobile. It was history repeating itself down to the anger expressed by Ned's wealthy parents who reacted much in the manner as Stevenson's father, Thomas when Stevenson courted Fanny. Like Thomas they thought their son was wasting his life with Fanny. Meanwhile, Fanny and Ned decided to splurge. They built an exquisite villa in the Santa Cruz mountains of California, an extravagant mansion outside of Santa Barbara, and a hacienda in Mexico. Parcels of land were bought in and around Los Angeles, for, unlike Mary Shelley's *Frankenstein* and Stoker's *Dracula*, *Jekyll and Hyde* had produced hefty royalties for the Stevenson heirs.

Finally, Fanny could indulge in the grand life of which she had always dreamed, beginning with the modest Bournemouth villa, Skerryvore, given to her by Thomas where *Jekyll and Hyde* had been born. She continued to be involved in perpetuating the Stevenson legend—for which she was in part responsible.

Fanny died on February 18, 1914, at the age of seventy-four, on a stormy California night, six months before the start of World War I, twenty years after the death of Stevenson, and thirty-six years after the writing of *Jekyll and Hyde*. The continuing profitability of the novella continued to influence Stevenson's heirs. Totally distraught by Fanny's death, Ned Field decided to marry Fanny's daughter Belle Strong. In a sense, Belle became, for him, Fanny's double, standing in for her mother. At the time Belle was fifty-six, Ned barely thirty-four. The money kept coming in. Ned Field had advised Fanny to invest some of the royalties from *Jekyll and Hyde* in buying real estate in the Los Angeles area; properties which Belle inherited. Luckily for them, in 1921 oil was discovered on these parcels and suddenly Belle and Ned became millionaires, one of the richest couples in Hollywood. These were the roaring twenties. Ned became a well-known scriptwriter of movies, such as George Cukor's *Little Women* (1933), and they lived a charmed life that lasted until the death of Ned on the eve of his seventy-eighth birthday. She survived him by fifteen years, just as Fanny had survived Stevenson and all her other men.

During World War I, Germany lost its preeminent position in Samoa and, as part of the British Empire, New Zealand took over the western portion of the Island. As a result, in 1915 the British flag at last flew over Vailima. The governor of the Island then placed Stevenson's property at the disposal of Belle. Together with Ned she immediately decided that Fanny's last resting place belonged to the site where Stevenson's ashes lay buried on the top of Mount Vaea facing the Pacific. The urn containing her mother's ashes was placed beside Stevenson's in a common tomb. On one side was the inscription from the book of Ruth. "Whither thou goest I will go, and where thou lodgest I will lodge, thy people shall be my people, and thy God, my God."

Adaptations—
Theater, Movies, Television, and Radio

---

*To know what you prefer, instead of humbly saying
Amen to what the world tells you you ought to
prefer, is to have kept your soul alive.*

—Robert Louis Stevenson, *An Inland
Voyage* (1878)

An analysis of the varying stage and film adaptations of the *Jekyll and Hyde* story shows us some of the ways the novella had such a profound and enduring effect on popular audiences. These changes often eclipsed the basic messages in the Stevenson work. Here we urge the reader to abandon preconceptions about the nature of literature, theater, and the motion pictures. Our main focus is whether a given theatrical or film adaptation seems to reflect *in a creative way* the *spirit* of the work of literature. We have restricted ourselves largely to important English and American theatrical productions and films in the English and German languages, because they have often exerted a very strong influence on one another.

Most of us like to be scared a little under controlled conditions. A little bit of horror is good, because it prepares most humans for the real horrors awaiting them in actual life. Most horror stories, plays, and movies are conservative; order is generally restored to the fictional world in the end. Evil is real, like original sin; one cannot, of course, ever fully conquer it. One can, however, put it to rest temporarily.

Modern theater and movies first and foremost reflect the changing interest and values of society, primarily because they have to sell their product in order to pay the many people involved in the production and performance. Modern theater and movies, therefore, must appeal to a wide range of persons. That is why theater and movies provide an important barometer of the changes in society. Once they become popularized, theater and movie products can then exert influences upon society as a whole. Thus, adaptations of *Jekyll and Hyde* often partake in, and accentuate, the social and cultural anxieties of their times.

During the early period of adaptation of Stevenson's *Jekyll and Hyde,* from 1886 to 1932, aside from the parodies of the hide-and-seek variety, the emphasis was upon concerns about Darwinian reversion to the ape stage of human evolution. Modern science was in serious conflict with traditional religious belief. Jekyll was given a fiancée, in order to present a domestic character with whom the average viewer could sympathize. In those adaptations Hyde was portrayed essentially as a sexual predator. In comedies the *Jekyll and Hyde* theme was satirized. The adaptations done during the Great Depression reflect fears and longings about economic matters. Movies of that period attempted to depict for viewers those who were worse off than they. It is not by chance, thus, that many classic horror movies were made during the 1930s.

Because motion pictures cannot portray thought the way one can in a novel, the story line must be simplified. Characters are usually combined, so as not to confuse the viewer. There is a need to have both a clear-cut hero and an obvious villain. Hence Jekyll as Mr. Good Guy is wholly the product of the theatrical and film adaptations. He is made into a medical doctor, a benefactor of mankind, and a heroic upholder of the theory of evolution. Whereas Jekyll deserves his fate in the novel, in the theater and in the movies he is habitually transformed into a noble victim who is tragically overwhelmed by Hyde, his evil alter ego.

After 1932 came films that embodied a pop-Freudian approach to Jekyll and Hyde. An Oscar was given to actor Fredric March for his portrayal of Jekyll and Hyde that year. The psychological duality of Jekyll is shown visually, along with a general distrust of science. Pop-Freudianism had become popular in the United States. In addition, one learns that Jekyll's obsession with science leads to a destruction of his personal life. The scientist is portrayed not as the usual apostle of social redemption but as untrustworthy. This trend reflected American (and, by extension, much of Western) society's fear of "scientific" socialism soon to be implemented in the Soviet Union under the five-year plans of Joseph Stalin and "scientific" racism being promulgated in Germany during the dictatorship (1933–1945) of Adolf Hitler. By 1941 Jekyll could be played by a benign, staid Spencer Tracy. The coming of World War II put an end to this bastardization of the theme until the 1950s.

During the post–World War II period, the Jekyll and Hyde theme was ready for transformation into major comic adaptations on film. Capitalizing on its successes with remakes of *Dracula* and *Frankenstein* in lurid gory color, Hammer Films of London turned to the notion of Jekyll being transformed into a handsome Hyde in 1960. But the epitome of adaptations came with Jerry Lewis's *The Nutty Professor* in 1963, which spawned a popular remake with Eddie Murphy in 1996 and a sequel in 2000. What had begun as a tragedy by Stevenson was turned into farce.

Gender-bending became fashionable for *Jekyll and Hyde*. Hammer Studios indulged in gender-bending as early as 1971 when Dr. Jekyll transformed into lovely Sister Hyde, a feature imitated in other subsequent films. By 1973 came a major musical on the theme made for TV, starring Kirk Douglas. Finally, by the 1990s the *Jekyll and Hyde* story had become so familiar to the public that it was turned into a series of musicals on stage. The previous sensational change from Jekyll into Hyde has become a subject of amusement, since the discovery of DNA has made the creation of a double or clone scientifically realizable. What follows here are the significant details behind the strange adaptations of the *Jekyll and Hyde* tale.

Theater

Only four months after Robert Louis Stevenson's *Jekyll and Hyde* story was published, a parody was performed at L. C. Toole's Theater in London on May 18, 1886, under the title *The Strange Case of a Hyde and Seekyl*. When Stevenson arrived in New York during the summer of 1887, just after the American publication of *Dr. Jekyll and Mr. Hyde,* his bestseller, the character actor Richard Mansfield had already portrayed Jekyll and Hyde in the first serious theatrical adaptation of the story.

Adapted by the Bostonian playwright Thomas Russell Sullivan (1854–1908), *Dr. Jekyll and Mr. Hyde* was first staged at the Boston Museum from May 9 through 13 in 1887, and at the Madison

Square Theater in New York City from September 12 through October 1 of that year. Audiences reputedly went away from *Dr. Jekyll and Mr. Hyde* so frightened that they were afraid later to enter their homes alone. Some also could not sleep in the dark, and some often had nightmares based on the play. Nonetheless, audiences were mesmerized by the crime and mystery, and many came again and again. But the desire for parody was not dead. On October 3, 1887, another satire entitled *Dr. Freckle and Mr. Snide* appeared on stage at Dockstadter's Minstrel Hall in New York City.

The Sullivan play, which was an obvious box office success, also enjoyed an American tour from October 3, 1887, to June 25, 1888. The handsome thirty-year-old actor Richard Mansfield was able to make the transformation from Jekyll into the ugly, frightening dwarf Hyde with body contortions and the use of relatively little makeup in full view of the astonished audiences. He was wrongly accused of using acids and other chemicals to complete the transformation; in fact, he simply modified the muscles in his face, his voice, and his posture, as he crouched down balancing back and forth on his toes to create an eerie effect. Instead of Stevenson's opening setting on dark streets with a strange door, Sullivan's play opened in a well-lit upper-class drawing room with the trees visible through the French doors.

Richard Mansfield as Jekyll and Hyde in his 1887–1888 stage adaptation. (LIBRARY OF CONGRESS)

Mansfield did not portray Jekyll as a simple hero but rather as a complex character haunted by the fiend Hyde. Sullivan delayed the transformation scene to the third act, so as to increase the realism of the plot and build the suspense. In this way Sullivan maintained Stevenson's sense of mystery; the play is like a detective story with Utterson as the intrepid investigator. The play represented a step away from the atmosphere of the Old Boys' Club into the realm of traditional domestic melodrama.

The role of the female as domesticator attempts to transform the selfish, neurotic Jekyll into a potential home provider. Later on in life, Stevenson objected to Mansfield's portrayal of Hyde as a sex fiend, because Stevenson looked upon Hyde as no more lecherous than any human being. The main message of the Stevenson story remained, in his mind, the fact that Jekyll was a hypocrite.

At the outset of the Sullivan play, Agnes Carew, daughter of Sir Danvers Carew, is seen as the fiancée of the nervous Dr. Jekyll. Jekyll confronts his fiancée, Agnes and Hyde's landlady. Sir Danvers Carew is called "General Sir" rather than just plain "Sir" to indicate both his upper-class status *and* military background, so that he can emerge as a doubly powerful father figure. Dr. Lanyon's wife, who never appears in Stevenson's novella, turns up as Agnes Carew's aunt, and Utterson is a Carew family friend, whereas in the novella he is a lonely bachelor and friend of Jekyll. Hyde emerges as a rather typical stage villain common to many melodramas of the time.

In the original novella, Hyde commits a crime "of singular ferocity," the white-haired genial Sir Danvers Carew has simply asked Hyde for directions. Hyde does not like him and covers poor Carew with abusive language. Carew expresses surprise and emotional hurt, whereupon Hyde "clubbed him to the earth . . .

with ape-like fury, he was trampling the body underfoot . . . the bones were audibly shattered and the body dumped upon the roadway . . . his victim . . . incredibly mangled." In Sullivan's play, however, Hyde slips into the Carew household and demands to see Agnes Carew. When Sir Danvers refuses, Hyde chokes him to death in the murder scene. Agnes spurs Jekyll on to help Utterson in his pursuit of Hyde after the death of her father. She cannot understand why Jekyll is not enthusiastic enough about the pursuit.

In the second act, a drunken Hyde, confronted by the ghost of Sir Danvers, escapes from the London police. Hyde enters Jekyll's laboratory but is confronted by Utterson. In the third act, Hyde swallows the potion and transforms into Jekyll in Dr. Lanyon's house. The last act has Jekyll pleading with Lanyon to bring Agnes to him. Involuntarily changing into Hyde, however, he is forced to commit suicide when discovered by Utterson and the London police.

The second serious adaptation written by Daniel Bandmann opened in New York City during Mansfield's tour on March 12, 1888, but it was a failure. Bandmann, the author of the play, also appeared in the title role, first at Niblo's Garden and then at Brooklyn's Amphion Academy on March 19. After a short run in New York City, the play opened in London's Opera Comique on August 6, but closed after only two performances. A review in the *London Theater* panned the Bandmann version.

During the late summer of 1888, Mansfield took his company to England, where Sullivan's *Jekyll and Hyde* play was produced by Howard Poole at Croyden's Theater Royal on July 26, attracting little attention. On August 4, 1888, the play moved to the Lyceum Theater, where it fared somewhat better. However, a review in London's *The Theater* asserted: "No one who has seen Mr. Sullivan's version of R. L. Stevenson's weird story will for a moment speak of it as making a good play—in fact it would have been almost impossible out of the material at command to produce an effective drama." Interestingly, the play was temporarily closed down by the authorities, because it was thought to have inspired the contemporary Jack the Ripper murders in the London slum of Whitechapel in 1888. Even Mansfield himself was one of the many persons suspected of being Jack the Ripper.

Mansfield revived the Sullivan play on May 7, 1888, at the Boston Museum, one year after the premiere of the play, staged at the same theater on May 9, 1887. (This fact is confirmed here for the first time by one of the present authors who consulted the notes and program preserved among the Sullivan papers presently located at the American Antiquarian Society archives in Worcester, Massachusetts. Most previous sources erroneously place the revival on January 1, 1890.) Mansfield continued to play in the Sullivan version until his final curtain call as Jekyll and Hyde on March 21, 1907, at New York's New Amsterdam Theater.

Though Sir Henry Irving, the noted English actor, purchased the theatrical rights for a *Jekyll and Hyde* production in 1893, he did not put on the play. An adaptation was performed by J. Comyns Carr at London's Queen Theater on January 29, 1910. Irving's son, the actor H. B. Irving, appeared as Dr. Jekyll along with Dorothea Baird playing his wife in a 1910 Queen's Theater production that ran for ninety-eight performances.

Playwrights Luella Forepaugh Fish and George F. Fish created another theatrical version in 1904, specifically for the stock company Forepaugh's Theater, Philadelphia, Pennsylvania. The play bore the morally revealing title *Dr. Jekyll and Mr. Hyde or a Mis-Spent Life.*

The curtain opened not on the bleak, brown-colored back streets in Stevenson's story but rather on a lovely garden set between a church and the local vicar's house with a church looming in the distance. In this way a religious theme is introduced into the story in more ways than one. The father of Jekyll's fiancée turns out to be the vicar himself, who later also becomes Hyde's murder victim.

Writers Forepaugh and Fish wrote the following instructions for the critical transformation scene: "Dr. Jekyll writhes as though in physical pain; assumes crouching position; during this with one hand he pulls a portion of the wig which is brought forward and falls in a tangled mass over his forehead and eyes."

The Fish version has a murder scene different from that in the Sullivan play, in that the vicar is killed by Hyde after a confrontation with the heroine, Alice. Before dying the Vicar names Hyde as his killer. Later in the Fish play, Hyde recounts his main motives for killing the vicar and also his hatred for Jekyll. In comparing the Sullivan play with the Fish play, we feel that the Sullivan version is the superior work. The Fish play is more of a simple, melodramatic adaptation designed clearly for a regional theatrical audience and contains heavy racist overtones.

Thirteen years passed between the Fish adaptation in 1904 and the Lena Ashwell and Roger Pocock adaptation, which opened at the Century Theater (London, England) on March 28, 1927. Wilfred Fletcher starred in the drama. Four years later, at the Savoy Theater (London, England), William Senior's version of the play debuted on July 14. Starring Arthur Phillips, it lasted for forty-six performances. Four years later, the William Senior adaptation, again starring Arthur Phillips, played on London's West End.

The next major stage rendition came in 1941. A theatrical adaptation by Richard Abbott entitled *Dr. Jekyll and Mr. Hyde* was produced in that year and demonstrated the common worries about modern science peculiar to the period that began with World War II in 1939. Abbott's theater piece represents one of the last major attempts to use the theater for the *Jekyll and Hyde* tale until one reaches the transformation of Stevenson's story into several musicals. The Abbott version begins not in the dark street behind Dr. Jekyll's laboratory, as in Louis's novella, but, rather, is set in Jekyll's elegant home, as in the Sullivan adaptation. Thus, the emphasis is once again upon the domestic surroundings of Dr. Jekyll. The opening scene of the room in Jekyll's house sets the main mood of the entire Abbott play, as it depicts the house as gloomy and depressing.

Jekyll is in an intimate relationship with the daughter of Sir Danvers Carew, named Diana, whom Enfield also loves. Much is made of the notion that Jekyll is too old for Diana, because she is only nineteen or twenty and Jekyll is forty-five or older. Young Enfield is closer in age to Diana. There is no laboratory scene in which Jekyll transforms into Hyde. Jekyll simply turns into Hyde and takes center stage. Hyde's laugh temporarily disrupts the action, but Jekyll unexpectedly appears. He scolds his house-keeper for suggesting to his guests that he is not at home or in his laboratory. He is there but has become a recluse and lost contact with his old friends. The basic message is that scientific research of a bizarre nature leads to danger.

Since World War II, there have been various stage adaptations of Stevenson's classic on both sides of the Atlantic Ocean. For example, The Drury Theater in Cleveland, Ohio, produced a version in December 1975 written and directed by Paul Lee, with

Jonathan Farwell (Dr. Henry Jekyll) and Robert Snook (Dr. Lanyon). In the Down Center Stage (Dallas, Texas) adaptation by Jim Marvin in April 1980, the lead assignments were split, with Wayne Lambert as Jekyll and Jeffrey Kinhorn as Hyde. Stage and TV veteran Orson Bean was Jekyll for the Apple Corps Theater (New York City) production of the *Strange Case of Dr. Jekyll and Mr. Hyde* (August 1983). In December 1989, the iconoclastic Ridiculous Theatrical Company based at the Charles Ludham Theater in Manhattan offered its take of Stevenson's famed story, with Everett Quinton in the lead.

In 1990 *Jekyll and Hyde,* the musical, was performed at the George Street Playhouse in New Brunswick, New Jersey. Directed by Gregory S. Hurst, it boasted John Cullum in the title parts and utilized a book by Leonora Thuna, music by Norman Sachs, and lyrics by Mel Mandel. During that same season, the Promenade Theater (New York City) presented *Jekyll and Hyde,* a musical "loosely based" on the Stevenson work. David Crane and Marta Kauffman provided the book and lyrics, Michael Skoff did the music, and Jay Harnick directed. It featured Christopher Scott (Henry), Amanda Green (Marissa/Mother), Eric Ruffin (Stuart), Emily Gear (Chelsea), and Frederck Einhorn (Vernicker/Father).

In London during November 1991, the Royal Shakespeare Company offered David Edgar's adaptation of Stevenson's drama. It featured Roger Allam (Dr. Henry Jekyll), Simon Russell Beale (Mr. Hyde), Alec Linstead (Dr. Hastie Lanyon), Pippa Guard (Katherine Urquahart), and Ellie Beaven or Lilly Gallafent (Lucy Urquhart). Yet another full-length modern melodrama titled simply *Jekyll and Hyde* was written by Leonard H. Caddy for four actors, four actresses, and one child. Dr. Jekyll appears on the verge of uncovering a scientific method to tap into human inner reality. He experiments upon himself and discovers that his serum works, but trouble comes from the fact that his real inner self is the cruel Mr. Hyde. In continuing his research, Jekyll succumbs increasingly to his inner Hyde. His fiancée and his friends notice the personality changes coming over Jekyll but can do nothing to save him. Although he had at first delighted in becoming Hyde, Jekyll is gripped with fear and loathing for him. After Hyde cruelly murders one of the maids, Jekyll realizes that his experiment has gone too far and he commits suicide.

Another modern musical comedy called *Jekyll Hydes Again!* appeared with book, music, and lyrics by Jack Sharkley and Dave Reiser. The story revolves around the son of Jekyll, a recent medical school graduate. He wishes to settle his father's estate and comes across Formula Number One, the potion that initially changed his father into Mr. Hyde. Like his late father, Junior is in deep trouble: He is poor, wanted by the police, and engaged to marry a fat slob. He is really in love with his lovely lab assistant. Junior meets a salon singer who just happens to know the secret of Jekyll's Formula Number Two. Near the end of the show, Jekyll's Formula Number Three is discovered, which allows for a happy ending to the musical, as Jekyll is united with the beautiful lab assistant.

Most important of all these modern adaptations is the current *Jekyll and Hyde,* a musical with lyrics by Leslie Bricusse and music by Frank Wildhorn "from the novella the *Strange Case of Dr. Jekyll and Mr. Hyde* by Robert Louis Stevenson," which opened on Broadway in 1997. Wildhorn and Steve Caden had the original idea for this musical during the 1960s and recruited Leslie Bricusse to write the lyrics. The show was first performed in 1990 at the Alley Theater in Houston, Texas, with Chuck Wagner in the title role and Linda Eden as Lucy, the prostitute.

By 1992 disagreements arose between the creative staff and the producers, which

The marquee for Jekyll and Hyde, the musical. Plymouth Theatre, New York City. (MICHAEL MCNALLY)

resulted in a Broadway production being abandoned. The creative staff won control of the project in 1994, and the show was revived and new songs added. The musical opened again in Seattle, Washington in 1996, and, after a short hiatus, went on tour that spring. After the tour, Gregory Boyd, the original artistic director of the world premiere at the Alley Theater in Houston, signed on again, and Robin Phillips, the original Broadway director and scenic designer also helped. Phillips was the recipient of The American Theater Wing Design Award for *Jekyll and Hyde*. On April 26, 1997, the show began its present long run at the Plymouth Theater in New York City. The musical marked its five hundredth performance in July 1998, and, as of this writing, is still going strong. It is supported by self-proclaimed "Jekkies" who have seen the production countless times in New York City and elsewhere.

This hit version of the musical also went on tour in October 1999. Chuck Wagner, who originated the dual role in the World Premiere at the Houston Alley Theater, gave a particularly powerful performance. Directed by David Warren and choreographed by Jerry Mitchell in Boston, the road show version was based primarily on Robin Phillips's original Broadway production. Characters from the Stevenson story, such as John Utterson and Sir Danvers Carew, also appear in the stage production. Starting January 25, 2000, Jack Wagner (from TV's *Melrose Place*) took over the title role. By June of the year 2000, Jack Wagner handed the title role over to a rock star named Sebastien Bach.

The musical opens with a prologue on a London Street and moves to "The Violent Ward" (The Insane Asylum) at St. Jude's Hospital. Dr. Jekyll broods over trying to cure an insane patient with two arias, "Lost in the Darkness" and "I Need to Know." The board of governors of St. Jude Hospital meet to criticize the scientific views and experiments of Dr. Jekyll, with Jekyll arguing in favor of pure scientific research with his aria, "Pursue the Truth," but the hospital authorities reject him.

At the engagement party of Emma Carew and Dr. Jekyll at the home of Sir Danvers Carew, Regents Park in London, Jekyll sings to Emma "Take Me as I Am." The scene shifts to the Red Rat Café, where the sexy prostitute Lucy is introduced and intones, "Bring On the Men." Outside of his laboratory Jekyll performs "This Is the Moment" and "The Transformation." Then, inside his laboratory Jekyll injects himself and becomes the sinister Hyde. As Hyde he glories in his bizarre new life in an aria called "Alive."

In the second act, people in the streets of London vocalize about "Murder, Murder." In brief sequences Hyde is seen cutting the throats of victims without any clear motive. Jekyll dreams of finding his way back to normalcy, but as Hyde he pursues Lucy to her room above the Red Rat Café and murders her. In the final scene at St. Anne's Church in Westminster, Jekyll sings his "Final Transformation," turns into Hyde, and is killed.

The actor Chuck Wagner commented on his performance as both the nice Dr. Jekyll and the evil Mr. Hyde, "I feel that you can't play one without the other. In fact, even in Stevenson's novel [sic], it talks about how he recognized the dark side within him and realized that there was such a dual nature to his own personality. . . ." He sees the musical as "Definitely a fusion of Jack the Ripper and Jekyll and Hyde."

The review in the *Boston Globe* of Thursday, September 30, 1999, labeled the musical a *popera*. Ed Siegel, the reviewer, places the musical not in the Broadway musical tradition, but rather in those of pop operas in the style of Andrew Lloyd Weber. He compares Chuck Wagner's portrayal to that of Dan Akroyd's characterization of Richard Nixon, made popular on TV's *Saturday Night Live* and concludes, "One wonders what it is thought about *Jekyll and Hyde* that keeps Jekkies coming back time and again. A second viewing seems far more tedious than it did the first sight. Any show, no matter what its genre, that deals with the extremes of good and evil should not hew so closely to the middle of the road."

Marc J. Goldman, who is co-president of the Jekyll & Hyde Fan Club explains why self-proclaimed Jekkies return again and again to see it, some more than a hundred times. He first asks, "Why is *Jekyll and Hyde*—years in the making, bashed by New York critics, and snubbed by the Tony committee—the only musical from its season still running on Broadway?" He asserts, "It comes down to four basic things: the music, the journey, the Internet, and the people." He declares, "From 1994 (when the first e-mail list was set up by *Jekyll* veteran Phillip Hoffman) to today (when there are show, cast, composer, role playing, and fan club Web sites to view) the Internet has played a major role in Jekyll's popularity. With a few keystrokes and a quick click of the mouse—to www.jekyll-hyde.com—fans can discuss, criticize, and publicize the show across states, time zones, and even countries." Goldman concludes, "I have friends from all over the country whom I would never have met if it were not for this show."

The Jekyll & Hyde Fan Club e-mail address is: JHFC@aol.com. Regular mail (termed "snail-mail") can be sent to:

> The Jekyll & Hyde Fan Club
> P.O. Box 116962
> Carrollton, Texas 75011–6962

Movies and Television

The visual imagery of Jekyll and Hyde was bound to inspire filmmakers. The setting of the story—the foggy, shadowy streets of Victorian London—is a dreamscape in which the battle for Dr. Jekyll's soul is played out. In Stevenson's tale, Utterson, who has been influenced by Richard Enfield's account of Mr. Hyde, falls asleep and has a powerful dream which almost reads as if it were written to be part of a script for a movie:

"Six o'clock struck on the bells of the church that was so conveniently near to Mr. Utterson's dwelling, and still he was digging at the problem. Hitherto it had touched him on the intellectual side alone, but now his imagination also was engaged, or rather enslaved; as he lay and tossed in the gross darkness of the night and the curtained room, Mr. Enfield's tale went by before his mind in a scroll of lighted pictures."

Further visions from Utterson's dream also seem made for the movies, though no one has ever put them on film:

In summoning up his image of Hyde brooding over Dr. Jekyll in his dream, Utterson would see a room in a rich house, where his friend lay asleep, dreaming and smiling at his dreams; and then the door of that room would be opened, the curtains of the bed plucked apart, the sleeper recalled, and lo! there would stand by his side a figure to whom power was given, and even at that dead hour he must rise to do his bidding. The figure in these two phases haunted the lawyer all night; and if at any time he dozed over, it was but to see it glide more stealthily through the sleeping houses, or move the more swiftly and still more swiftly, even to dizziness, through wider labyrinths of the lamp lighted city, and at every street corner crush a child and leave her screaming.

Most of the movie scriptwriters doing their adaptations have depended on the theatrical version of Thomas Russell Sullivan or the version by Luella Forepaugh and George F. Fish rather than Stevenson's novella itself. In 1908 Colonel William Selig at his Polyscope Company had his actors turn the stage play by Forepaugh and Fish into a short silent movie in a version severely condensed from the Forepaugh-Fish four-act play. In it Dr. Jekyll and Alice, the vicar's daughter, swear eternal love to one another. There follows the transformation of the upright gentleman Dr. Jekyll into the hideous maniacal brute known as Mr. Hyde. Hyde is addicted to ingesting a strange potion. He eventually kills the vicar only to disappear and then reappear as the genial Dr. Jekyll. Colonel Selig enlisted some of the same actors from the Fish theatrical version for his movie, such as Hobart Bosworth and Betty Harte, though the main actor who played Jekyll and Hyde in the Selig production actually went unbilled. The Polyscope Company released the film for the nickelodeons; it was entitled *Dr. Jekyll and Mr. Hyde,* and is also known as *The Modern Dr. Jekyll.* Another film adaptation by the Kalem Company was also released in 1908.

Mention must be made of the version by The Nordisk Company of Copenhagen, Denmark, in 1909, because it introduced the notion that Jekyll only *imagines* turning into Hyde. The director of *Den Skaebnesv Angre Opfindelse* was August Bloom, with Alwin Neuss in the title role and Oda Alstrup as Agnes Carew. Later some American-made films would imitate the notion that the change from Jekyll into Hyde took place only in a nightmare from which Jekyll awakens in the end.

A British film company named Wrench brought out its own silent screen production of the Stevenson story in 1910 in a movie called *The Duality of Man.* Hyde is depicted as a criminal on a rampage and pursued by detectives. In order to thwart the police, Hyde enters Jekyll's laboratory and changes into Jekyll. As Jekyll he courts his fiancée Hilda. In the closing scene, just as Hilda enters with her father, Jekyll involuntarily turns back into Hyde, so he kills Hilda's father. The police arrive and Hyde swallows a fatal dose of poison.

The first overtly popular movie adaptation of Stevenson's novella was the one produced by Edwin Thanhouser and released as *Dr. Jekyll and Mr. Hyde* in 1911 according to one source (or 1912, or even as late as 1913, according to other sources). This one-reeler was modeled very closely on both the Sullivan and Forepaugh plays. James Cruze portrayed Dr. Jekyll and Harry Benham was Mr. Hyde, with Cruze's real-life wife, Marguerite Snow, portraying Jekyll's sweetheart. She is simply called "the

Minister's daughter" in the silent movie's subtitles, so the religious theme is heralded again as in the Forepaugh play.

In this version, white-haired Dr. Jekyll ingests a steaming potion in his laboratory. He slumps down and in a sudden quick-dissolve frame-cut Mr. Hyde rises up with curly black hair. His eyeballs are popping out, and he has fangs at the corners of his mouth. Hyde is given a woman, but Jekyll stands between them. Hyde attacks a small girl as well as Jekyll's fiancée and kills her father. When the police arrive at his laboratory, Hyde wrecks the laboratory and destroys himself.

In 1913 Imp/Universal Pictures offered *Dr. Jekyll and Mr. Hyde* as directed by King Baggot and produced by Carl Laemmle, who was head of the studio. King Baggot himself played Hyde covered with crepe hair and greasepaint. Baggot was a former stage star who had begun appearing in Laemmle productions after his own theatrical company failed. Baggot achieved international fame, and he was supported by a fine cast including Jane Gail, Matt Snyder, Howard Crampton, and William Sorrell.

Charles Urban's Kineto-Kinemacolor Company was one of the first to photograph the horror story in color (albeit rather primitive hues). For the two-reel *Dr. Jekyll and Mr. Hyde* (1913), the company used a double-speed projector fitted with red-green revolving filters. Few people saw the film, because theaters had to buy costly, crude, bulky equipment, such as a special projector running at twice the normal speed and filters that had to be installed before the presentation. In this two-reeler directed by Frank Woods, Murdock J. MacQuarrie played the dual roles.

Lubin's *Dr. Jekyll and Mr. Hyde,* directed by Arthur Hotaling with Jerold T. Horner in the title role, came out in 1915. Billy Reeves and Mae Hotely were also in the cast. Vitagraph's *Miss*

Jekyll and Madame Hyde (1915) was the first known film to change Dr. Jekyll's gender. As we shall see later, it would be not the last such gender-bending regarding Stevenson's novella.

The year 1920 can be seen as a watershed time for *Jekyll and Hyde* on film. Liptow Films's *Der Januskopf* (the American titles were *Janus-Faced, The Head of Janus,* or *Love's Mockery*) was directed by "German genius" Friedrich W. Murnau. The reckless Murnau did not secure copyright for the Stevenson tale, so he altered the original story and the names of the characters in much the way he would do two years later with Bram Stoker's *Dracula,* renamed *Nosferatu.*

The title *Der Januskopf* (Janushead) came from the ancient two-faced Roman god with different faces mounted on opposite sides of doorways. The star who played the dual role of "Dr. Warren and Mr. O'Connor" was Conrad Veidt who had scored such a success in the now classic horror film, *The Cabinet of Dr. Caligari* (1919).

In this adaptation there is no potion or drug used to transform the main character. Dr. Warren is fixated on his bust of the Roman god Janus and inadvertently transforms into the

John Barrymore committing murder as Hyde. (JOHN SPRINGER COLLECTION/CORBIS)

villainous O'Connor. O'Connor tramples a diminutive girl in the street as in Stevenson's story; he also forcibly drags Warren's fiancée, portrayed by Margaret Schlegel, to a whorehouse. At the conclusion of Murnau's story,

Warren poisons himself. The screenplay was written by Hans Janowitz who had co-authored *The Cabinet of Dr. Caligari* with Carl Mayer. Apparently, only the original script and a few stills have survived.

The most famous of all the *Jekyll and Hyde* silent movies is the 1920 black-and-white release with tints by Paramount-Artcraft Production. Directed by Sheldon Lewis, it starred the famous American actor known as "The Great Profile," John Barrymore (1882–1942). Barrymore, who was born John Blyth in Philadelphia, led a controversial, tempestuous life. At the time of this filming, he was riding the crest of his popularity as an actor. On April 9, 1919, he joined his elder brother, Lionel, on the stage of Broadway's Plymouth Theater. There they began a seventy-seven performance run of a play called *The Jest*. The opening night review in the *New York Times* gushed, "*The Jest* has fallen across the sky of the declining season like a burst of sunset color."

In this new movie version of Stevenson's novella, Clara Beranger's script insists again upon a decidedly traditional sexual bent for Jekyll, by giving him a fiancée named Millicent, while Hyde is provided with a prostitute girlfriend, called Gina. Martha Mansfield played Millicent, the daughter of Sir George Carew, and Nita Naldi portrayed the sexy Miss Gina. This is the film that established the common image of Dr. Jekyll as Mr. Nice Guy and set the formula for many of the screen adaptations to follow.

In this silent picture, Dr. Jekyll runs a free clinic for the poor. Thus, the scenarist transforms Stevenson's creation into a medical doctor rather than a chemical researcher. Behind Jekyll in the first hospital scene is conservative Dr. Richard Lanyon who objects to Jekyll's idealistic notions about scientific research.

While dining at the home of the rakish Sir George Carew, the father of his fiancée Millicent, it is the cynical Carew who insists on "man's dual nature" and advises Jekyll to spend less time on charity work and more on personal pleasure. Dissipated Carew lures Jekyll to a local music hall to meet a seductive dancer. Jekyll's libido is aroused, and he has her become his mistress. Here heterosexual sex is again introduced as a central feature in the *Jekyll and Hyde* story. Jekyll takes a drug, which turns him into Hyde. As Hyde, Jekyll is not only vicious but also sexually depraved, and he tries to seduce Millicent in Jekyll's study.

Like Mansfield before him, Barrymore did not rely on any excessive makeup for his transformation, but the claim that the Great Profile wore no makeup on camera at all is merely legend. The use of filters and other camera techniques of the time aided in making the initial visual transformation from Jekyll into Hyde. After the transformation scenes, however, rather heavy makeup was, in fact, gradually applied to Barrymore as Hyde.

Barrymore played Hyde on film not as an ape, but as a kind of huge spider with a pointed head. One can see in Barrymore's Hyde something of Shakespeare's hunchback Richard III, a role that Barrymore, who was thirty-eight years old at the time, happened to be playing on Broadway during the filming of this movie. His elongated hands, pointed head, and long, glistening hair make him visually monstrous even for today's audience. Some film historians claim that, in his efforts to elongate his face, Barrymore hurt his jaw during the shoot. It is a fact that Barrymore was so exhausted by the filming of his Jekyll and Hyde portrayal, his acting as Richard III, and his studying for a new stage production of *Hamlet,* all three at the same time, that he had a nervous breakdown.

In this movie adaptation, Millicent's father Sir George Carew figures out Jekyll's secret, but when Carew confronts Jekyll about his connection with the uncouth Hyde and threatens to cut off his engagement to Millicent, Jekyll goes wild. Accusing Carew himself of leading him into temptation, Jekyll turns into Hyde without any dependency on the drug. He chases old Carew into the courtyard, bites the old man like a vampire, and viciously bludgeons him to death. This scene is one of the most frightening in the history of horror films to that date.

Having turned back into Jekyll by using up all of the remaining potion, Jekyll realizes that he cannot control his Hyde. As Millicent apprehensively approaches the laboratory door from the courtyard, Jekyll feels an inadvertent transformation into Hyde beginning to work on him. He suddenly downs a slow-working poison from his old Italian Borgialike ring before changing fully into Hyde. As Millicent enters, Hyde crouches behind the door, springs up, and chases Millicent around the room but soon falls dead into a chair. As Millicent runs from the room, Lanyon arrives in time to see Hyde turn back into Jekyll. Lanyon consoles Millicent with the text, "Hyde has killed Dr. Jekyll."

The critic Edward Weitzel claimed in his 1920 review of Barrymore's part in the film that his performance "is worthy to rank alongside of the Mephistopheles of Henry Irving and the Bertuccio of Edwin Booth (two of the most famous actors of the late nineteenth century). The screen has never before known such great acting." Most of the other critics agreed. The *New York Times* pointed out that, "While Mr. Barrymore is achieving greatness as Richard III on the stage . . . a great many more people will see *Dr. Jekyll and Mr. Hyde,* and have through it their only opportunity of knowing what Mr. Barrymore can do. This is true today and more importantly for the future."

In that same year, 1920, Pioneer Films released its own version of *Dr. Jekyll and Mr. Hyde*. Producer Louis B. Mayer made what amounted to a trashy remake of the Barrymore entry. It is in fact a boldfaced rip-off. The picture owes much to the Thomas Russell Sullivan play and previous movie scripts. The setting is moved from London to America. Normally, in the opinion of the present authors, the attempt to transform a horror story from the past into the contemporary world often produces good results, by making the tale more immediate and plausible. In this film the actors do use telephones rather than transmitting carried messages, and they drive in automobiles rather than horse-drawn hansom carriages. They live in the then-present, but the film is a disaster, because the script is so inane.

The movie opens with Dr. Jekyll, portrayed by Sheldon Lewis, caring for children. He is a medical doctor. A group of Jekyll's friends, relatives, and acquaintances are shown playing cards as handsome young Danvers Carew (Leslie Austen) arrives. Meanwhile, Lanyon's niece and Jekyll's fiancée, Bernice (Gladys Fields), wanders into Jekyll's laboratory to remind him that he had promised to play golf with her! Jekyll expounds a bit on his duality theory, which is based on his personal atheism. The moral comment in this movie is that Jekyll's declaration of atheism drives his fiancée into the arms of another lover named Enfield. This is the only adaptation in which Jekyll's fiancée does not stick by her Jekyll through thick and thin.

Jekyll drinks a billowing potion and transforms into Hyde. Forsaken, Bernice calls off her engagement to Jekyll, and, in retaliation, Hyde burns down the Lanyon mansion. Hyde finds that

Danvers Carew has proposed marriage to Bernice, so he beats Carew to death.

When Hyde briefly turns into Jekyll, he writes a confession to Bernice, who arrives only to be warned by the butler that "Dr. Jekyll is not himself." Inexplicably the police arrive and arrest Hyde, and he is condemned to die in the electric chair. As Hyde is strapped to the electric chair, the camera dissolves to Jekyll asleep in his armchair. It has all been but a nightmare. "I believe in God," Jekyll screams, "I have a soul—and I shall have *you!*" So, the viewer is left with a typical Hollywood happy ending, as Jekyll smiles. The producer of this junky film, Louis B. Mayer, went on to become one of the most powerful forces in the Hollywood movie business.

Contemporary reviews of the 1920 Mayer version differ from the existing prints, as the reviews refer to the dance hall performer, played by Nita Naldi, as "Therese" rather than "Gina." The film opened in New York on March 28, 1920. According to a promotional news release, Charles J. Hayden, who wrote and directed the movie, claimed that he based his adaptation upon "the novelette the *Strange Case of Dr. Jekyll and Mr. Hyde* by Robert Louis Stevenson (London 1886)." Hayden also admitted that his version was strongly influenced by the performance of "that great stage actor Richard Mansfield. . . ."

Later, in 1925, comedian Stan Laurel made the satirical *Dr. Pyckle and Mr. Pride,* which poked fun at Stevenson's much-adapted tale. (Over the years there would be several live-action and animated short subjects satirizing, parodying, or relying on Stevenson's novella for their plot-line inspiration. Such entries would include: *Dr. Jekyll and Mr. Zip* [1918], *Doctor Jekyll's Hyde* [1932], a ten-minute short directed by Albert DeMond for

Universal; *Mighty Mouse Meets Jekyll and Hyde Cat* [1944], a Terry-toon cartoon from Twentieth Century-Fox; *Dr. Jekyll and Mr. Mouse* [1947], from the Joseph Barbera–William Hanna animation division at MGM; David Bairstow's *Gentleman Jekyll and Driver Hyde* [1950]; the British *Teenage Jekyll and Hyde* [1963], and so forth.)

In 1931, after the successful release of Universal's *Dracula*, and the beginning of production of James Whale's *Frankenstein* at Universal Pictures, studio executives began to note that cinematic adaptations of nineteenth-century Gothic literature could be great moneymakers. On April 15, 1931, David O. Selznick, executive assistant to B. P. Schulberg, wrote a memo to Schulberg, the then-managing director of production at Paramount Studios, suggesting that the famed German actor, Emil Jannings, be cast in the title role for a new film on the *Jekyll and Hyde* theme. The communication was never sent, but during that summer of 1931, Rouben Mamoulian was given the task of directing such a movie. The project was destined to become a screen classic.

The Paramount director Robert Lee ceded his position and became assistant director to Mamoulian for this single production. According to the official press release, Mamoulian had thirty-five sets built specifically for 216 scenes in the film. The *New York Times* reported that Robert Louis Stevenson, the nephew of the author, appeared in the film only as an extra, because he could not speak with the correct cockney accent.

The director, Rouben Mamoulian, who had been born in Tbilisi, Georgia, within the Russian Empire in 1898, was one of the few well-educated film directors of that time. He had studied criminology at Moscow University and the famed Stanislavsky method of acting at the Moscow Art Theater. In 1922 he studied drama at the University of London, and, in 1923 he emigrated to America, where he directed operas and operettas at the George Eastman Theater in Rochester, New York. Mamoulian then landed a position with the New York Theater Guild in 1926. He was intensely interested in films and looked to use new film techniques. In particular, he freed the camera from the microphone "stranglehold," which was so usual during the early days of sound films. He was also a pioneer in the use of the fluid camera, later made famous by Karl Freund and Alfred Hitchcock under the name "the inquisitive camera technique," in which the camera functions as a *voyeur.* In addition, Mamoulian developed the use of the voiceover to communicate what he called "audience thoughts."

Rouben Mamoulian only credits Stevenson's story as the source for the movie plot, but in fact he was highly influenced by Thomas Russell Sullivan's play. The story line of the Paramount production was also indebted to the studio's 1920 silent version. By the 1930s pop interpretations of Freudianism became especially widespread, particularly in America, and this trend is reflected in Mamoulian's movie with its probing into the unconscious. In addition, both the Mamoulian production and the later Fleming MGM version emphasize sadism as a release of the unconscious desires of Jekyll, which had been repressed by civilization.

At the outset of the Mamoulian adaptation, the cameraman Karl Struss has the audience see what is going on through the eyes of Dr. Jekyll, who is played by handsome Fredric March. This in and of itself is an unusual twist to Stevenson's narrative in which the action was viewed mostly through the eyes of Utterson, Jekyll's friend who investigates the matter of Hyde.

In the movie one first sees slender male hands playing the Prelude and Fugue in D Minor of Johannes Sebastian Bach on a

Frederic March as Jekyll and Hyde. (JOHN SPRINGER
COLLECTION/CORBIS)

pipe organ. The viewer learns that the hands are those of Jekyll, when Poole, his butler (portrayed by Edgar Norton, who played Dr. Jekyll's butler on stage) interrupts his employer and reminds him that it's time to leave for his lecture. The image of the cleancut Dr. Jekyll is reflected in the hall mirror, as he adjusts his clothing before venturing outside. The camera is still acting as *voyeur,* because the audience sees the action through Jekyll's own view of things as he rides in a horse-driven carriage through London. In his provocative lecture at St. Simon's Hospital, Jekyll holds that there are two distinct selves within a person and that soon one should be able to separate out these two persons within oneself. The older professors are skeptical of this young upstart. Thus the theme of the scientist who defies conventional wisdom becomes a part of Mamoulian's celluloid retelling of the *Jekyll and Hyde* story.

Jekyll wishes to be married to Muriel Carew (played by Rose Hobart), daughter of Brigadier General Carew (played by Halliwell Hobbes), as soon as possible, but her father, a conservative, sees no rush. As in the Sullivan theatrical version of 1887, Carew's title indicates that he not only belongs to the upper class but also has ties to the military, unlike Stevenson's original novella. As Jekyll and Lanyon, his friend, leave from a house party at the Carew's, Jekyll hears a woman's scream and saves her from the clutches of a street ruffian. He carries her to her room, where the flirtatious streetwalker, named Ivy Pierson (played by Miriam Hopkins), gives Jekyll a passionate kiss, as Lanyon enters aghast at Jekyll's ungentlemanly conduct.

In his laboratory, amid Bunsen burners and test tubes, Jekyll drinks the potion and convulsively turns into Hyde. (This is accomplished on screen here through the use of film lighting and filters.) When Jekyll turns into Hyde his first words are, "Free, free at last! . . ." In this screen version, Hyde is depicted as a crouching figure with thick lips, a broad fat nose, and very prominent buck teeth, and he walks with a lurch.

Hyde returns soon to the dance hall where he demonstrates his interest in Ivy. Eventually, Hyde dominates and tortures Ivy physically. In turn, Jekyll tries to free himself from Hyde's influence and sends money to Ivy. He assures her that she won't be troubled by Hyde again. Later, Jekyll turns involuntarily into Hyde. Hyde taunts Ivy for falling for a gentleman (namely, Jekyll), so unlike himself, and then he kills her and escapes. Unable to get into the laboratory (he has lost the key to the back door), Hyde tries unsuccessfully to get into the house by the front door. When Jekyll is late for the Carew dinner party, the General orders his daughter never to see Jekyll again.

Hyde sends a message begging his friend Dr. Lanyon (played by Holmes Herbert) to get him a vial from his laboratory and have it ready for him. When Hyde arrives at Lanyon's place, however, Lanyon demands to see Jekyll. Hyde reluctantly opens the package, mixes the chemicals, and drinks the potion. To the amazed Lanyon, wild Hyde turns into gentle Jekyll and promises Lanyon that he will never take the potion again.

When Jekyll reads about Ivy's murder, he realizes the enormity of his misdeeds and frees Muriel from any commitment to him. Once again transformed against his will into Hyde, the madman returns to the Carew's where he murders Carew. Back at Jekyll's laboratory, Hyde transforms into Jekyll. Thereafter, Lanyon arrives with the police and points to Jekyll as the culprit. Jekyll turns into his evil alter ego for the last time, and the police shoot him down. The dying Hyde reverts back into a serene Jekyll. This ending is in sharp contrast to Stevenson's original plot in which Hyde dies as Hyde with *no* transformation into Jekyll, because Jekyll has, in fact, ceased to exist. The movie finale is reminiscent of countless endings of werewolf movies in which the werewolf, once dead, turns back into a smiling, benevolent character. The final release from torment . . . real death!

Fredric March, who had to spend four hours each morning in the makeup chair of Wally Westmore for the Hyde sequences, won an Academy Award as Best Actor to become the only actor in a horror movie to win an Oscar over subsequent years. (Such genre specialists as Boris Karloff, Bela Lugosi, and Peter Lorre never accomplished this feat.) For the Paramount release, Karl Strauss was Oscar-nominated for cinematography, and Samuel Hoffenstein and Percy Heath were nominated for writing, that is, "adaptation" as it was then called. When the picture was released on December 26, 1931, a Detroit critic praised it by claiming the 1931 *Frankenstein* movie was but "a comedy" in comparison with Mamoulian's *Jekyll and Hyde* entry. Movie theaters at the time sponsored *Jekyll and Hyde* contests and gave prizes to children who did the best impersonations of the vivid main characters.

"I think the destiny of mankind lies in our ability to control certain basic elements in our nature. We seem to succeed in all sorts of miraculous achievements, but we fail to dominate ourselves—which is why we have murders and war—because it's difficult to control the primitive elements in ourselves." As for Jekyll, in the opinion of Mamoulian, "His experiment failed, but his aim was noble." Director Rouben Mamoulian revealed this personal viewpoint on the movie's theme in an interview with Thomas R. Atkins (published in *Film Journal,* January–March 1973, and cited on page 182 in Scott Allen Nollen's *Robert Louis Stevenson: Life, Literature, and the Silver Screen,* published in 1994).

The Hays Office, official censors of the movies at the time, cautioned Paramount's then–studio chief B. P. Schulberg against using the lines in which Ivy says to Hyde, "Take me!" and Hyde responds, "I am going to take you." Objections were also raised that the movie dialogue was "overly brutal" and "too suggestive." Specific objections were cited about Hyde's lines, as he fondles Ivy's garter, "Look, my darling, how tight your garter is. You mustn't wear it so tight. It will bruise your pretty, tender flesh." The Hays Office also complained about the on-screen reference to Ivy's "customers" and to the scene of Ivy undressing before Jekyll.

Most critics agreed that the Mamoulian screen version was closest to the spirit of Stevenson's masterpiece. RLS's niece, Sally Fields, went to see the film with reservations, because she knew how difficult it was to render justice to her uncle's novella on screen. After viewing the movie, however, she wrote to Mamoulian, "Dear Sir, as a member of the Stevenson family, I went to see your film on *Jekyll and Hyde* with a certain apprehension, because I knew that it needed a great genius to render justice to this great work. You have shown it Mr. Mamoulian, because it is a magnificent film, and my only regret when I saw it was that Mr. Stevenson was no longer alive to see it."

Unfortunately for film buffs, Metro-Goldwyn-Mayer acquired the screen rights to *Dr. Jekyll and Mr. Hyde* from Paramount and consigned the Mamoulian classic to the archives for the next thirty years, in order to release their own version without competition. Initially, Victor Fleming the director and producer of MGM's new adaptation, wanted to cast the suave English actor Robert Donat in the title role, but Donat dropped out of consideration and Spencer Tracy replaced him. At the time Tracy was very much a marketable star. Nonetheless, Tracy was sorely miscast as Jekyll and Hyde. He himself did not enjoy playing the roles. Tracy used so little makeup that the writer Somerset Maugham, upon viewing Tracy's performance, wryly asked director Fleming, "Which one is he now, Jekyll or Hyde?" Tracy's Hyde is human, not apelike. He does not appear much different from Jekyll, so it is hard for the viewer to believe that characters in the movie do not recognize him at once.

In the maudlin opening of this black-and-white film, which is set in London in 1887, Dr. Harry Jekyll is seen praying in church with his fiancée Beatrix Emery (Lana Turner) and her

Spencer Tracy with beakers.
(BETTMANN/CORBIS)

father Sir Charles (Donald Crisp). The sermon by the bishop is disrupted by a violent man who grabs Jekyll and declares that Jekyll shares his views concerning the hypocrisy of the Church and acceptable social practices. Jekyll takes this madman back with him to his clinic for treatment. But the insane man dies and Jekyll, now unable to try out the new drug on a patient, takes it himself. As he chokes, the scene

IN SEARCH OF DR. JEKYLL AND MR. HYDE

quickly dissolves to show him in a pop-Freudian pose of wildly whipping horses that transform into the prostitute, Ivy, and Jekyll's fiancée, Beatrix. As Hyde, Jekyll soon meets the music hall girl, Ivy Peterson (her last name was changed from Pierson to account for Ingrid Bergman's Swedish accent in the film).

When Jekyll and Beatrix are found kissing by Sir Charles, the baronet packs her off to the Continent. The depressed Jekyll drinks the potion and turns into Hyde. As Hyde he visits the frightened Ivy and strangles her. Hyde then reverts into Jekyll in front of Dr. Lanyon (Ian Hunter). Hyde next visits Beatrix and kills her father. The police arrive at the Jekyll mansion just after Hyde has changed back into Jekyll, who claims that Hyde had indeed been seen there, but has left. Now frightened himself, Jekyll transforms involuntarily into Hyde. While fighting off the police, he is mortally wounded and dies, whereupon Hyde's face turns back into that of the serene Jekyll.

Ingrid Bergman stated to her co-author Alan Burgess in *Ingrid Bergman: My Story* (1980) that:

> Spencer didn't like some of the scenes, especially the one where he had to race up the stair carrying me off to the bedroom for his immoral purposes. Victor Fleming demonstrated. Big and strong, he picked me up and ran up the stairs as if I weighed nothing. Spencer wailed, "What about my hernia?" So, they rigged up a sling which supported me so they could hoist me upwards while Spencer hung on and raced up behind me looking as if he were carrying me. But it wasn't that easy. First they hauled me up so fast that Spencer could not keep up, and Victor Fleming said, "Take her up at a natural

pace. Let's try it again." It was most difficult. Up and down, for the whole rehearsal time. Then, on the twentieth attempt, the rope broke. I dropped into Spencer's arms. He couldn't hold me, and we went head over heels to the bottom of the stairs.

This MGM entry is interesting in that it shows that Jekyll had actually been leading a secret double life of vice *before* he took the potion. The Hays Office censorship group objected to Hyde's words to Ivy: "I'm hurting you, because I *like* to hurt you." After some minor changes, the script was approved.

Aside from Ingrid Bergman's sensitive performance as Ivy, the 1941 film is truly bad. The *New York Times* review declared, "Mr. Tracy has taken the short end of the stick by choice. . . . Mr. Tracy's portrait of Hyde is not so much evil incarnate as it is the ham rampant. When his eyes roll in a fine frenzy, like loose marbles in his head, he is more ludicrous than dreadful." Without proper makeup, Tracy as Hyde actually looks more sick than scary.

The final word on this disappointing celluloid adaptation belongs to the *New York Times* review, which correctly concludes, "Out of ham and hokum the adapters have tried to create a study of a man caught at bay by the devil he has released within himself. And it doesn't come off either as hokum, significant drama, or entertainment." Thanks, however, to the studio's politicking, the movie earned three Academy Award nominations.

World War II, which formally began for the United States on December 7, 1941, led to a number of remakes based on the made-up "lives" of the sons and daughters of Frankenstein, Dracula, and Jekyll and Hyde during the forties, as audiences sought rather primitive escapism. The son of Dr. Jekyll, however, had to await his incarnation until after the end of World War II, perhaps because the horrors of the real war and the revelations of the Holocaust were enough for most people.

In 1951 Columbia Pictures released *The Son of Dr. Jekyll* with the aging romantic lead actor Louis Hayward appearing in the title role, actually as the son of Hyde, not Jekyll. Hence, logically, Hyde had to have been given a wife, which is weird, because in previous movies both Jekyll and Hyde died before being able to marry. The written prologue of this black-and-white entry states, "Hyde, the monster, terror of all London, climaxed his many acts of violence by murdering his wife in their Soho flat." The feature then opens with a mob pursuing Hyde, a scene that looks as if it has been taken from the numerous mob pursuits in many Frankenstein films, and the mob burns Hyde to death in 1860. Then two of Jekyll's friends decide to help raise Hyde's son as Edward Jekyll. The movie subsequently jumps from 1860 to 1890, when Edward Jekyll is thirty years of age and a student at the Royal Academy of Science. He goes to medical school but is booted out because of his strange theories and "experiments bordering on witchcraft."

Dr. Lanyon (Alexander Knox) tells him the story of his real background, and young Jekyll, of course, decides to try to prove that his father was not a monster. Young Jekyll restores his father's old laboratory and tries to re-create the transformation drug. Lanyon has secretly added an ingredient to the drug, so when Jekyll drinks the drug it does not work. Nevertheless, the blame for some murders falls on young Jekyll, and Lanyon is able to certify Jekyll as insane.

While in Lanyon's sanitarium, Jekyll figures out that the real murderer is Lanyon. The two grapple with one another. Jekyll escapes, and Lanyon is forced by an angry mob to jump to his death from his laboratory roof. Ultimately, this is a very silly film.

After the American comedy team of Abbott and Costello met Dracula, the Wolfman, and the Frankenstein creature on the silver screen in the late 1940s and early 1950s, it was almost inevitable that Hollywood would compel the comedy duo to meet the legendary Jekyll and Hyde. Thus, in 1953, came Universal's *Abbott and Costello Meet Dr. Jekyll and Mr. Hyde.* It is included here, because despite a sometimes silly script, it is visually a good movie. In it two bungling detectives, Slim and Tubby, played by Abbott and Costello, appear as two American officers sent to London to learn British police procedures. The film, scripted by Lee Loeb and John Grant, opens imaginatively in the early 1890s with a women's suffragette rally in Hyde Park ending in a fight between the women campaigning for the right to vote and some male bystanders.

After failing to quell the riot, the British inspector, portrayed by Reginald Denny, has the two American detectives thrown in jail, and then officially dismissed from his British police force. Trying to vindicate themselves, the two Americans track down the murderous monster Mr. Hyde, played very effectively by the veteran star Boris Karloff.

Abbott and Costello put Hyde in jail in a wax museum. By the time the inspector comes to get Hyde, he has changed into the mild-mannered Dr. Henry Jekyll. Now employed as a body-guard for Dr. Jekyll, Tubby drinks a drug from Jekyll's laboratory and turns into a large rat. The climactic police chase ends with the death of Dr. Jekyll, the capture of Tubby, and the transformation of all of the British police officers into monsters, because the infected Tubby had bitten them and transmitted the effects of the drug onto them. The film was a box-office winner.

The 1955 TV adaptation of Stevenson's tale, written by Gore Vidal and starring Michael Rennie, was produced as part of the CBS-TV series *Climax!* The story was played out for suspense as a modern melodrama. Though it was long missing, a video has since emerged intact. This was not the first TV presentation of the classic story. As early as 1940, NBC-TV telecast a one-hour adaptation of Stevenson's work, starring Winfield Hoeny in the dual lead roles. Nine years later, CBS-TV offered a thirty-minute rendition on its *Suspense* series with Ralph Bell in the lead. In 1951 *Suspense* again presented the *Jekyll and Hyde* tale. Once again it was directed by Robert Stevens, but this time Basil Rathbone played the title parts. NBC-TV's *Matinee Theater* provided a one-hour version of the property on March 8, 1957; Douglas Montgomery starred in that project.

In 1957 came the ludicrous *Daughter of Dr. Jekyll* directed by Edgar G. Ulmer, who helmed many budget adventure films. This threadbare variation on the *Jekyll and Hyde* theme opens with a hairy face intoning the following silly words labeling the narrative about Dr. Jekyll and Mr. Hyde as "the thought-provoking story of how a strange experiment transforms a benevolent old doctor into Mr. Hyde, a human werewolf. When the news of the death of this monster came, there was a nationwide sigh of relief. . . . The evil thing would never prowl the dark again." Then the grimacing face warns, "Are you sure?"

The incompetent script, written by Jack Pollexfen, did not even cite the full title of Stevenson's story, and the use of the words *human werewolf* is a tautology, because the word *werewolf* actually signifies "human wolf" all by itself. Young Janet Smith (Gloria Talbott), an English orphan, returns home to gain her sizeable inheritance. Her guardian Dr. Lomas (Arthur Shields), looking like a zombie, informs her that her father was the infamous Dr. Jekyll who was rumored to have been a werewolf named Hyde.

After a number of werewolflike killings occur in the neighborhood, Janet dreams that she has become a werewolf, feels guilty about it, and contemplates suicide. Fortunately, her boyfriend George (John Agar) discovers that Dr. Lomas is the real werewolf who killed her father. George rallies the villagers who chase Lomas into a cave, where the villagers impale Lomas, the werewolf, on a wooden stake. *Variety* put the production in its place very well by saying, "At one point, co-star John Agar declares, 'This is ridiculous.' That sums up the cheapie horror pic for the exploitation market."

The British film company, Hammer Films, which had turned out successful horror movies since the late 1950s, released *The Two Faces of Dr. Jekyll* (aka *House of Fright*) in 1960. The plot, written by Wolf Mankowitz, involves a kind of inversion of the *Jekyll and Hyde* theme in which Dr. Jekyll is a dull, drab character who transforms into the handsome womanizer Mr. Hyde in anticipation of Jerry Lewis's *The Nutty Professor*. The setting is London in 1874, where Jekyll's colleagues ridicule his theories about the duality of man.

In this color feature, when Dr. Henry Jekyll (Paul Massie) turns into the good-looking Mr. Hyde, he finds out that his wife Kitty (Dawn Adams) is having an affair with his friend Paul Allen (Christopher Lee). As Hyde, he rapes Kitty and causes her death. As for her lover, Paul, he is smothered to death by a python. Hyde then takes up with snake dancer Maria (Norma Marla) but later murders her. Hyde also kills a stable boy who has found out his secret, and then declares, at the resultant inquest where Jekyll is found guilty of all the murders, that Jekyll has committed suicide. In the end Hyde involuntarily turns into an aged, spent, over-the-hill Jekyll, rejoicing in Hyde's destruction but realizing also that, as Jekyll, he has destroyed himself as well.

Paul Massie, who played both Jekyll and Hyde was a comparatively unknown actor, so, when the role was offered to him, he said, "I fairly jumped at the opportunity," as quoted in the film's press book. The director Terence Fisher said, "Massie understood the role and felt it. There was not one redeeming character—it was an exercise, rightly, or wrongly, in evil." Christopher Lee, who played the scoundrel Paul, friend of Dr. Jekyll, felt that "The part was written for me. I think it was one of the best performances I've given."

Nevertheless, the best actor in the project was the python. Margaret Robinson who provided the masks used in the movie also took care of the snake. She said that the actress playing the snake charmer could not dance very well, so another woman who knew how to handle the snake was in some of the takes disguised behind a mask. Besides, Christopher Lee "wasn't too keen on snakes, so I had to make two—one to look alive, one to look dead." But when the producer Michael Carreras accidentally picked up the real snake, thinking it was the fake, the two-snake notion was scrapped.

The Times (London) characterized the movie as "an ingenious, though repellant variation." *The Observer* called it, "a vulgar, intentionally foolish work." In contrast, the *New York Herald Tribune* wrote that it was "a colorful, ingenious remake." In any case, the film did poorly at the box office.

The Stevenson novella, which began as serious tragedy, was turned into farce when *The Nutty Professor*, a Jerry Lewis comedy, appeared in 1963. In this expansive, 107-minute Paramount release, Lewis plays a wacky, unattractive professor called Ferris Kelp, who turns into the seductive Buddy Love (a supposed takeoff on Lewis's former partner Dean Martin). His love interest is the aptly named Stella Purdy, portrayed by Stella Stevens. The color feature did very well at the box office and became a popular item in later television airings. A dissenter at the time of its initial release was *Variety*, whose reviewer (Tube) complained: "Too often the film bogs down in pointless, irrelevant or repetitious business, nullifying the flavor of the occasionally choice comic capers . . ."

An ABC network, made-for-TV movie, entitled the *Strange Case of Dr. Jekyll and Mr. Hyde*, was produced by Dan Curtis and had Jack Palance in the title role. The two-and-half-hour saga was telecast in 1967. Jekyll, the researcher who has no traditional fiancée for a change, claims that, by separating the two selves in one person, one can speed up evolution. Yet Palance was about fifty years of age at the time, the same age as Jekyll in Stevenson's story. As an athletic Jekyll, Palance seems to have fun fencing and fighting street hoodlums. The good doctor continues his experiments with drugs, gleefully becomes Hyde, and kills his lab assistant Dr. Stryker (Oscar Homolka).

After that Jekyll is determined to halt his experiments and become a philanthropist. Upon receiving a charitable contribution from Jekyll, the prostitute Gwyn (Billie Whitelaw) arrives to thank Jekyll for the money. She lures him to her boudoir and takes off her clothes, while awaiting a passionate embrace from Jekyll. Instead, it is Hyde who strangles her. Pursued by the police, Jekyll is shot to death. The show was nominated for six Emmy awards.

In 1971 the British Amicus Studio released *I, Monster*. The film was directed by Stephen Weeks and starred veteran British horror actor Christopher Lee in the dual lead assignment. The script, by Milton Subotsky, relied closely on the Stevenson tale. Here, however, the dual character is called "Dr. Marlowe" and "Mr. Blake." Like Stevenson's original Dr. Jekyll, Dr. Marlowe is a middle-aged, apparently asexual researcher. In addition, his other self, Mr. Blake also has no evident interest in traditional sex.

Marlowe attempts to pick up a slut in a lowlife tavern. He pursues her through the streets and when he corners her in an alley beats her to death with his walking stick. The next day the police discover a piece of the murder weapon, which is identified by Utterson as belonging to Marlowe. Meanwhile, Marlowe injects one of his female patients, Diane (Susan Jameson), with a drug to cure her neurosis, which he is convinced comes from her sexual repression. She offers herself to Marlowe, but, because he is not interested, he simply injects her with an antidote.

Then Marlowe takes some of the serum himself, which releases his secret desires, and, as Blake, he happily smashes his laboratory. Blake gets an apartment in Soho, but, in the end, Blake attacks Dr. Lanyon and is thrown down the stairs to his death. At that point Marlowe's facial features reappear, and the movie ends. In an interview in the 1980s, Christopher Lee claimed, "It was probably the most difficult picture I've ever done" and "one of the best performances I've given." It's actually not a bad movie compared to many others of its ilk. Originally, it was planned to distribute the seventy-four-minute color feature in the 3-D process, which is the reason for many of the strange camera shots that seem somewhat out of place in the "flat" release version.

The Hammer film *Dr. Jekyll and Sister Hyde* released in mid-October of 1971 became the first *major* motion picture to feature Hyde as a woman and to portray Jekyll as a kind of bisexual, as well as a variation of the Jack the Ripper character. The usual transformation of Jekyll into Hyde is completely absent from the screenplay.

Set in the late 1800s, Dr. Henry Jekyll, played by Ralph Bates, is in search of an elixir that can keep people young. One of Dr. Jekyll's colleagues, Professor Robinson, enacted by Gerald Sim, advises Jekyll to get more joy out of life. By utilizing female hormones taken from bodies, Dr. Jekyll eventually discovers a life-prolonging drug that transforms him temporarily into a lovely but evil woman, portrayed by the beautiful Martine Beswick.

Because he requires bodies for further experimentation, Jekyll hires two body snatchers named Burke (Ivor Dean) and Hare (Tony Calvin) to get them, but a mob kills Burke and throws Hare into a lime pit. Jekyll, therefore, becomes another Jack the Ripper–type murderer in order to further his experiments. Professor Robinson becomes suspicious when he examines the body of a murder victim and finds that the sex glands have been removed. Robinson recommends that the police watch Jekyll's apartment. Jekyll, however, as Sister Hyde, kills Robinson who knows too much and attempts to murder Jekyll's neighbor Susan Spenser (Susan Broderick). A mob closes in on Jekyll. To his horror, he observes that Sister Hyde is trying to come out of him. Before this can occur, Jekyll commits suicide. As he expires, the transformation into lovely Sister Hyde occurs one final time.

By throwing Burke and Hare into the plot, the screenwriter, Brian Clemens, introduces Jekyll as the re-embodiment of Dr. Knox from the Stevenson story *The Body-Snatchers*. *The London*

Times of October 15, 1971, proclaimed the movie to be "quite a nicely kinky idea." Nevertheless, theater attendance slipped quickly, largely because the average viewer found the screenplay too puzzling, as the two leads were never seen together in the same scene. Actually photos in the press release show the two of them, Bates and Beswick, side-by-side with a resemblance that is uncanny, if confusing. On the heels of *Dr. Jekyll and Sister Hyde* came the silly *The Man with Two Heads* (1972), with Denis De Marne as Dr. William Jekyll and Mr. Blood. As adapted, directed, and photographed by Andy Milligan it was very low-rate fare.

In 1973 Kirk Douglas appeared in an NBC network made-for-TV musical, *Dr. Jekyll and Mr. Hyde,* set to the usual *Jekyll and Hyde* story line in a performance nothing short of shameful. This musical was indebted to a theatrical musical called *After You, Mr. Hyde,* which was performed on June 24, 1968, at the Goodspeed Opera House in East Haddam, Connecticut. Music for that song-and-dance rendition was by Norman Sachs and Lee Thuna, and was "based on *Dr. Jekyll and Mr. Hyde* by Robert Louis Stevenson."

Lionel Bart added several lyrics and music for the 1973 TV adaptation of that stage rendition. Utilizing Sherman Yellen's new script, the 1973 TV offering is set in 1887 London, and features Kirk Douglas as a singing Jekyll and Hyde. Jekyll is trying to find a drug that will cure insanity, because he disagrees with usual diagnoses of mental problems as that of diabolical possession. Because Jekyll is not allowed to experiment on humans, at the suggestion of a pickpocket (Donald Pleasance), he experiments upon himself. He ingests the drug and transforms into Hyde. As Jekyll, he is involved with his virgin girlfriend Isabel (Susan Hampshire) and with a streetwalker called Annie (Susan George), whom he injects with the serum, literally driving her crazy.

Meanwhile, Jekyll arrives at the home of Danvers, Isabel's conservative father, on a bicycle, which he rides inside the solarium as he sings requesting an earlier wedding date from Danvers. He later involuntarily turns into Hyde and smashes Danvers's skull. Pursued by the police, Hyde transforms suddenly back into Jekyll. Then, enraged, he turns back into Hyde yet again and climbs a wall only to slip and fall to his death on his laboratory table.

Variety (March 14, 1973) was not impressed by the Kirk Douglas TV production of the Stevenson classic. Summing up its disappointment, the trade paper concluded, "Problem is that almost anything can be forgiven a rehash of Jekyll-Hyde except a lack of dramatic fun and gusto."

Three years later, a 1976 release, originally titled *Dr. Black and Mr. White,* and then *Dr. Black and Mr. Hyde* (and also *The Watts Monster*), was essentially part of Hollywood's black exploitation trend in horror movies dating back at least to the 1972 *Blackula.* In *Dr. Black and Mr. Hyde,* Dr. Henry Poole (played by ex–Los Angeles football running back Bernie Casey) is experimenting on a drug that turns dark animals white. He takes the potion and turns into a livid gray zombie who goes on a rampage and murders several prostitutes. In the end the police trap him atop of the Watts Tower in Los Angeles and shoot him in a final scene vaguely reminiscent of the 1933 movie *King Kong.*

In 1980 a bleak Hollywood low-budget comedy entitled *Dr. Heckyl and Mr. Hype,* written "with apologies to Robert Louis Stevenson" and directed by Charles D. Griffin, a protégé of Roger Corman, was inflicted on the filmgoing public. In it a very unsightly podiatrist, named Dr. Heckyl, played by Oliver Reed, swallows a potion in order to kill himself. Instead, he transforms into Mr. Hype, a handsome but violent killer. Next produced was the November 20, 1980, BBC-TV production of *Dr. Jekyll and Mr. Hyde*. The two-hour rendition was directed by Alistair Read and used Gerald Savory's adaptation of Stevenson's original. David Hemmings starred as Jekyll and Hyde. The supporting cast included Ian Bannen (Oliver Lutterson), Lisa Harrow (Ann), Toyah Willcox (Janet), and Diana Dors (Kate Winterton). On January 6 and 13, 1981, as part of the PBS *Mystery!* series, the show aired in the United States.

Shot in 1978 but not released until 1982 was *Dr. Jekyll's Dungeon of Death,* an entry set in San Francisco in 1959 (for no apparent reason). James Matheers is seen as Jekyll's great-grandson, who goes afoul when he experiments with a mind-control serum that his ancestor had developed and which Nazi scientists had toyed with during World War II. Most unusual about this screen misadventure was the fact that the New Age Jekyll does not turn into a Hyde, but rather is sinister enough on his own to commit a rash of misdeeds. *Variety* (February 17, 1982) complained, "Helmer James Wood displays an unhealthy preoccupation with oncamera injections and stages the kung fu material listlessly . . . and his lighting is so bad that when the thespians miss their marks, they are swallowed up in total darkness."

In 1982 Paramount Pictures brought out *Jekyll and Hyde . . . Together Again*. It was directed by veteran comedy writer Jerry Belson. The R-rated production starred Mark Blankfield as Dr. Daniel Jekyll, who is developing a drug that will make most surgery unnecessary. By error, he mixes a concoction that transforms him from a timid physician into an untamed, sex-crazy party animal. The concept was very reminiscent of the same studio's earlier and superior *The Nutty Professor* and Jerry Lewis's Buddy Love.) In this new excursion, the surgeon-researcher is romancing wealthy Mary (Bess Armstrong) while lusting for punk vocalist Ivy (Krista Errickson). Here Dr. Lanyon (Tim Thomerson) is presented as an egotistical plastic surgeon who is his own best patient. *Variety* (September 1, 1992) enthused that "*Jekyll and Hyde . . . Together Again* is an irresistible title and so is the picture, a bizarre comedy that should wow hip kids of all ages. . . . Suffice to say, this is one for those who dip toward the daffy." Unfortunately the filmgoing public did not agree and the movie soon was relegated to TV airings.

Made directly for TV, was *O. G. Readmore Meets Dr. Jekyll and Mr. Hyde* (1986), an animated cartoon written by Malcolm Marmorstein and directed by Rick Reinert. It featured the voices of Lucille Bliss, Stanley Jones, Ilene Latter, Neil Ross, and Hal Smith. On a grander scale was the syndicated-for-TV *Dr. Jekyll and Mr. Hyde* (1986). Made in Australia, the 75-minute production had the voice of Max Meldrum for Dr. Jekyll with David Nettheim speaking for Mr. Hyde.

In 1988, a few weeks after reaching his fifty-sixth birthday, the actor Anthony Perkins, most famous for his screen portrayal of the mother-obsessed Norman Bates in Alfred Hitchcock's classic *Psycho* (1960), traveled to Budapest to star in yet another strange adaptation of Stevenson's novella. The project was directed by Gerard Kikoine, who had made his reputation primarily with soft- and hard-core pornographic movies.

In the final cut, given the title *Edge of Sanity* and released in 1989, Perkins is seen as a seemingly respectable medical doctor, who hobbles around on a cane by day but transforms at night into the dashing Mr. Hyde as a kind of red-eyed, spiky-haired punk clad in fashionable clothing. Jekyll is already married in this version of the story, and his wife recognizes Hyde as Jekyll, because they both look somewhat alike. The Jekyll and Hyde character is, in fact, simply a crack addict who turns into a kind of Jack the Ripper when he takes his cocaine. The feature proved to be yet another poor R-rated screen outing.

Also in 1989 came the *Strange Case of Dr. Jekyll and Mr. Hyde*, part of *Shelley Duvall's Nightmare Classics* series for Showtime cable television. Directed by Michael Lindsay-Hogg with a teleplay by J. Michael Straczynski, it featured Anthony Andrews in the dual lead parts, with Laura Dern as Rebecca Laymon, Rue McClanahan as a madam, Nicholas Guest as Fred Morley, and George Murdoch as Professor Laymon. The next year, 1990, there was a British made-for-TV adaptation for the ABC network of the familiar story, starring Michael Caine; it emphasized the eighteen years of research Dr. Jekyll has put into his startling experiment. This time around, Jekyll is a university lecturer who misses dates and parties in order to care for the poor. To his university students, Dr. Jekyll argues in favor of the power of drugs to transform human behavior. Except for Caine, this two-hour offering which featured Cheryl Ladd (Sara Crawford), Joss Ackland (Dr. Lanyon), and Kim Thomson (Lucy) was just another mediocre production.

In 1995 came the Hollywood movie *Dr. Jekyll and Ms. Hyde,* a puerile comedy in which Dr. Jekyll's grandson (Tim Daly) ingests the potion and turns into a female seductive killer named Ms. Helen Hyde (Sean Young). Unfortunately, after killing several men, there are unanticipated and unwanted return trips as prominent female parts burst out of the embarrassed Jekyll's male body in public. The special effects concentrate upon Helen Hyde's emerging burgeoning breasts in several asinine sequences. The ninety-two-minute, PG-13-rated entry boasted a very eclectic supporting cast, including Harvey Fierstein, Polly Bergen, and Jane Connell.

A remake of Jerry Lewis's *The Nutty Professor* was released in 1996 by Universal Pictures in which the Jekyll and Hyde character, this time named Professor Sherman Klump and played by comedian Eddie Murphy, appears first as a milquetoast, obese science teacher. When Klump takes the magic potion, however, he transforms into the suave Buddy Love, a slimy ladies' man who finds romance with Carla Purty (Jada Pinkett).

The PG-13-rated feature is interesting, particularly in the way that Eddie Murphy successfully plays all adult members of the professor's family in a memorable dinner scene. *The New York Times* review (June 28, 1996) trumpeted, "Eddie Murphy makes his overdue comeback—with a vengeance. Thanks to the mind-boggling morphing and makeup effects that are the film's impressive highlight, Mr. Murphy is able to become Sherman Klump, a shy, gentle, 400-pound lonely guy." The movie was a big hit, grossing more than $128.8 million at the box-office in its domestic release.

Also in 1996 came *Mary Reilly*. The R-rated, Tristar release centered on the *Jekyll and Hyde* story as seen through the eyes of an Irish maid. Joan Didion's screenplay is based on a 1990 novel entitled *Mary Reilly* by Valerie Martin; this feature took a minor character from the original *Jekyll and Hyde* story and turned her into a main participant. According to the narrative, Mary Reilly was abused by her sadistic drunken father (Michael Gambon), who placed a rat in a sack in the cupboard with the frightened child; the rodent bit through the sack and scarred Mary for life. Throughout the story line, Dr. Jekyll preys on this innocent, psychologically maimed Irish servant girl. Unfortunately, as directed by Stephen Frears, John Malkovich as Jekyll and Hyde is not very scary, and Julia Roberts (as Mary) loses her fake Irish accent very soon into the movie, which makes it difficult to believe her character as genuine. (Far more interesting are the supporting characters, played by such talents as George Cole, Glenn Close, and Kathy Staff.)

Made on a budget of $47 million, the R-rated release grossed only $5.6 million in its U.S. release. It won no critical plaudits either. Mike Clark, writing in *USA Today* (February 23, 1996) observed, "Film critic Andrew Sarris once despaired that 1957's *Daughter of Dr. Jekyll* took 40 minutes to establish the truth of the title. This is peanuts compared with the belabored obviousness in Julia Roberts' long-delayed Mary Reilly . . . a perversely coura-geous disaster that audiences will simply hate." Walter Addiego of the *San Francisco Chronicle* (February 23, 1996) pointed out that the filmmakers "seem much impressed with the notion that nine-teenth century Britain was a place where an exceedingly rigid social system caused countless injustices and cruelties. No doubt—but in 1996 this is hardly a novel insight . . . We're left to conclude that the filmmakers took on the project before they imagined any new spin for the material."

A champion of the much-maligned release was the *Chicago Sun-Times's* Roger Ebert, who wrote on February 23, 1996: "*Mary Reilly* is in some ways more faithful to the spirit of Robert Louis Stevenson's original story than any of the earlier films based on it, because it's true to the underlying horror. This film is not about makeup or special effects, or Hyde turning into the Wolf Man. It's about a powerless young woman who feels sympathy for one side of a man's nature, and horror of the other. . . . *Mary Reilly* is a dark, sad, frightening, gloomy story. . . . Of course there can be no happy ending, because what Hyde has done, Jekyll has done—that's the whole point, in a way. But the movie does provide a satisfactory ending, in that Mary is able to comprehend the nature of the man's two personalities, and to pity him."

Additionally in 1996, a video recording (really a docudrama, not a documentary, because historical fact and fiction are blended together), called *Deacon Brodie* was made for BBC-TV in England by Videorecording Tiger Aspect. The Scottish/British ninety-minute production was directed by Philip Saville, written by Simon Donald, and starred Billy Connolly, Patrick Malahide, Catherine McCormack, and Lorcan Canitch. Because it is the only account of the Deacon Brodie case on film to date, it is worth noting in some detail here.

It begins with Brodie's burglary of William Creech's office, from which Brodie steals some poems written by Creech. The stealing of the silver mace of Edinburgh University is depicted before the scene shifts to pretty Anne Grant, the first of Brodie's two mistresses, who declares her love for Brodie and for their young son. When William Creech appears, warning her against Brodie, he attempts to sodomize her, but she pokes him in the eye.

The next several scenes depict Brodie's financial difficulties, his love of gambling, and his other mistress Jenny Watt. With his creditors pursuing him, Brodie faces financial ruin unless he can get money from the city council to back his new gallows plan. When Creech opposes him once again, and the gallows apparatus fails, the council members ridicule him.

On a snowy night in Edinburgh, Brodie and his gang plan the burglary of the Excise Office. On the night of the scheduled break-in, Brodie appears drunk and his fellow conspirator, John Brown, takes over the robbery, shooting a guard. The burglars find little money at the Excise Office, and Brown turns himself in, accusing George Smith and Andrew Ainslie of participating in the robbery. After being promised a pardon by Creech, he implicates Brodie directly. Brodie is tried and sentenced to hang on his own gallows. A French doctor rigs an apparatus so that the condemned man will not die on the gallows. In this television presentation, Brodie survives, and, with Anne Grant escapes to France to start life anew.

Finally, following up on the hugely successful 1996 *The Nutty Professor,* Universal Pictures released *Nutty Professor II: The Klumps* during the summer of 2000. This sequel centers on Dr. Klump's family, and again all the adult members are played by Eddie Murphy (who benefits from the magical special makeup effects devised by Rick Baker). In the plot, Dr. Klump has discovered a youth serum and is successful and happy except for the fact that Buddy Love, his twenty-year-old suave but sleazy alter ego, continues to plague him. Janet Jackson as Denise Gains is Dr. Klump's fiancée, a highly intellectual DNA researcher, and she is the one he turns to for help in eliminating his dark alter ego (Buddy) from his DNA structure. Unfortunately, the experiment goes awry, and it unleashes the scheming Buddy who intends to gain control of the marvelous youth serum. Eddie Murphy again turns in a brilliant comic variation on the *Jekyll and Hyde* theme.

Beyond a 1999 documentary *(Mr. Jekyll & Dr. Hyde),* one new project, still to be completed on the theme of *Jekyll and Hyde,* is being done by New Regency Films. Harold Becker is set to direct the big screen production under the helm of producer Art Linson, and David Mamet is writing the film adaptation, to be based very closely on the novella by Robert Louis Stevenson. American film and theater star Al Pacino is set to play the dual role of Jekyll and Hyde. For further information about this project, interested readers can consult the Internet Web site: www. corona.bc.ca/films/details/drjekyllandmrhyde.html.

If the past century is any indication, there are surely to be many more new adaptations in a variety of film/TV formats. Some may even add the Brodie connection to enhance the verisimilitude of the plot. Present-day filmmakers are bound to delve into the lore of Stevenson's *Strange Case of Dr. Jekyll and Mr. Hyde* and correlate its plot, truths, and conundrums to the philosophies, lifestyles, and urgencies of the twenty-first century.

Chronology and Works of Robert Louis Stevenson

Introduction

The chronology of Stevenson's life and works is an extraordinarily difficult task in part because of his constant travels and the sheer number and variety of works he has left, far surpassing anything that Mary Shelley and Bram Stoker wrote. Stevenson became one of the most widely read authors of his time. The list of his writings provides an excellent introduction to what can truly be described as "Stevenson country." One could, as some have done, tackle his life story by way of his books, which provide all the essential ingredients for a biography.

First, because of the diverse genres of writing, listing his work is a complex task. He has written novels and novellas (some of them

Statue of RLS inside the Edinburgh City Library. (RAYMOND T. MCNALLY)

unfinished fragments), plays, fables, poetry, travelogues, biographies, innumerable letters (some of them unintelligible, even to his friends), articles for journals, and magazines. He left behind many manuscripts now housed at the Huntington Library, the Silverado Museum, Yale, Princeton, Harvard, the Isabella Strong Center in California, and so forth, many of which are not yet published. To compound the difficulty, RLS would begin a piece in one year, set it aside for months and even years, going to some other work, then, finally, finishing the initial piece much later, if at all. One of his greatest works, *The Weir of Hermiston* was published unfinished. Often, he would also co-author work with W. E. Henley (mostly plays), his son-in-law Lloyd Osbourne, his wife Fanny, and, at the end of his life, even with Isabelle Strong, his stepdaughter, whom he hired as his secretary after her divorce from her husband. The total oeuvre is impressive enough: novels and novellas, twenty-eight; plays, seven; fables, eighteen; travelogues, seven; poem collections, six; biographies, two; historical works, one; essays and articles, 152; as well as innumerable letters edited by Ernest Meyhew among others (*Selected Letters of Robert Louis Stevenson*, Yale University Press, London 1997).

In this appendix we will focus first on Stevenson's whereabouts from 1850 to 1894, making each year correspond to each work when he began writing it, and then listing the dates of publication.

Only his principal works will be included, because listing them all would represent a book unto itself. Each title will be italicized, whether a story, poem, play, novel, novella, work of nonfiction, and so on for the sake of consistency. For each year, we shall also include the principal political, cultural, or artistic events that took place in the world, particularly those that affected his life and his writings, which could be useful as a background for the reader.

Year	RLS Chronology	Writings	Events
1850	Born November 13 at 8 Howard Place, Edinburgh, Scotland, north of Leith Estuary. Baptized Robert Lewis Balfour Stevenson.		English physicist William Thompson (future Lord Elgin) invents the thermometer.
1852	Alison Cunningham "Cummy" hired as nurse.		May 1— Inauguration in London of first Universal Exhibition of industrial arts.
1853	Moves to 1 Inverleigh Terrace (now 9) across from Royal Botanical garden in New Town.	RLS dictates *History of Moses* to his mother, November 21.	First Congress of International Hygiene regarding salubrity of cities such as Edinburgh.
1856	First schooling at the Preparatory School for Boys in Cannonmills, Edinburgh, on Rodney Street.		March 30— Signature of Treaty of Paris ends Crimean War between Britain, France, Turkey, and Russia. Allied Victory.
1857	January 1, moves to 17 Heriot Row in Edinburgh, New Town, bought by	Dictates *Book of Joseph* and *The American Traveler* to his mother.	June 26—Prince Albert of Saxe Coburg Ghota, Queen Victoria's

Year	RLS Chronology	Writings	Events
1857 (cont'd)	his parents. Attends Mr. Henderson's Preparatory School on East India Street, Edinburgh. Spends summer at Presbytery of Colinton, his paternal grandfather's place.	Privately printed at Edward Nelson, London.	husband, is elevated to the title of Prince Consort.
1859	After staying home two years, returns to prep school. When Colinton cottage is sold after death of Uncle Balfour, his widow Auntie Jane moves to Perthshire, Scotland.	Dictates *Travels to Perthshire* to his mother.	Charles Darwin (1809–1882) publishes *On the Origin of Species*.
1861	Enrolls at Edinburgh Academy (stays fifteen months).	Dictates *The Antiquities of Midlothian* to his mother.	Outbreak of U.S. Civil War. British Parliament passes Homestead Act for Ireland.
1862	In company of mother Maggie, Cummy, and cousin Margaret (Isabella Balfour), visits London, Southern England,		

Year	RLS Chronology	Writings	Events
1862 (CONT'D)	Stonehenge, and Isle of Wight. In summer travels to Hamburg (a German spa), then back to Scottish coast, North Berwick, and Firth of Forth.		
1863	First travel to French Riviera because of Maggie's poor health, accompanied by Thomas (father), Cummy, and cousin Margaret. Then to Rome, Florence, Venice, and, finally, Cologne, Germany. Late summer accompanies father on trip on Scottish coast (Fife). In fall enrolls at Burlington Lodge Academy, Spring Grove, Isleworth, Middlesex, in England. Later joins his mother on Riviera.	Founds and edits *School Boys Magazine*. In it he writes *The Adventures of Jan van Steen, The Wreckers, Adventures in the South Seas*. All were to be continued but died with the magazine.	May 15—Eduard Manet, French Impressionist painter, scandalizes art world by showing a naked woman with clothed men in his painting, "Luncheon on the Grass."
1864	Returns to Riviera where Maggie	Writes *The Inhabitants of Peebles,*	September 28— First International

Year	RLS Chronology	Writings	Events
1864 (cont'd)	resides. Goes back to Scotland by way of Fontainebleau and Paris. Then to Peebles in Scotland. Enrolls in Mr. Thompson's private school in Edinburgh (New Town) and spends vacations in Scotland at Bridge of Allan, Duncan, Rothesay, North Berwick, and especially Peebles. Also, accompanies father on tours of Scottish coast. In England he visits Torquay, Devon, on the English Riviera.	later inserted in *A College Magazine* (1887). *The Plague Cellar,* his first novel, is never published. Writes the first draft of his play *Deacon Brodie,* and reads it to his friend H. B. Baildon. Manuscript evidently destroyed.	Union of Workers founded in Ireland.
1865	Spring in Torquay, England. Mother in poor health.	Starts *The Trial Magazine* with H. B. Baildon. June 3—Writes two serial tales *The Count's Secret* and the *Convicts.* Writes a novel *Hackton of Rathillet* (unpublished).	April 14—President Lincoln assassinated shortly after victory over Southern Confederacy in American Civil War.
1866	Roams around Edinburgh country	January—Publishes *Sunbeam Magazine,*	July 3—Prussia defeats Austria at

Year	RLS Chronology	Writings	Events
1866 (CONT'D)	side. Summer vacation at Torquay with his mother, Maggie.	only two issues. Writes essays and poems, all unpublished. Writes *The Pentland Rising in Edinburgh: A Page of History 1666,* a short essay on a seventeenth-century Puritan revolt. Father pays to print one hundred copies in Edinburgh.	battle of Sadowa in six-week war.
1867	Father, Thomas rents Swanston Cottage in Pentland Hills near Edinburgh, which becomes RLS's favorite refuge. In November—RLS enrolls in School of Science and Technology at Edinburgh University to study engineering. Summer is spent with Thomas inspecting lighthouses off northern Scottish coast.	Writes eleven unproduced plays.	December 13— while attempting to liberate prisoners held at Clerkenwell jail in London, the Irish Fenians cause the deaths of twelve Londoners.
1868	RLS now a student at Edinburgh	Writes a play with cousin Bob,	First Disraeli Conservative

Year	RLS Chronology	Writings	Events
1868 (CONT'D)	University; rarely attends courses.	*Monmouth: A Tragedy*, published privately in New York by William Edward Rudge (1928).	government oversees the extension of British colonies.
1869	Member and later president of the Speculative Society of Edinburgh. Accompanies father on trip to Orkneys on SS *Pharos*. Discovers the Old Town of Edinburgh with its lowlife of prostitutes and Bohemians.	Writes a series of essays and sketches. Writes a novel, *Covenanting Story Book,* as well as speeches for the Speculative Society. Journal of his trip to Orkneys, published in *Scribner's Magazine,* January 2, 1899. Most of these essays represent material for future books.	Anglican Church is disestablished in Ireland. Beginning of home rule agitation.
1870	With friends he inaugurates *Edinburgh College Magazine*. Often uses "jink," a coded language.	Begins writing essays for *Edinburgh College Magazine* (*Children, Games, Reminiscences of Colinton Manse*). Many are rejected.	July 19—Outbreak of Franco-Prussian War. September 2— Emperor Napoleon III capitulates at Sedan.
1871	Receives Silver Medal from Royal Scottish Society of Arts for paper on lighthouse	*Notice of a New Form of Intermittent Light for Lighthouses, Transactions of the Royal Scottish Society*	January 18— Foundation of German Empire. May 10—Hall of Mirrors in Palace of

Year	RLS Chronology	Writings	Events
1871 (CONT'D)	construction (never built). Abandons engineering. Thomas persuades RLS to enroll at Edinburgh law faculty.	*of Arts,* 8, iii, 1870–71. *Parochial Work and Organization* published in the Church of Scotland Home and Foreign Missionary Record.	Versailles, signature of Peace between France and Prussia. The former loses Alsace-Lorraine.
1872	Joins Conservative Club but also turns to left wing politics and, together with Bob, founds society called Liberty, Justice, and Reverence in Edinburgh. Finishes law school and is admitted to the bar.	*Journal Written as Law Clerk,* published by *Scribner's Magazine.*	Karl Marx's *Das Kapital Volume 1* published.
1873	Visits cousin Maud Babington at Presbytery of Cockfield in England. Falls in love with Frances Sitwell. Visits Sidney Colvin, Professor of Art at Cambridge University. Spring in Menton, French Riviera, with Colvin at Hotel Mirabeau. By	Writes *The New Lighthouse on the DhuHartach Rock, Argyllshire; Law and Free Will.* Notes on the Duke of Argyle delivered to the Speculative Society (unpublished).	In Ireland Isaac Butt founds the Home Rule League. Jules Verne writes *Around the World in Eighty Days.*

Year	RLS Chronology	Writings	Events
1873 (CONT'D)	April joins cousin Bob who studies art in Paris. Returns to Edinburgh.		
1874	Is elected to Saville Club in London. Travels off the Scottish coast on Schooner *Heron*. Accompanies parents to Wales (Llandudno) and returns to Edinburgh in September. At Swanston in October, later walks across Chiltern Hills in England. Returns to London, and then back in Edinburgh in November.	*Roads* written late August for Journal *Portfolio*. *Planned at Cockfield* (first paid writing, three pounds, eight shillings); *Ordered South* for *MacMillan Magazine*; *Lord Lytton's Fables in Song,* for *Fortnightly Review*; *Notes on the Movement of Young Children* for *Portfolio*. RLS writes many other unpaid essays for *Portfolio* journal, *The Academy* (of Edinburgh), William Blackwood and Sons, and so on.	Impressionist Exhibition in Paris opens. The painters exhibited had regrouped as a society of artists after their work was criticized.
1875	RLS travels to Paris and then to Barbizon to join cousin Bob. Passes Bar in Edinburgh in June. In July he returns to Barbizon and Chatillon. With	Writes a number of prose pieces and poems from May to June. Also various reviews (*Vanity Fair* magazine), reference to which can be found in RLS	Benjamin Disraeli's Conservative government replaces that of William E. Gladstone's Liberals.

Year	RLS Chronology	Writings	Events
1875 (CONT'D)	parents travels to Germany (Wiesbaden, Hamburg, and Mainz). Begins legal career in Edinburgh at the end of the year.	letters to Mrs. Sitwell.	
1876	Back in Scotland, walks through Ayrshire and visits village of Ballantrae. Trip to France at Grez-sur-Loing art colony near Barbizon in forest of Fontainebleau (summer). In August undertakes canoe trip on rivers and canals in Belgium and Holland. Back in France meets Fanny Osbourne and daughter Isobel (Belle) and son Lloyd. Back in Edinburgh but Christmas in Paris with Fanny.	Writes travel and nature articles (*Forest Notes,* May, *Walking Tours,* June) for *Cornhill Magazine.* Pens *Virginibus Puerisque* (in Tusitala Edition of Complete Works, Volume 25). Does a review of eight novels by Jules Verne for *The Academy.*	First representation of Goethe's *Faust* at Weimar. Mark Twain writes *The Adventures of Tom Sawyer.* Queen Victoria is proclaimed Empress of India.
1877	Back to Edinburgh (February), and then leads truant	*An Apology for Idlers,* printed in *Cornhill Magazine; Falling in*	Outbreak of Russo-Turkish War in Balkans (April).

Year	RLS Chronology	Writings	Events
1877 (CONT'D)	life in London and Paris. Founds Asthetic Community. In Paris buys a barge with Fanny. Then to Grez (August). In Paris they stay at 5 rue Ravignan. In Edinburgh for short stays (marriage of Charles Baxter) to recover from con-junctivitis. Back in Paris in December.	*Love,* printed in *Cornhill Magazine*; *An Old Song,* (RLS's first novella) in four weekly installments, London, 24–27; *Francois Villon, Student, Poet, House Breaker, Cornhill Magazine.*	German Government signs treaty of friendship with Samoa. Britain and France form defacto Protectorate. Sculptor Auguste Rodin exhibits his "Age of Steel."
1878	Ill in Dieppe, France. Spring in Edinburgh and at Garlrock on Clyde (Easter), but fails to reconcile parents to Fanny. Accompanies Fleeming Jenkins (a juror during Paris Exhibit) as translator. In September, travels through Cèvennes with Donkey Modestine. Ends year with Colvin at Trinity College, Cambridge.	*Inland Voyage* (canoe trip in low coun-tries) is published by C. Kegan Paul and Co., London. For first travel book, RLS gets paid twenty pounds. Only forty-eight copies sold the first year. *Travels with Donkey in the Cèvennes* is pub-lished by C. Kegan Paul and Co., London, 1879. Seven hundred fifty copies sold, paid thirty pounds.	Congress of Berlin. Serbia and Romania become independent from Turkey. Henry James writes *The Europeans,* focusing on European sophis-tication versus American innocence.

Year	RLS Chronology	Writings	Events
1878 (cont'd)		*Edinburgh: Picturesque Notes,* initially seven essays in *Portfolio* (June to December), published by Seeley, Jackson, and Halliday, London, 1879 (has some material on Brodie).	
1879	In London at Savile Club, then Edinburgh. On August 7, embarks on SS *Devonia,* as second-class passenger and reaches New York August 17. Thence by wagon convoy to Monterey, California, August 30. Stays at French Hotel owned by Madame Girardin. RLS is sick (pleurisy) and is nursed by a French innkeeper Jules Simoneau.	RLS writes an early version of the play titled *Deacon Brodie, or The Double Life: a Melodrama, Founded on Facts in Four Acts and Ten Tableaux,* printed by T. and A. Constable in Edinburgh, December 1879. It has its origins in youthful writing by RLS aged fourteen. With the help of W. E. Henley, it is rewritten in January 1879. Revised again in 1880 by Henley, though not printed. In 1888 a version is published under the same title by William Ernest	Auguste Rodin attains International recognition with his statue of John the Baptist. The Fenian militant James Davitt founds the Irish Land League.

Year	RLS Chronology	Writings	Events
1879 (CONT'D)		Henley and Robert Louis Stevenson, T. and A. Constable: Edinburgh University Press, 1888. *The Amateur Emigrant* written for *Longman's Magazine* printed in several installments. Finally published under title *Across the Plain with Other Memories and Essays,* Chatto and Windus, 1892, London. *The Pavillion on the Links* published in *Cornhill Magazine.* Works on a number of articles for the *Monterey Californian* to survive.	
1880	Moves to San Francisco, resides in Irish Hostel on Bush Street (now the RLS museum) to be closer to Fanny, who is seeking a divorce from her husband. Catches malaria in March. Tuberculosis diag–nosed for the first	*Memoirs* of *Himself* for private distribu–tion (later published in *The Cornhill Booklet,* Christmas 1914). *Samuel Pepys* written in June *Cornhill Magazine.* Completes *Virginibus Puerisque,* late 1880, published as *Virginibus Puerisque*	Gladstone's second ministry (April 15) succeeds Disraeli.

Year	RLS Chronology	Writings	Events
1880 (CONT'D)	time. Moves to Fanny's home in Oakland. After divorce (May 19) and marriage in San Francisco, RLS and Fanny spend honeymoon in abandoned gold mining town, Silverado. July 29, RLS, Fanny, and Lloyd take train to New York. August 17, embark on SS *City of Chester* for Liverpool. Back to Edinburgh and Strathpeffer in Highlands of Scotland. Doctors recommend Davos, Switzerland, for treatment of tuberculosis. RLS and Fanny leave Scotland for Davos in October.	*and Other Papers,* London, C. Kegan Paul and Co., 1881.	
1881	Tuberculosis sanatorium with Fanny and Lloyd at Davos. In April moves to Barbizon and Paris, rue St. Roche, then Edinburgh and summer at		British Parliament votes Irish Land Act.

First electric tramway in Berlin. |

Year	RLS Chronology	Writings	Events
1881 (CONT'D)	Pitlochry in Highlands (Kinnaird Cottage). July at Braemar, Scotland. Autumn back at Davos. Depressed, they return to Edinburgh end of May. Because of RLS's ill health, are compelled to return to Davos during winter.		
1882	RLS at Davos during spring with Lloyd where they play "war games." Late spring, back to London, Surrey, and Edinburgh. Summer is spent at Strobo Manse in Peebleshire, then at Kingussie Speyside (Scotland). In fall back to France: Montpellier and Marseilles and stays in working-class district of St. Marcel at Campagne. Typhoid epidemic forces them to leave.	*New Arabian Nights* (story collection), two volumes, published in the spring by Chatto and Windus, London. (They succeeded C. Kegan Paul and Co. as RLS's regular publisher.) *The Treasure of Franchard,* finished in October, is published in *Longman's Magazine,* April 1883. *A Gossip on Romance* appears in *Longman's Magazine,* November 1882.	Victor Hugo publishes *The Four Winds of the Spirit.* Robert Koch, German physicist, discovers bacilli of tuberculosis. Lord Frederick Cavendish, Secretary of Ireland, assassinated in Dublin.

Year	RLS Chronology	Writings	Events
1883	RLS and Fanny move to Nice on Riviera in January, then to Hyères, where they rent a villa, La Solitude, and stay sixteen months. After journey to Lyon, Vichy, and Clermont Ferrand, they are joined by RLS's parents at Royan, France. They hire Valentine Roch. Then, back to Hyères.	*Treasure Island* begun in Highlands for Lloyd and finished at Davos (September–November), written in fifteen days. First published in *Young Folks* in seventeen episodes. Published by Cassell and Co., London, 1883. Initially titled *Treasure Island: or the Mutiny of the Hispaniola by Captain George North,* Stevenson's first successful book. He's paid one hundred pounds. *The Body Snatchers* is written at Braemar, Scotland. *Thrawn Janet,* also written at Braemar, is published in *Cornhill Magazine.* *The Merry Men* published by *Cornhill Magazine.* *Young Rob Roy,* printed in *Stirling Observer,* October 21, Edinburgh. *The Silverado Squatters:*	John Singer Sargent establishes his reputation as portraitist for his portrait of Mrs. Gautreau. Inaugural run of Orient Express train from Paris to Constantinople.

Year	RLS Chronology	Writings	Events
1883 (CONT'D)		*Sketched from a California Mountain* appears in *Century Illustrated Monthly Magazine,* November 1883, pp. 27–39, and is published in book form by Chatto and Windus (London, 1883).	
1884	January—Henley and Baxter accompany RLS from Nice to England to nursing home, then back to Nice and Hyères, with RLS in poor state of health. He is nursed by cousin Bob, and they return to England in June, at Richmond with Fanny before proceeding to Bournemouth.	*More New Arabian Nights* and *The Dynamiter* are begun at Hyères, spring 1883, but completed in Bournemouth and published by Longmans, Green, Co., London, 1885. *Prince Otto: A Romance* is printed in *Longman's Magazine,* and then published in seven installments by Chatto and Windus for one hundred pounds in 1885. *The Black Arrow, a Tale of Two Roses* begun in the spring, published in New York by Charles Scribner's and Sons, 1888. *A*	Mark Twain's *The Adventures of Huckleberry Finn* is published.

Invention of fountain pen by the American, Lewis Edson Waterman.

Oscar Hammerstein invents the first practical cigar-rolling machine. (RLS is an inveterate smoker.)

Death of Victor Hugo in Paris.

Conservative Ministry of Lord Salisbury replaces the Liberal Gladstone. |

Year	RLS Chronology	Writings	Events
1884 (CONT'D)		*Humble Remonstrance* (written in autumn) is printed by *Longman's Magazine,* December 5, 1884. *Admiral Guinea* and *Beau Austin* are published privately in *Three Plays* by W. E. Henley and R. L. Stevenson, London, 1892. *The Bell Rock Lighthouse* is published in *The Athenaeum,* October 1884. *The Body Snatchers* (written in 1881) is published in the *Pall Mall Christmas Extra,* No. 13, December, pp. 2–12. *Macaire: A Farce in Three Acts,* with Henley, is privately printed by R. and R. Clark, Edinburgh, 1885. *The Great North Road* (late 1884) is published in 1895 in *Illustrated London News. Fontainebleau, a Village Community of Painters,* printed in *The Magazine of Art,* and published	British Parliament passes Land Bill easing purchase of land in Ireland.

Death of General Charles "Chinese" Gordon at Khartoum in the Sudan, occupied by the Mahdi's insurrectionary forces. |

Year	RLS Chronology	Writings	Events
1884 (CONT'D)		privately. *A Child's Garden of Verses,* published by Chatto and Windus, 1885, London.	
1885	After lodging in several hostels in Bournemouth, England, settles at Skerryvore Villa at Easter time. Has a few escapades with Colvin to British Museum and Dorchester (August), where RLS meets Thomas Hardy. In Paris RLS visits sculptor Auguste Rodin, befriends painter John Singer Sargent and William Archer. Henry James, the American writer, comes to visit in Bournemouth.	*Memoir of Fleeming Jenkin* begun in autumn 1885, completed in 1887, and published in two volumes in 1887 by Charles Scribner's and Sons in New York and Longman's, Green, Co. in London. Begun in spring, finished in May 1886, *Kidnapped* published by Cassell and Co., London, under the title, *Kidnapped: Being Memoirs of the Adventures of David Balfour in the Year 1751.* Written at Skerryvore September–October 1885, *Strange Case of Dr. Jekyll and Mr. Hyde* published in book form in London by	

Year	RLS Chronology	Writings	Events
1885 (CONT'D)		Longman's, Green, Co., January 1886.	
1886	Joins ailing father at Matlock in England. Sees Auguste Rodin in Paris in company of Colvin. Visits Cambridge University and British Museum in London again with Colvin.	*The Merry Men and Other Tales* (which include *Will o' the Mill, Markheim, Thrawn Janet, Olalla, The Treasure of Franchard*) published by Chatto and Windus, London, 1887. *The Hanging Judge, a Drama in Three Acts* and *Six Tableau* (written with Fanny) printed by R. and R. Clark, 1887. *The Misadventures of John Nicholson* published in *Cassell's Christmas Annual*, December 1887.	Gladstone introduces Home Rule Bill for Ireland Gottlieb Daimler and his son Adolf invent first gas-propelled car. Edouard Drumont publishes his pamphlet *Jewish France*, beginning the Dreyfuss and anti-Semitism crisis in France. Sexual relations between males made a criminal offense under English law. Oscar Wilde is convicted and goes to jail.
1887	Death of Thomas Stevenson in Edinburgh, May 8. Louis arrives from Bournemouth May 6 too ill to attend the funeral. Leaves Skerryvore in the	*The Day After Tomorrow*, published in April in *The Contemporary Review. The Manse: A Fragment* printed in *Scribner's Magazine,* May	The U.S. establishes its first naval base in the Pacific at Pearl Harbor in Honolulu.

Year	RLS Chronology	Writings	Events
1887 (CONT'D)	hands of Mrs. Boodle, the neighbor. RLS, his mother Maggie, Fanny, Lloyd, Belle (Strong), and Valentine Roch sail to Le Havre and embark on SS *Ludgate Hill* for New York where they arrive September 7. Louis stays with Charles Fairchild (Boston Banker and businessman) at Newport, Rhode Island. Fanny finds house in upper New York State in Adirondack Mountains on Saranac Lake, recommended by Dr. Edward Livingstone, a specialist in tuberculosis. Baker's Cottage where they stayed is today an RLS museum.	1887. *Thomas Stevenson: Civil Engineer* published in *The Contemporary Review* in June 1887. RLS later rewrites it as *Records of a Family of Engineers,* August 1891–1893 (complete works, Edinburgh edition). Both *A Chapter on Dreams* and *The Lantern Bearers* published in *Scribner's Magazine,* February 2, 1888. *Pulvis et Umbra* printed in *Scribner's Magazine,* April 3, 1888. *The Master of Ballantrae: A Winter's Tale* begun in December. First published in twelve episodes in *Scribner's Magazine* from November 1888 to October 1889, then in book form by Charles Scribner's and Sons, New York, 1889.	The opening of the first telephonic line between Paris and Brussels is established on February 24. Queen Victoria's Golden Jubilee.
1888	Fanny leaves Saranac (due to	*Some Gentlemen in Fiction* printed in	A socialist Scottish miner declares

Year	RLS Chronology	Writings	Events
1888 (CONT'D)	illness) for San Francisco to see daughter, Belle Strong. Louis goes to New York with Maggie and Valentine Roch. RLS stays at Union House, a picturesque inn at Manasquam, New Jersey. Fanny rents schooner SS *Casco* and persuades RLS to sail to South Seas with Lloyd, Maggie, and Valentine. They leave June 26 with a crew of four for Marquesan Islands. They anchor at Anaho Bay on Island of Nuka Hiva on July 21, then Fakarava on September 4, Tapeete in Tahiti in October, Tautira on Sandwich Island, and, finally, Honolulu in Hawaii, where Valentine gives notice and mother Maggie returns, temporarily, to Scotland.	*Scribner's Magazine,* June 3. *Popular Authors* published in *Scribner's Magazine,* July 4. *The Wrong Box,* begun by Lloyd, his stepson, previous year, is rewritten in 1888 by RLS. Published by Charles Scribner's and Sons, New York, 1889.	himself first socialist and labor candidate to British Parliament (April). Inauguration of Universal Exhibit in Barcelona, Spain (May). Gladstone's Home Rule Bill for Ireland defeated in English Parliament.

Year	RLS Chronology	Writings	Events
1889	Rents a sturdy schooner *Equator* in Honolulu, and leaves Honolulu for Gilbert Islands. Stops at Butaritari and Apemama (June, July). Reaches Apia, capital of Upolu in Samoan archipelago. Buys property, Vailima, twenty hectares (2000 acres) of jungle. Island under German, British, and American protectorate. (Vailima is in German section.)	*The Ebb Tide,* begun by Lloyd in spring (finished by RLS in 1893). Published in thirteen weekly installments in *Magazine Today.* Published in book form under title *The Ebb Tide: A Trio and Quartet,* William Heinemann, London, 1894. *The Wrecker* (summer) published by Charles Scribner's and Sons, New York, and Cassell and Co., London, both in 1892. *The South Seas* (autumn during cruises), published under title *The South Seas: A Record of Three Cruises,* Cassell and Co., London, 1890. *The Bottle Imp* (December) printed in *New York Herald* in four weekly installments, February 8 to March 1, 1891.	Universal Exhibition held in Paris, resulting in building of Eiffel Tower on schedule. Condominium status established in Samoa by Germany, France, and Britain. Bismarck forbids establishment of naval bases on the island. Rudolph Hapsburg commits suicide at Mayerling, together with his mistress Marie Vetsera.

Year	RLS Chronology	Writings	Events
1890	RLS travels to Sydney, Australia, onboard SS *Lubeck* (February). Falls sick and then sails to Auckland, New Zealand, on SS *Janet Nichol* (April). Mid-June goes on to Apemama, and Gilbert, and then settles in at his house at Vailima in Samoa.	*Father Damien: An Open Letter to the Reverend Dr. Hyde of Honolulu* printed by Ben Franklin printing office, Sydney, Australia, 1890. *The Beach of Falesa,* published by Cassell and Co., London, 1892.	Auguste Rodin dedicates one of his sculptures to Victor Hugo. Kaiser William II dismisses Chancellor Bismarck. Parnell forced to resign as Irish leader due to a scandalous affair with a married woman.
1891	RLS returns to Sydney to join his mother Maggie, who has returned from Edinburgh. Takes her back to Vailima. RLS ill again but recovers in New Zealand. With help from natives, Fanny builds big mansion in Vailima with running water.	*Prayers* (summer), fourteen of these *Prayers Written for Family Use at Vailima* (in Edinburgh edition of *Complete Works,* 1896, volume 18, pp. 187–389). *A Footnote to History* (finished November) is published as *A Footnote to History: Eight Years of Trouble in Samoa* by Charles Scribner's and Sons, New York, 1892. *Across the Plains,* twelve essays, eight	Oscar Wilde writes *The Portrait of Dorian Gray.* Arthur Conan Doyle writes *The Adventures of Sherlock Holmes.*

Year	RLS Chronology	Writings	Events
1891 (CONT'D)		of which are printed in *Scribner's Magazine.* Finally published in book form as *Across the Plains with Other Memories and Essays,* Chatto and Windus, London, 1892.	
1892	RLS gets involved with Samoan politics. He supports legitimate King Mataafa and refuses to recognize German puppet ruler, Laupepa. Beginning of Fanny's depressions, some say lunacy. Belle, Fanny's daughter, divorces her husband, Joe Strong, (disliked by RLS) and becomes Stevenson's secretary.	*Catriona,* written February–September, is published in ten episodes in periodical *Atalanta* (December 1893), under title *David Balfour: Memoirs of His Adventures at Home and Abroad.* Then published in book form by Cassell and Co., London, 1893. *Scott's Voyage on the Lighthouse Yacht* (July) is published in *Scribner's Magazine,* October 14, 1893, pp. 492–494. *The Weir of Hermiston,* begun in October but never finished, is one of RLS's best books. Published in	Gladstone forms his third ministry, 1892–1894. Franco-Russian Military Alliance (August). Oscar Wilde's play *Salome* is banned in England.

Year	RLS Chronology	Writings	Events
1892 (CONT'D)		first four issues of *Magazine Cosmopolis* January–April 1896. *The Waif Woman* (autumn), initially printed under the title *The Waif Woman: A Cue from a Saga* printed in *Scribner's Magazine,* December 5, 1914 (pp. 687–701), is later edited by N. C. Wyeth as *The Waif Woman* and published by Chatto and Windus, London, 1916.	
1893	Flu epidemic at Vailima strikes RLS, Maggie, and Fanny. RLS leaves for Sydney, Australia. Doctors order him back to Vailima. RLS gets involved in Samoan politics. His protégé King Mataafa is exiled to the Marshall Islands by his enemy Laupepa (July). RLS leaves for Hawaii with Graham Balfour. Arrives on	*St. Ives* (September), the adventures of a French prisoner in England (and dictated to Isobel Strong in January), is never finished. First published in thirteen episodes from October 1896 to November 1897 by *Pall Mall Magazine*. It's finally published under title: *St. Ives: The Adventures of a French Prisoner in*	Return of the Conservative Unionists to power in England. Oscar Wilde rewrites his drama *Salome* in French, and it is played by French actress Sarah Bernhardt. Outbreak of civil war in Samoa.

Year	RLS Chronology	Writings	Events
1893 (CONT'D)	Island of Oatu (September). Fanny joins him. Both are back at Vailima in October. Fanny has a nervous break-down.	*England* by Charles Scribner's and Sons, New York, 1897 (in the same year as Bram Stoker's *Dracula*). *Fables* is published in *Longman's Magazine,* August 26, 1895. *Heathercat* (July) is left unfinished, abandoned for *St. Ives*.	
1894	RLS has a reconcil-iation with his political enemy in Samoa, Chief Laupepa, and suc-ceeds in freeing his protégé Mataafa from jail. By way of thanks, Mataafa's people build a road from RLS's house to Apia called "the road of gratitude." RLS dies December 3 from a stroke at the age of forty. RLS is cre-mated and his ashes are buried on the top of Mount Vaea facing the Pacific.	Charles Baxter publishes first complete edition of Robert Louis Stevenson's works in twenty-eight volumes (Edinburgh edition).	Rudyard Kipling writes *Jungle Book.* Lord Rosebery suc-ceeds Gladstone as head of the Liberal Party. Anti-Semitism and the Dreyfuss Affair in France nearly tear that country apart.

Year	RLS Chronology	Writings	Events
1894 (CONT'D)	(When Britain retakes possession over the western portion of the Island of Samoa in 1915, RLS's step-daughter, Belle, decides to take the urn containing Fanny's ashes to be placed beside those of RLS in a com-mon tomb on Mount Vaea.)		

Travel Guide—
In the Footsteps of Brodie and Stevenson

Our previous works *In Search of Dracula* and *In Search of Frankenstein* inspired successful travel tours to Romania, Switzerland, and Germany. So it seems appropriate for us to provide a short travel guide to the major places associated with William Deacon Brodie and Robert Louis Stevenson.

The famed Scottish writer loved to travel as evidenced by the many places he visited during his rather short lifetime. In particular, he liked the French Riviera and certain spots in America, but we shall not deal with them here. Furthermore, we presume that only the most devoted fans of RLS may travel to the island of Opolu in the Samoan Archipelago where Stevenson's tomb lies atop Mt. Vaea at Vailima. Also few may wish to travel to

Bournemouth, England, where RLS wrote the *Strange Case of Dr. Jekyll and Mr. Hyde,* because the house in which he lived there was destroyed by Nazi bombs and only a plaque remains. We confine our travel guide to the relevant places in Brodie's and Stevenson's native Edinburgh, Scotland, and Amsterdam, the Netherlands, because they can be easily reached. In addition, we do this for practical reasons because those locations offer excellent accommodations for the modern tourist.

London is technically the setting for Stevenson's novella, but you would never know it. We contend, as did the famous English writer Gilbert K. Chesterton (1834–1936), that the so-called

London of *Jekyll and Hyde* was, in fact, a camouflage for Edinburgh, the native city of both Robert Louis Stevenson and William Deacon Brodie, who inspired the story. The dank atmosphere of the *Jekyll and Hyde* tale is "brown" like

The street in Edinburgh where Brodie's mansion once stood, now called Victoria Street. (RAYMOND T. MCNALLY)

Edinburgh is when the cold mist (the *haar*) blows in from the Firth of Forth and envelopes the city. It is different from the pea soup London fog, which is usually impenetrable. In addition, Stevenson's main characters speak not like Londoners but rather like a kind of Scottish dialect put into English. In fact, Dr. Hastie Lanyon is clearly identified as Scotch.

So, the first stop on our tour is Edinburgh, which has the most dramatic setting of any European city. It is built on a weird landscape of extinct volcanoes. Above the old city looms Edinburgh Castle, which is perched on top of a large crag. In the distance one sees a huge hill jutting up, a former volcano, known as Arthur's Seat, which some attribute to the legendary King Arthur, whereas it actually has no relationship to Camelot.

It is fun to imagine Stevenson, awakened from a deep slumber by the medical marvels of DNA, journeying back to his native city. From the top of Corstorphine Hill (The Cross of Torphin), three miles west of the city, he would be able to see the vast panorama of Edinburgh all the way to Leith Harbor on a clear day. Very little of his beloved homeland has changed.

We recommend beginning our tour historically (see map on page 256) with the Brodie locations in the seedy, colorful alleyways of the Edinburgh Old Town. There is the classic Royal Mile, which extends as its name implies for a walkable mile stretching from the lofty Edinburgh Castle to Holyroodhouse, the Royal Palace at the far end. The city fathers have done a good job in preserving many of the eighteenth-century buildings from Brodie's day. At the Castle one can witness the changing of the guard with the kilted Scotch soldiers hamming it up with a heavy Scotch brogue meant for tourists.

As you walk along the Royal Mile from the Castle, the street changes almost immediately into the Lawnmarket, where cloth merchants once plied

The Deacon Brodie Tavern on High Street, Edinburgh. (RAYMOND T. MCNALLY)

their trade. (Lawnmarket is a corruption of the city of "Laon" a famous fabric center in France.) Along the main street lined with small shops, one usually spots a kilted bagpiper merrily squeezing his baggies for the tourists, even though the authorities have attempted to restrict the sound of bagpipes because it irritates some locals. If you wish to be photographed with the local bagpiper, he is usually agreeable.

As you continue your walk along the Royal Mile, on the left you will spot a sign indicating the Writers' Museum. Built in 1622 it is also called Lady Stair's House, named after a notorious eighteenth-century beautiful lady with a reputedly foul mouth. Inside is a separate, special room housing RLS memorabilia. There is the precious Brodie-designed cabinet, which once stood in the young boy's nursery and which gave his nurse Cummy the opportunity to relate to her impressionable little patient the story of the notorious Deacon Brodie. It is a genuine miracle that this Brodie cabinet has survived. There is also a small statue of RLS in an alcove and other related items in exhibit cases. It is worth a lengthy visit for the aficionado.

As the Lawnmarket imperceptibly merges into High Street, one must imagine the slums beneath the present George IV Bridge. Their homes fell victim to urban renewal long ago. However, the tiny streets are there: Niddry Street where Anne Grant once lived, and Libberton Wynd where Brodie's other mistress, Jean Watt, resided. At Fleshmarket Close, running into High Street, once stood Clarke's Tavern, one of Brodie's favorite haunts. Up above on what is now Victoria Street, one glimpses the remnants of Brodie's mansion.

Walking along High Street, you come across a movable statue of Brodie unmistakably clad in his elegant blue coat over his eighteenth-century lavish attire of matching pants and stockings with gold-buckled shoes. He seems to be inviting you into Brodie's Close. Within the alleyway you find a café with wall paintings depicting central events in the life of the notorious Deacon. This space currently occupied by the café was once the workshop of Brodie, where he also nurtured his cocks for cock-fighting contests.

You cannot miss Deacon Brodie's Tavern, which stands proudly on High Street at the corner of Bank Street. Outside are plaques and wall paintings, which reflect the double life of Brodie. You see him on one side of a plaque clad in his immaculate dandy clothing, and, on the other side, the burglar Brodie is dressed in black. There is also a depiction of the Deacon as a respectable citizen and as a criminal hanging from a gibbet. Here we recommend that you rest a bit and drink a pint of soothing Edinburgh lager beer.

Resuming your walk along High Street and the Royal Mile, you come across the heart of Brodie's Old Edinburgh. It is Parliament Square dominated by St. Giles Cathedral. In front of the cathedral, which was once the main city church, to the south-west is literally the heart of Old Town, a depiction of a heart made of cobblestones, where the Old Tolbooth Prison once stood (demolished in 1817) and where Brodie was held prisoner. This also marks the spot where Brodie was hanged in 1788.

Inside St. Giles Cathedral against the southside wall of the church is a remarkable bronze relief of Robert Louis Stevenson by the noted American artist Auguste St. Gaudens. It shows RLS resting on a chaise lounge with a quill pen in his hand. It is interesting that originally Stevenson had a cigarette in his hand, not a quill pen. Evidently some censor did not approve of having the Scottish writer viewed as the smoker that he was. To the southeast of the cathedral once stood the bookstore of William Creech, Brodie's archenemy.

As you proceed along High Street it turns into Canon Gate, which was once a separate city but is now part of Edinburgh. There was Chessel's Court, built in 1748, where the Excise Office was, which Brodie and his gang burglarized. At the end of Canon Gate is the Palace of Holyroodhouse, which is still used as a royal residence by the kings and queens of Britain on their rare visits to Edinburgh.

From the Palace you can take the Holyrood road toward Nicholson's Street by way of Cowgate, a place used to drive cattle to grazing land outside. This was also often a meeting-place for Brodie and his gang.

Take a bus to get to the southern edge of sprawling Edinburgh University and get off at the Buccleuch Street stop. There lies the Buccleuch cemetery where Brodie was buried. The university uses the Buccleuch chapel for storage and the cemetery yard is locked, so it is difficult to get a close look at Brodie's tomb. If you are athletic and daring, however, you may risk climbing the gate at the back of the chapel and the cemetery. (One of the wives of the current authors jumped over the fence to get clear photos of the Brodie tomb lodged inside the cemetery wall yard.)

For the true Brodie enthusiast, a visit to Amsterdam is a must. You will be one of the few tourists to view the place where Brodie was held prisoner until he was sent back to Edinburgh for trial. Amsterdam is easily accessible by plane from Edinburgh.

Go to the former city hall, now the Royal Palace, in the center of Old Amsterdam. Ask the director to view the fascinating prison cells in the lower part of the building. There you can see the cell where Brodie was incarcerated before being shipped back to Edinburgh for trial. The cells appear to have changed very little from the late eighteenth century. During the early nineteenth century, the cells were used as wine cellars. You can still see the signs on the cell doorways—one for the white wines and the other for the reds!

Now we will turn away from the Brodie places to go to the locations associated with Robert Louis Stevenson. To the southwest of Holyrood Park, which is located southeast of Holyroodhouse, is the main campus of Edinburgh University. There are most of the science and engineering departments, which Stevenson briefly attended before shifting to the study of law.

The major Stevenson places, however, are in the New Town. It is best to get there by bus from central Waverley Station. As you ride up from the Old Town to the New Town, a completely different environment engulfs you, which is probably one reason why RLS thought of his native city as having a double identity. In 1763 a young twenty-three-year-old architect named James Craig won the competition for the design of the New Town, but actual construction did not begin until the 1770s. The New Town was designed in Georgian style in geometric fashion with parallel streets ending in neat squares. On every block was a locked garden open only to the local residents. The New Town, lying north of the Old Town, was completed around 1840, ten years before the birth of RLS. At the southern boundary of the New Town is presently the chic Princes Street, named in honor of the future King George IV; it is now the main shopping center of Edinburgh.

To reach Stevenson's birthplace, you may take a bus or drive. Go along Dundas Street northward, cross one of the bridges over the Leith River, and proceed on to the Inverleith area near the

Botanical Gardens. There, on a small street called Howard Place, is where RLS was born at number 8 in 1850. The *terraced* (a fancy word for a side-by-side row building) house still stands. In 1853 the family moved to Inverleith Terrace number 1 (now number 9) when RLS was two years old. The Stevensons lived there until 1857.

But the main family residence was at number 17 Heriot Row where the Stevensons moved to in January 1857. So, from the age of six onward, Louis called this home until 1881 when he left to marry Fanny Osbourne. Graham Gillespie built this lovely home. One can still admire the elegant look of the place with it iron gatepipes and lampholders. There is a plaque on the house. It is currently a private residence. Some critics believe that Stevenson's famous bestseller *Treasure Island* was inspired by a decorative pool located on Queen Street, gardens which he viewed from his bedroom window.

To complete your tour of Stevenson's New Town, we recommend walking along George Street, one of the finest in the city,

Jekyll and Hyde Pub, Hanover Street, Edinburgh. (CAROL MCNALLY)

where at number 45, the *Blackwood Magazine* was published, to which RLS contributed essays. It is also the home of the *Royal Society of Edinburgh,* founded in 1793, of which RLS was a member. Walking west on George Street, you come to St. Andrew's Square. In the center you'll find a prominent fourteen-foot statue created by Robert Forrest, dedicated to the powerful Viscount Melville, Henry Dundas. Stevenson's father,

Thomas, the lighthouse engineer, designed the foundation of the statue. You can also visit the Jekyll and Hyde Pub at 112 Hanover Street in the New Town.

One of the locations of which RLS was fondest as a youth was the old village of Colinton, a few miles south of the city. This was the home of his uncle, the local minister Lewis Balfour. The manse, church, and cemetery so vividly described by RLS in his Pentland essays has not changed much.

After his uncle died, Stevenson's father, Thomas bought a house in the village of Swanson on the Pentland Peaks. You will need to take a taxi to get you close, then walk the rest of the way. Built in 1761, the former Stevenson cottage has been much altered. It was here that young RLS liked to spend his summers far above Auld Reekie.

In the United States, the following are RLS sites to visit: Deacon Brodie's, a tavern at 2512 North Halsted Street in Chicago, Illinois; the Jekyll and Hyde Club, 140 Avenue of the Americas, New York, New York, which opened January 1995; the Jekyll and Hyde Club, 51 East Ohio Street, Chicago, Illinois, which opened August 1999; and the Jekyll and Hyde Club, Grapevine Mills Mass, Grapevine, Texas. Also, the Stevenson Museum in Monterey, California, and Stevenson's cottage in Sarnac, New York, may well be worth a visit.

Edinburgh

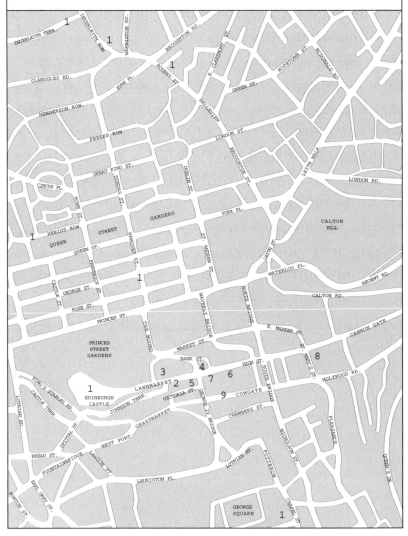

1. Edinburgh Castle
2. Brodie's Close
3. The Writers' Museum
4. Deacon Brodie's Tavern
5. Victoria Street
6. St. Giles' Cathedral
7. Heart of Edinburgh
8. Chessel's Court

9. Cowgate
10. Buccleugh Cemetary
11. Howard Place
12. Rodney Street School
13. Inverleith Terrace
14. Heriot Row
15. Jekyll and Hyde Pub

Bibliography

Most of the Stevenson letters are in the Beinecke Collection at Yale University and the National Library of Scotland at Edinburgh. Sidney Colvin, who was Stevenson's literary mentor, censured Stevenson's letters in various publications.

Aldington, Richard. *Portrait of a Rebel—The Life and Works of Robert Louis Stevenson*. London: Evans, 1957.

Baildon, H. Bellyse. *Robert Louis Stevenson. A Life Study in Criticism*. London: Chatto and Windus, 1901. One of RLS's intimate friends to whom he dictated an early version of his Brodie tale.

Balfour, Graham. *The Life of Robert Louis Stevenson,* 2 vols. London: Methuen & Co., 1901. The official biography largely responsible for legends about RLS.

Beinecke, E. J., ed. *A Stevenson Library Catalogue of a Collection of Writings by and about Robert Louis Stevenson*. New Haven, CT: Yale University Press, 1958.

Boodle, Adelaide A. *RLS and His Sine Qua Non. Flashlights from Skerryvore by the Gamekeeper*. New York: Charles Scribner's & Sons, 1926. A good look into the daily life at Skerryvore as seen through the eyes of his neighbor, friend, and admirer.

Booth, Bradford A. and Ernest Mehew (eds.). *The Letters of Robert Louis Stevenson,* 8 vols. New Haven, CT: Yale University Press, 1994–95.

Buckley, Jerome Hamilton. *William Ernest Henley. A Study in the Counter Decadence of the Nineties*. Princeton, NJ: Princeton University Press, 1945. The best study of the stormy relationship between RLS and William Henley.

Calder, Jenni. *RLS—A Life Study*. London: Richard Drew Publishing Ltd., 1980. Refutes the rumor that RLS married a prostitute.

Calder, Jenni, ed. *Stevenson and Victorian Scotland*. Edinburgh: Edinburgh University Press, 1981.

Chesterton, Gilbert Keith. *Robert Louis Stevenson*. London: Hodder and Stoughton, 1927. Still one of the most insightful studies of Stevenson, in general, and the *Strange Case of Dr. Jekyll and Mr. Hyde* in particular.

Colvin, Sidney. *Robert Louis Stevenson: His Work and Personality*. London: Hodder and Stoughton, 1924. Friend and ardent defender of RLS.

Creech, William. *An Account of the Trial of William Brodie and George Smith*. Edinburgh: William Creech, second edition, 1788.

Cunningham, Alison. *Cummy's Diary*. Preface and Notes by Robert T. Skinner. London: Chatto and Windus, 1926. A diary kept by RLS's nurse while traveling with him on the Continent during 1863.

Eigner, Edwin. "The Double in the Fiction of R. L. Stevenson." Unpublished doctoral dissertation, State University of Iowa, 1963.

———. *Robert Louis Stevenson and the Romantic Tradition*. Princeton, NJ: Princeton University Press, 1966. A seemingly quick reworking of his dissertation.

Elwin, M. *The Strange Case of Robert Louis Stevenson*. London: Macdonald, 1950.

Evans, Hilary. *John Kay of Edinburgh*. Edinburgh: Paul Harris Publishing, 1980.

Field, Isobel Osbourne Strong. *The Life I've Loved*. London: Longmans, Green, Co., 1936. Initially hostile to RLS but eventually gave into his charm and became his secretary in Samoa.

Forbes, Bramble. *The Strange Case of Deacon Brodie*. A novel. London: Hamish Hamilton, 1975.

Furnas, J. C. *Voyage to Windward*. New York: William Sloane Associates, 1951. An excellent, reliable biography.

Geduld, Harry M. *The Definitive Dr. Jekyll and Mr. Hyde Companion*. New York: Garland Publishers, 1983.

Gibson, John S. *Deacon Brodie, Father to Jekyll and Hyde*. Edinburgh: Paul Harris, 1977. Badly organized work centering mostly on the trial of Deacon Brodie.

Grossfurth, Phyllis, ed. *The Memoirs of John Addington Symonds: The Secret Homosexual Life of a Leading Nineteenth-Century Man of Letters*. Chicago, IL: University of Chicago Press, 1984.

Hennessey, James Pope. *Robert Louis Stevenson*. London: Jonathan Cape and Cassell Publishers Ltd., 1974.

Henley, William Ernest H. and Robert Louis Stevenson. *Deacon Brodie*, printed as *Deacon Brodie or the Double Life*. Edinburgh: T. and A. Constable, 1880.

Henley, William Ernest H. written in collaboration with Robert Louis Stevenson. *Plays*. London: Macmillan & Co., 1921.

Herdman, John. *The Double in Nineteenth Century Fiction*. Edinburgh and London: Macmillan, 1990.

Kent, Harold Winfields. *Dr. Hyde and Mr. Stevenson; the Life of Rev. Dr. Charles McEwen Hyde, including a discussion of the open letter of Robert Louis Stevenson*. Rutland, VT. C. E. Tuttle, [1973?].

Kiely, Robert. *Robert Louis Stevenson and the Fiction of Adventure*. Cambridge, MA: Harvard Univ. Press, 1965. Limited by a Freudian perspective.

Lang, Robert. *Gender, Identity, and Madness in the Nineteenth Century Novel*. Leviston, N.Y.: Edwin Mellon Press, c. 1998.

Lapierre, Alexandra. *Fanny Stevenson*. Paris: Robert Laffont, 1993. The best biography of Fanny. In French.

Le Bris, Michel. *R. L. Stevenson. Les années bohémiennes, 1850/1880, Volume I*. Paris: Nil Editions, 1994. The best book on the subject of RLS's early Bohemian life. He criticizes McLynn's biography of RLS.

Maixner, Paul, ed. *RLS: The Critical Heritage.* London: Routledge and Paul Kegan, 1981. Reviews of the *Strange Case of Dr. Jekyll and Mr. Hyde* and a reproduction of Stevenson's manuscript of the *Jekyll and Hyde* novella with his annotations.

Mansfield, Richard. *Unpublished Notes to His Interpretation of Dr. Jekyll and Mr. Hyde.* Pasadena, CA: Henry Huntington Library, n.d.

Masson, Rosalind. *A Life of Robert Louis Stevenson,* Edinburgh and London: T. C. and E. C. Jack, n.d.

McKay, George L., ed. *The Stevenson Library of E. J. Beinecke,* 6 vols. New Haven: Yale Library, 1951–64. The catalogue of the largest collection of Stevenson materials in the world. Essential for Stevenson research.

McLynn, Frank, *Robert Louis Stevenson, a Biography.* London: Hutchinson, 1993. and Pimlico, 1994. McLynn blames much of RLS's problems on the rapacity of the Osbourne family, including Fanny.

Miller, Karl. *Doubles. Studies in Literary History.* Oxford: Oxford University Press, 1985.

Miyoshi, Masao. *The Divided Self: A Perspective on the Literature of the Victorians.* New York: New York University, 1969.

Morison, Aeneas. *The Trial of William Brodie, Wright and Cabinet Maker in Edinburgh and of John Smith, Grocer There Before the High Court of the Justiciary.* Edinburgh: Aeneas Morison, 1788.

Nollen, Scott Allen. *Robert Louis Stevenson, Life, Literature, and the Silver Screen.* Jefferson, N.C.: McFarland & Co., 1994. Good work on the adaptations of Stevenson's stories to the theater and the movies.

Osbourne, Lloyd. *An Intimate Portrait of R. L. S.* New York: Charles Scribner's & Sons, 1924. RLS's stepson is especially good on the setting of Skerryvore and the creation of the *Jekyll and Hyde* novella.

Prideaux, W. F. *A Bibliography of the Works of Robert Louis Stevenson.* London: F. Hollings, 1917.

Rankin, Nicholas. *Dead Man's Chest: Travels after Robert Louis Stevenson*. London: Faber & Faber, 1988.

Rose, Brian A. *Jekyll and Hyde Adapted*. Dramatizations of Cultural Anxiety. Westport, CT: Greenwood Press, 1996. Analytical study of the adaptations of the *Jekyll and Hyde* novella.

Roughead, William. *Classic Crimes*. London: Cassell, 1951.

Sanchez, Nellie Van de Grift. *The Life of Mrs. R. L. Stevenson*. New York: Charles Scribner's & Sons, 1920. Outdated.

Simpson, Eve Blantyre. *Robert Louis Stevenson's Edinburgh Days*. London: Hodder and Stoughton, 1898.

———. *The Robert Louis Stevenson Originals*. New York: Charles Scribner's & Sons, 1913.

Stevenson, Robert Louis. "A Chapter on Dreams." New York: *Scribner's Magazine*, no. 3, January, 1888, reprinted in *The Works of Robert Louis Stevenson*, Tusitala edition, volume 30, 1924.

———. *Edinburgh*. New York and London: The Co-Operative Publications Society, n.d. (1904?).

———. *Dr. Jekyll and Mr. Hyde and Other Stories.* New York: Alfred A. Knopf, Everyman's Library, 1992.

———. *Selected Letters of Robert Louis Stevenson*. Ernest Mehew, ed. Yale University Press, 1997.

———. *The Strange Case of Dr. Jekyll and Mr. Hyde and Weir of Hermiston*. Emma Letley, ed. Oxford: Oxford University Press, 1987.

———. *The Works of Robert Louis Stevenson*. The Edinburgh Edition, 28 vol. London: Chatto and Windus, 1894–98. The first collected edition.

———. *The Works of Robert Louis Stevenson*. The South Seas Edition, 32 vol. New York: Scribner's & Sons, 1925. Fairly complete.

————. *The Works of Robert Louis Stevenson.* The Tusitala Edition, 35 vol. London: Heinemann, 1923–27.

————. *The Works of Robert Louis Stevenson.* The Vailima Edition, 26 vol. London: Longman's, Green, Co., 1922–23. Contains newly found poetry, the story "The Hanging Judge," and other source materials missing from the previous edition.

Swearingen, Robert. *The Prose Writings of Robert Louis Stevenson: a Guide.* London: The Macmillan Press Ltd., 1980. and Hamden, CT: Archon Books, 1980.

Veeder, William and Gordon Hirsch, eds. *Dr. Jekyll and Mr. Hyde after One Hundred Years.* Chicago: Univ. of Chicago Press, 1988. Especially Veeder, William. "Children of the Night: Stevenson and Patriarchy," pp. 107–160.

Wilde, Oscar. *The Complete Works*, 12 vols. New York: Collins, 1927.

Filmography and Videography

[Abbreviations: b/w=black and white; c=color; cam.=camera; dir.=director; ed.=editor; mak.=makeup; mus.=music; prod.=producer; scr.=screenplay; sp. eff.=special effects; tel.=teleplay]

SILENT MOVIES

Dr. Jekyll and Mr. Hyde, aka *The Modern Dr. Jekyll* (Selig Polyscope, 1908), b/w, one reel.

CREDITS: Prod.: Colonel William Selig; dir.: Otis Turner; based on the novella *Strange Case of Dr. Jekyll and Mr. Hyde* by Robert Louis Stevenson and the play by Luella Forepaugh.

CAST: Hobart Bosworth, Betty Harte.

Den Skaebnesvangre Opfindelse (Nordisk, 1909; Danish), b/w, one reel.

CREDITS: Prod.: Ole Olson; dir.: August Bloom; scr.: August Bloom, based on the novella *Strange Case of Dr. Jekyll and Mr. Hyde* by Robert Louis Stevenson.

CAST: Alwin Neuss (Dr. Jekyll and Mr. Hyde), Emilie Sannon, and Oda Alstrup.

The Duality of Man (Wrench Films, 1910; Great Britain), b/w, one reel.

CREDITS: Based on the novella *Strange Case of Dr. Jekyll and Mr. Hyde* by Robert Louis Stevenson.

CAST: Unavailable.

Dr. Jekyll and Mr. Hyde (Thanhouser, sometime between 1911 and 1913), b/w, one reel.

CREDITS: Prod.: Edwin Thanhouser; dir.: Lucius Henderson; based on the novella *Strange Case of Dr. Jekyll and Mr. Hyde* by Robert Louis Stevenson.

CAST: James Cruze (Dr. Jekyll), Marguerite Snow (Muriel Carew, the minister's daughter), Harry Benham (Mr. Hyde).

Dr. Jekyll and Mr. Hyde (Imp/Universal, 1913), b/w, two reels.

CREDITS: Prod.: Carl Laemmle; dir. and scr.: Herbert Brenon; based on the novella *Strange Case of Dr. Jekyll and Mr. Hyde* by Robert Louis Stevenson.

CAST: King Baggot (Dr. Jekyll and Mr. Hyde), Jane Gail (Alice), Matt Snyder (Alice's father), Howard Crampton (Dr. Lanyon), William Sorrell (Utterson).

Dr. Jekyll and Mr. Hyde (Kineto-Kinemacolor Corp., 1913; Great Britain), c, two reels.

CREDITS: Prod.: Charles Urban; dir., Frank Wood; based on the novella *Strange Case of Dr. Jekyll and Mr. Hyde* by Robert Louis Stevenson.

CAST: Murdock, J. MacQuarrie (Dr. Jekyll and Mr. Hyde).

Ein Seltsamer Fall (Vitascope, 1914; Germany), b/w, 50 minutes.

CREDITS: Dir.: Max Mack; based on the novella *Strange Case of Dr. Jekyll and Mr. Hyde* by Robert Louis Stevenson; scr.: Richard Oswald.

CAST: Alwin Neus (Dr. Jekyll and Mr. Hyde).

Dr. Jekyll and Mr. Hyde, or Horrible Hyde (Lubin, 1915), b/w, two reels.

CREDITS: Dir.: Arthur Hotaling; based on the novella *Strange Case of Dr. Jekyll and Mr. Hyde* by Robert Louis Stevenson.

CAST: Jerold T. Horner (Dr. Jekyll and Mr. Hyde), Billy Reeves, May Hotely.

Miss Jekyll and Madame Hyde (Vitagraph, 1915), two reels.

CREDITS: Dir.: Charles L. Gaskill; based on the novella *Strange Case of Dr. Jekyll and Mr. Hyde* by Robert Louis Stevenson.

CAST: Helen Gardner, Paul Scardon.

Der Januskopf, aka *The Head of Janus; Janus-Faced; Love's Mockery* (Decla-Bioscope, 1920; Germany), b/w, 107 minutes.

CREDITS: Dir.: Friedrich W. Murnau; scr.: Hans Janowitz, based on the novella *Strange Case of Dr. Jekyll and Mr. Hyde* by Robert Louise Stevenson; cam.: Karl Freund, Carl Hoffman, and Carl Weiss.

CAST: Conrad Veidt (Dr. Warren and Mr. O'Connor), Margarete Schlegel (Grace and Jane), Bela Lugosi (Dr. Warren's valet), Magnus Stifter (Dr. Warren's friend), and Willi Kaiser-Heyl, Margarete Kupfer, Gustav Botz, Jaro Furth, Danny Guertler, Hans Lanser-Ludolff, Mara Reuter.

Dr. Jekyll and Mr. Hyde. (Paramount, early April 1920), b/w, 96 minutes.

CREDITS: presenter: Adolph Zukor; dir.: John S. Robertson; scr.: Clara S. Beranger, based on the novella *Strange Case of Dr. Jekyll and Mr. Hyde* by Robert Louis Stevenson; cam.: Ray Overbough.

CAST: John Barrymore (Dr. Henry Jekyll and Mr. Oscar Hyde), Nita Naldi (Miss Gina), Brandon Hurst (Sir Richard Carew), Martha Mansfield (Millicent Carew), Louis Wolheim (cabaret manager), Charles Lane (Dr. Richard Lanyon), George Stevens (Poole), Malcolm J. Dunn (John Utterson), Cecil Clovelly (Edward Enfield).

[Available in a Kino video edition from Republic Pictures Home Video, Sinister Cinema, including scenes from the movie cited, which was directed by Lucius Henderson, as well as scenes that are different from the 1920 release cited following.]

Dr. Jekyll and Mr. Hyde. (Pioneer, Film Corp., late April 1920,), b/w, five reels.

CREDITS: Prod.: Louis B. Mayer; dir. and scr.: Charles J. Hayden, based on the novella *Strange Case of Dr. Jekyll and Mr. Hyde* by Robert Louis Stevenson.

CAST: Sheldon Lewis (Dr. Jekyll and Mr. Hyde), Alexander Shannon (Dr. Lanyon), Dora Mills Adams (Mrs. Lanyon), Gladys Field (Bernice Lanyon), Harold Forshay (Edward Utterson), Leslie Austin (Danvers Carew); available on video cassette.

SOUND FILMS

Dr. Jekyll and Mr. Hyde (Paramount, 1932, released on December 26, 1931), b/w, 97 minutes.

CREDITS: Presented by Adolph Zukor; dir.: Rouben Mamoulian; scr.: Samuel Hoffenstein and Percy Heath, based on the novella *Strange Case of Dr. Jekyll and Mr. Hyde* by Robert Louis Stevenson; mak.: Wally Westmore; cam.: Karl Struss; ed. William Shea.

CAST: Fredric March (Dr. Jekyll and Mr. Hyde), Miriam Hopkins (Ivy Pearson), Rose Hobart (Muriel Carew), Halliwell Hobbes (Brigadier-General Carew), Holmes Herbert (Dr. Lanyon), Edgar Norton (Poole), Arnold Lucy (Utterson), Tempe Pigott (Mrs. Hawkins), Colonel McDonnell (Hobson), Eric Wilton (Briggs), Douglas Walton (student), John Rogers (waiter), Murdock MacQuarrie (doctor), Major Sam Harris (dance extra).

[Available on video with whipping scenes restored, MGM Home Entertainment. Beware of the 82-minute reissued version.]

Dr. Jekyll and Mr. Hyde (Metro-Goldwyn-Mayer, 1941), b/w, 114 minutes.

CREDITS: Prod. Victor Fleming and Victor Saville; Victor Fleming, scr: John Lee Mahin, based on the novella *Strange Case of Dr. Jekyll and Mr. Hyde* by Robert Louis Stevenson; mus.: Franz Waxman; mak., Jack Dawn, sp. eff.: Warren Newcombe; cam.: Joseph Ruttenberg; ed. Harold F. Kress.

CAST: Spencer Tracy (Dr. Harry Jekyll and Mr. Hyde), Ingrid Bergman (Ivy Peterson), Lana Turner (Beatrix Emery), Donald Crisp (Sir Charles Emery), Ian Hunter (Dr. John Lanyon), Barton MacLane (Sam Higgins), C. Aubrey Smith (the bishop), Peter Godfrey (Poole), Sara Allgood (Mrs. Higgins), Frederic Worlock (Dr. Heath), William Tannen (Fenwick, the intern), Frances Robinson (Marcia), Denis Green (Freddie), Billy Bevan (Dr. Weller), Forrester Harvey (Old Prouty), Lumsden Hare (Colonel Weymouth), Lawrence Grant (Dr. Courtland), John Barclay (Constable), Doris Lloyd (Mrs. Marley), Gwen Gaze (Mrs. French), Hillary Brooke (Mrs. Arnold), Mary Field (wife), Aubrey Mather (Inspector).

[Available in video along with two scenes deleted from the released movie in which Tracy viciously beats his girlfriend Ivy Peterson played by Ingrid Bergman; computer-colored version available from MGM Home Entertainment.]

The Son of Dr. Jekyll (Columbia, 1951), b/w, 77 minutes.

CREDITS: Dir.: Seymour Friedman; scr.: Mortimer Braus, Jack Pollexfen, and Edward Huesbsch (uncredited); based on the novella *Strange Case of Dr. Jekyll and Mr. Hyde* by Robert Louis Stevenson; mus., Paul Sawtell; mak., Clay Campbell; cam.: Henry Freulich; ed.: Gene Havlick.

CAST: Louis Hayward (Edward Jekyll and Dr. Henry Jekyll), Jody Lawrence (Lynn), Alexander Knox (Dr. Curtis Lanyon), Lester Matthews (Sir John

Utterson), Gavin Muir (Richard Daniels), Paul Cavanagh (Inspector Stoddard), Rhys Williams (Michaels), Doris Lloyd (Lottie Sarelle), Claire Carleton (Hazel Sarelle), Rhys Williams (Michaels), Patrick O'Moore (Joe Sarelle), Olaf Hytten (prosecutor), Guy Kingsford and Ottola Nesmith (nurses), Bruce Lister (reporter), Phyllis Morris (tea woman), Leonard Mudie (pharmacist). Stapleton Kent (Mr. Arnim), Benita Booth (woman), David Cole (copy boy), Holmes Herbert and Keith Hitchcock (constables).

Abbott & Costello Meet Dr. Jekyll and Mr. Hyde (Universal, 1953), b/w, 77 minutes.

CREDITS: Prod.: Howard Christie; dir.: Charles Lamont; scr: Lee Loeb and John Grant, based on the screen story by Sidney Fields and Grant Garrett and the novella *Strange Case of Dr. Jekyll and Mr. Hyde* by Robert Louis Stevenson; mus. supervisor: Joseph E. Gershenson; mak., Bud Westmore; sp. eff. David S. Horsley; cam,: George Robinson, ed. Russell Schoengarth.

CAST: Bud Abbott (Slim), Lou Costello (Tubby), Boris Karloff (Dr. Henry Jekyll), Eddie Parker (Mr. Hyde—stunt double), Craig Stevens (Bruce Adams), Helen Westcott (Vicky Edwards), Reginald Denny (inspector); John Dierkes (Batley), Arthur Gould-Porter (bartender), Judith Brian (woman on bike), Hilda Plowright (nursemaid), Keith Hitchcock (jailer); Donald Kerr (chimney sweep), Lucille Lamarr and Patti McKay (dancers), John Rogers (drunk), Herbert Deans (victim), Carmen de Lavallade (Javanese).

The Daughter of Dr. Jekyll (Allied Artists, 1957), b/w, 71 minutes.

CREDITS: Prod.: Jack Pollexfen; dir.: Edgar G. Ulmer; suggested by the novella *Strange Case of Dr. Jekyll and Mr. Hyde* by Robert Louis Stevenson; scr.: Jack Pollexfen; mus.: Melvyn Leonard; cam.: John F. Warren; ed.: Holbrook N. Todd.

CAST: Gloria Talbott (Janet Smith), John Agar (George Hastings), Arthur Shields (Dr. Lomas), John Dierkes (Jacob), Martha Wentworth (Mrs. Merchant), Mollie McCart (Maggie, the maid), Rita Greene (young woman), Marel Page (young man).

Grip of the Strangler aka *The Haunted Strangler; Stranglehold* (Eros, 1958; Great Britain; Metro-Goldwyn-Mayer; United States, 1959), b/w, 81 minutes.

CREDITS: Prod.: John Croydon; dir.: Robert Day; scr.: Jan Read, John C. Cooper, and Lionel Baines; mus.: Buxton Orr; mak.: Jim Hydes; sp. eff.: Les Bowie; cam.: Lionel Banes; ed.: Peter Mayhew.

CAST: Boris Karloff (James Rankin), Jean Kent (Cora Seth), Elizabeth Allan (Barbara Rankin), Anthony Dawson (Superintendent Burke), Vera Day (Pearl), Timothy Turner (Kenneth McColl), Diane Aubrey (Lily), Dorothy Gordon (Hannah), Peggy Ann Clifford (Kate), Leslie Perrins (prison governor), Michael Atkinson (Styles), Desmond Roberts (Dr. Johnson), Jessie Cairns (maid), Roy Russell (medical superintendent), Derek Birch (superintendent), George Spense (hangman), Joan Elvin (can-can girl), John Fabian (Pearl's boyfriend).

Le Testament du Docteur Cordelier aka *The Will of Doctor Cordelier* (Pathe, 1959; France), c, 95 minutes.

CREDITS: Dir. and scr.: Jean Renoir, an updated adaptation of the novella *Strange Case of Dr. Jekyll and Mr. Hyde* by Robert Louis Stevenson; mus.: Joseph Kosma. cam.: Georges Leclerc; ed. Renee Lichtig.

CAST: Jean-Louis Barrault (Dr. Cordelier and Mr. Opale), Michel Vitold (Severin), Teddy Bilis (Joly), Jean Topart (Desire), Gaston Modot (Blaise), and Micheline Gary.

The Two Faces of Dr. Jekyll (Hammer Films, 1960; Great Britain), aka *House of Fright* (1961, American International), c, 88 minutes.

CREDITS: Prod.: Michael Carreras; dir.: Terence Fisher; scr: Wolf Mankowitz, based on the novella *Strange Case of Dr. Jekyll and Mr. Hyde* by Robert Louis Stevenson; mus.: Monty Norman and David Heneker; mak.: Roy Ashton; cam.: Jack Asher; ed.: Eric Boyd-Perkins.

CAST: Paul Massie (Dr. Henry Jekyll and Mr. Edward Hyde), Dawn Addams (Kitty Jekyll), Christopher Lee (Paul Allen), David Kossoff (Ernest Litauer), Francis De Wolfe (inspector), Norma Marla (Maria), Magda Miller and Joy Webster (sphinx girls), William Kendall (clubman), Oliver Reed (nightclub bouncer), Helen Goss (nanny), Pauline Shepherd (Mary, a young prostitute), Percy Cartwright (coroner), Joe Robinson (Corinthian), Arthur Lovegrove (cabby), Douglas Robinson (boxer).

The Nutty Professor (Paramount, 1963), c, 107 minutes.

CREDITS: Prod.: Jerry Lewis and Ernest D. Glucksman; dir.: Jerry Lewis, scr.: Jerry Lewis and Bill Richmond; based on a story by Jerry Lewis; mus.: Walter Scharf; mak.: Wally Westmore; sp. eff.: Paul K. Lerpal; cam.: W. Wallace Kelley; ed. John Woodcock.

CAST: Jerry Lewis (Professor Ferris Kelp and Buddy Love), Stella Stevens (Stella Purdy), Del Moore (Dr. Hamius R. Warfield), Kathleen Freeman (Millie Lemmon); Ned Flory, Skip Ward, and Norman Alden (football players), Howard Morris (Mr. Kelp); Elvia Allman (Mrs. Kelp), Milton Fromm (Dr. Leevee), Buddy Lester (bartender), Marvin Kaplan (English boy), Doodles Weaver (rube), Mushy Callahan (cab driver), Gary Lewis (boy), Les Brown and His Band of Renown (themselves).

I, Monster (British Lion-Amicus Pictures, filmed in 1970 in England, released in Great Britain in 1971 and in the United States in 1973), c, 74 minutes.

CREDITS: Prod.: Max J. Rosenberg and Milton Subotksy; dir.: Stephen Weeks; scr.: Milton Subotsky, based on the novella *Strange Case of Dr. Jekyll and Mr. Hyde* by Robert Louis Stevenson; mak.: Harry Frampton and Peter Frampton; cam.: Moray Grant; ed.: Peter Tanner.

CAST: Christopher Lee (Dr. Charles Marlowe and Mr. Edward Blake), Peter Cushing (Utterson), Susan Jameson (Diane), Mike Raven (Dr. Enfield), Richard Hearndell (Lanyon), George Merritt (Poole), Marjie Lawrence (Annie), Kenneth J. Warren (Deane), Aimée Delamain (landlady), Michael Des Barres (tough boy in alley).

Dr. Jekyll and Sister Hyde (Hammer Films, 1971; Great Britain; American International, 1972), c, 94 minutes.

CREDITS: Prod.: Albert Fennell and Brian Clemens; dir.: Roy Ward Baker; scr.: Brian Clemens, suggested by the novella *Strange Case of Dr. Jekyll and Mr. Hyde* by Robert Louis Stevenson; mus.: David Whittaker; mak.: Trevor Crole-Rees; cam.: Norman Warwick; ed.: James Needs.

CAST: Ralph Bates (Dr. Jekyll), Martine Beswick (Sister Hyde), Gerald Sim (Professor Robertson), Lewis Flander (Howard), Dorothy Alison (Mrs. Spencer), Neil Wilson (older policeman), Ivor Dean (Burke), Paul Whitsun-Jones

(Sergeant Danvers), Philip Madoc (Byker), Tony Calvin (Hare), Susan Broderick (Susan), Dan Meaden (town crier), Virginia Wetherell (Betsy), Geoffrey Kenion (first policeman), Irene Bradshaw (Yvonne), Anna Brett (Julie), Jackie Poole (Margie), Rosemary Lord (Marie), Petula Portell (Petra), Pat Brackenbury (Helen), Liz Romanoff (Emma), Will Stampe (mine host), Roy Evans (knife grinder), Jeannette Wild (Jill), Bobby Parr (young apprentice), Julia Wright (street singer).

The Man with Two Heads (Mishkin, 1972), c, 80 minutes.

CREDITS: Prod.: William Mishkin; dir. and scr.: Andy Milligan; based on the novella *Strange Case of Dr. Jekyll and Mr. Hyde* by Robert Louis Stevenson; mus.: David Tike; mak.: Lois Marsh; cam.: Andy Milligan.

CAST: Denis De Marne (Dr. William Jekyll and Mr. Blood), Julia Stratton (April Conners), Gay Feld (Mary Ann Marsden), Jacqueline Lawrence (Carla), Berwick Kaler (Smithers), Bryan Southcombe (Oliver Marsden), Jennifer Summerfield (Vicky).

Dr. Black, Mr. Hyde, aka *Dr. Black & Mr. White; The Watts Monster* (Dimension Pictures, 1976), c, 87 minutes.

CREDITS: Prod.: Charles Walker; dir.: William Crain; scr.: Larry LeBron, suggested by the novella *Strange Case of Dr. Jekyll and Mr. Hyde* by Robert Louis Stevenson; and screen idea by Lawrence Woolner; mus.: John Pate; mak.: Harry Woolman; sp. mak: Stan Winston; cam.: Tak Fujimoto; ed.: Jack Horger.

CAST: Bernie Casey (Dr. Pride and Mr. Hyde), Rosalind Cash (Dr. Billie Worth), Marie O'Henry (Linda), Ji-Tu Cumbuka (Lieutenant Jackson), Milt Kogan (Lieutenant O'Connor), Stu Gilliam (Silky).

Dr. Heckyll and Mr. Hype (Cannon Films, 1980), c, 99 minutes.

CREDITS: Prod.: Menahem Golan and Yoram Globus; dir. and scr.: Charles B. Griffith; mus.:Richard Band; cam.: Robert Carras and Hal Trussell; ed.: Skip Schoolnik.

CAST: Oliver Reed (Dr. Heckyll and Mr. Hype), Sunny Johnson (Coral Careen), Maia Danziger (Miss Fineburn), Mel Welles (Dr. Hinkle), Virgil Frye (Lieutenant MacDruck, "Il Topo"), Kedrick Wolfe (Dr. Lew Hoo);

Jackie Coogan (Sergeant Fleacollar), Corinne Calvet (Pizelle Puree), Sharon Compton (Mrs. Quivel), Deniose Hayes (Liza), and: Charles Howerton, Dick Miller, Jack Warford, Lucretia Love, Ben Frommer, Micky Fox, Lisa Zebra, Stan Ross, Joe Anthony Cox, Duane Thomas, Michael Ciccone, Steve Ciccone, Randi Brough, Herta Ware, Carin Berger, Ed Randolph.

Doctor Jekyll and Miss Osbourne, aka *Docteur Jekyll et les Femmes,* aka *The Blood of Dr. Jekyll* (1981, France), c, 92 minutes.

CREDITS: Prod.: Ralph Baum, Robert Kuperberg, and Jean-Pierre Labrande; dir. and scr.: Wladimir Borowczyk; mus.: Bernard Parmegiani; mak.: Christine Fornelli, cam.: Noel Very; ed.: Kadicha Bariha.

CAST: Udo Kier (Dr. Henry Jekyll), Marino Pierro (Fanny Osbourne), Patrick Magee (general), Howard Vernon (Dr. Lanyon), Clement Harari (Rev. Donald Regan), and: Rita Maiden, Gisèlle Preville, Gerard Zaleberg, Michèle Maze, Agnès Daems, Magali Noaro, Dominque Andersen, Isabelle Cagnat.

Dr. Jekyll's Dungeon of Death. (New American, [made in 1978] 1982), c, 90 minutes.

CREDITS: Prod. and dir.: James Wood; scr.: James Mather; mus.: Marty Allen; cam. and ed.: James Wood.

CAST: James Mathers (Dr. Jekyll), John Kearney (Professor Atkinson), Tom Nicholson (Boris), Dawn Carver Kelly (Julia), Nadine Kalmes (Helga), and Jake Pearson.

Jekyll and Hyde . . . Together Again (Paramount, 1982), c, 87 minutes.

CREDITS: Prod.: Lawrence Gordon; dir.: Jerry Belson; scr.: Monica Johnson, Harvey Miller, Jerry Belson, and Michael Lesson; based on the novella *Strange Case of Dr. Jekyll and Mr. Hyde* by Robert Louis Stevenson; mus.: Barry De Vorzon; mak.: John M. Elliott Jr.; sp. mak.: Mark Bussan; sp. eff.: Dewey Gene Grigg; cam.: Philip Lathrop; ed.: Billy Weber.

CAST: Mark Blankfield (Dr. Jekyll and Mr. Hyde), Bess Armstrong (Mary), Krista Erickson (Ivy), Tim Thomerson (Dr. Lanyon), Michael McGuire (Dr. Carew), Neil Hunt (Queen), Cassandra Peterson (Busty Nurse), Jessica Nelson (Barbara Blau), Peter Brocco (Hubert Howes), Michael Klingher,

Noelle North, and David Murphy (Students), Mary McCusker (Patient), Liz Sheridan (Mrs. Larson), Alison Hong (little Asian girl), Walter Janovitz (elderly man in charity ward), Ann M. Nelson (hunchback nurse), Belita Moreno (Nurse Gonzales), Leland Sun (Wong), George Wendt (injured man), Glen Chin (sushi chef), Peter Ivers (bandleader), David Ruprecht (Brigham), Barret Oliver (child in supermarket), Sheila Rogers (woman in Jaguar car), Madelyn Cates (Helen Schneider), George Chakiris (himself).

Strannaya Istoriya Doktora Dzhekila I Mistera Hayda aka *The Strange Case of Dr. Jekyll and Mr. Hyde* (Sovfilms, [made in 1985] 1987; USSR), c. 85 minutes.

CREDITS: Dir.: Aleksandr Orlov; scr.: Georgi Kapralov, and Aleksandr Orlov; based on the novella *Strange Case of Dr. Jekyll and Mr. Hyde* by Robert Louis Stevenson.; mus: Eduard Artemyev; cam.: Valeri Shuvalov.

CAST: Innokenty Smoktunovksy (Dr. Henry Jekyll), Aleksandr Feklistovh (Hyde); Allan Budnitskaya (Diana), Alexander Lazarev (Lanyon), Anatoliy Adoskin (Utterson), Bruno Freyndlikh (Poole), and: Eduard Martsevich, Leonid Satanovsky, Alexander Vokacy, Alexandr Kirillov, Tatyana Okunevskaya.

Edge of Sanity (1989, Millimeter Films; Great Britain/Hungary), c, 86 minutes.

CREDITS: Prod.: Edward Simons and Harry Alan Towers; dir.: Gerard Kikoine; scr.: J. P. Felix and Ron Raley; music.: Frederic Talgorn; mak.: Gordon Kay; cam.: Tony Spratling; ed.: Malcolm Cooke.

CAST: Anthony Perkins (Dr. Jekyll and Mr. Hyde), Glynis Barber (Elizabeth Jekyll), Sarah Maur-Thorp (Susannah), David Lodge (Underwood), Ben Cole (Johnny the pimp), Ray Jewers (Newcomen), Jill Melford (Flora); Lisa Davis (Maria), Moel Coleman (Egglestone), Briony McRoberts (Ann Underwood), Mark Elliot (Lanyon), Harry Landis (coroner), Jill Pearson (Mrs. Egglestone), Basil Hoskins (Mr. Bottingham), Ruth Burnett (Margo), Carolyn Cortez (Maggie), Cathy Murphy (cockney prostitute).

Dr. Jekyll and Ms. Hyde (Savoy, 1995), c, 90 minutes.

CREDITS: Prod.: Robert Shapiro and Jerry Leider; dir.: David F. Price; scr.: William Davies, William Osborne, Tim John, and Oliver Butcher; based on the novella *Strange Case of Dr. Jekyll and Mr. Hyde* by Robert Louis Stevenson; mus.: Mark McKenzie; mak.: Diane Simard; mak. eff.: Kevin Yagher; sp. eff.: Louis Craig; cam.: Tom Priestley; ed.: Tony Lombardo.

CAST: Tim Daly (Richard Jacks; Dr. Jekyll's great grandson), Sean Young (Helen Hyde), Lysette Anthony (Sarah Carver), Stephen Tobolowsky (Oliver Mintz), Harvey Fierstein (Yves DuBois), Thea Vidale (Valerie), Jeremy Pivens (Pete), Polly Bergen (Mrs. Unterveldt), Stephen Shellen (Larry), Sheena Larkin (Mrs. Mintz), John Franklyn-Robbins (Professor Mannings), Aron Tager (lawyer), Jane Connell (Aunt Agatha), Robert Wuhl (man with lighter), Mike Hodge (Eagleton), Michael Rudder (Nose), Mark Camacho (waiter).

The Nutty Professor (Universal, 1996), c, 95 minutes.

CREDITS: Prod.: Brian Grazer and Russell Simmons; dir.: Tom Shadyac; scr.: David Sheffield, Barry W. Blaustein, Steve Oedekerk, and Tom Shadyac; based on the 1963 motion picture written by Jerry Lewis and Bill Richmond; mus.: David Newman; mak.: Geri B. Oppenheim; special mak. eff.: Rick Baker; sp. eff.: Burt Dalton; camera, Julio Macat; ed.: Don Zimmerman.

CAST: Eddie Murphy (Professor Sherman Klump, Buddy Love, Lance Perkins, Papa Klump, Mama Klump, Grandma Klump, and Ernie Klump), Jada Pinkett (Carla Purty), James Coburn (Harlan Hartley), Larry Miller (Dean Richmond), Dave Chappelle (Reggie Warrington), John Ales (Jason), Patricia Wilson (Dean's secretary), Jamal Mixon (Ernie Klump Jr.), Nichole McAuley (fit woman), Hamilton Von Watts (health instructor), Chao-Li Chi (Asian man), Tony Carlin (host), Quinn Duffy (bartender), Doug Williams (bandleader), Lisa Halpern (sad fat girl), Mark McPherson, John Prosky, and Michael Rothhaar (doctors), Sara Ballantine (nurse), Greg Natale (cop), Joe Greco (security guard), Nick Kokotakis (waiter), Julianne Christie (sporting goods clerk), Christie Blanchard-Power (woman dignitary), Ned von Leuck (construction worker).

Mary Reilly: The Untold Story of Dr. Jekyll and Mr. Hyde (TriStar, 1996), c, 108 minutes.

CREDITS: Prod: Ned Tanen, Nancy Graham Tanen, and Norma Heyman; dir. Stephen Fears; scr.: Christopher Hampton, based on a novel by Valerie Martin; mus.: George Fenton; mak.: Jenny Shircore; sp. eff.: Richard Conway; cam.: Philippe Rousselot; ed.: Lesley Walker.

CAST: Julia Roberts (Mary Reilly), John Malkovich (Dr. Henry Jekyll and Mr. Hyde), George Cole (Mr. Poole), Michael Gambon (Mary's father), Kathy Staff (Mrs. Kent), Glenn Close (Mrs. Farraday) Michael Sheen (Bradshaw), Bronagh Gallagher (Annie), Linda Bassett (Mary's mother), Henry Goodman (Haffinger), Ciarán Hinds (Sir Danvers Carew), Sasha Hanau (young Mary), Moya Brady (young woman), Emma Griffiths Malin (young whore), David Ross (doctor), Tim Barlow (vicar), Stephen Boxer (inspector), Bob Mason (policeman).

Mr. Jekyll & Dr. Hyde: A Documentary (Basecamp Entertainment Group, LLC/Great Guns Prods, 1999).

CREDITS: Prod.: Robert Nackman; dir.: Liam Kan and Grant Hodgson; scr.: Philip Lawrence.

CAST: Steven Lesser.

Nutty Professor II: The Klumps (Universal Pictures, 2000).

CREDITS: Prod.: Brian Grazer; dir.: Peter Segal; scr.: Barry W. Blaustein and David Sheffield, and Paul Weitz and Chris Weitz; based on characters created by Jerry Lewis and Bill Richmond; mus.: David Newman; sp. mak. eff.: Rick Baker; sp. eff.: Daniel Sudick; cam. Dean Semler; ed.: William Kerr.

CAST: Eddie Murphy (Sherman Klump, Buddy Love, Mama Klump, Papa Klump, Ernie Klump, and Grandma Klump); Janet Jackson (Denice Gains); John Ales (Jason), and: Larry Miller, Jamal Mixon, Melinda McGraw, Gabriel Williams, Anna Maria Horsford.

TELEVISION

Special "Dr. Jekyll and Mr. Hyde" (NBC, June 4, 1940), b/w, 60 minutes.

CREDITS: Tel.: Warren Wade; based on the novella *Strange Case of Dr. Jekyll and Mr. Hyde* by Robert Louis Stevenson.

CAST: Jack Cherry (Dr. Jekyll and Mr. Hyde); Paula Stone (Elizabeth), Judson Laire (Utterson), Jack Cherry (vicar/detective), Anne Crosby (prima donna).

Suspense "Dr. Jekyll and Mr. Hyde" (CBS, September 20, 1949), b/w, 30 minutes.

CREDITS: Prod. and dir.: Robert Stevens; tel.: Hasted Welles; based on the novella *Strange Case of Dr. Jekyll and Mr. Hyde* by Robert Louis Stevenson.

CAST: Ralph Bell (Dr. Jekyll and Mr. Hyde), Pamela Conroy (Esther), Ivan Simpson (Poole), Gage Clarke (Smudge).

Suspense "Dr. Jekyll and Mr. Hyde" (CBS, March 6, 1951), b/w, 30 minutes.

CREDITS: Based on the novella *Strange Case of Dr. Jekyll and Mr. Hyde* by Robert Louis Stevenson.

CAST: Basil Rathbone (Dr. Jekyll and Mr. Hyde).

Climax! "Dr. Jekyll and Mr. Hyde" (CBS, July 28, 1955), b/w, 60 minutes.

CREDITS: Prod.: Edgar Peterson; dir.: Allen Reisner; tel.: Gore Vidal, based on the novella *Strange Case of Dr. Jekyll and Mr. Hyde* by Robert Louis Stevenson.

CAST: Michael Rennie (Dr. Jekyll and Mr. Hyde), Sir Cedric Hardwicke (Dr. Lanyon), Mary Sinclair, (Agnes), Lowell Gilmore, John Hoyt.

Matinee Theatre "Dr. Jekyll and Mr. Hyde" (NBC, March 8, 1957), b/w, 1957.

CREDITS: Prod.: Albert McCleary; dir.: Alan Buckhantz; tel.: Robert Esson; based on *Strange Case of Dr. Jekyll and Mr. Hyde* by Robert Louis Stevenson.

CAST: Douglas Montgomery (Dr. Jekyll and Mr. Hyde), Lisa Daniels (Polly Bannon), Chester Stratton (Utterson), Lumsden Hare (Poole), Patrick Macnee (Peter).

The Strange Case of Dr. Jekyll and Mr. Hyde (ABC, January 7, 1968), color, 150 minutes.

CREDITS: Prod.: Dan Curtis; dir.: Charles Jarrott; tel.: Ian McLellan Hunter, based on the novella *Strange Case of Dr. Jekyll and Mr. Hyde* by Robert Louis Stevenson; mus. Robert Cobert; mak. Dick Smith.

CAST: Jack Palance (Dr. Jekyll and Mr. Hyde), Denholm Elliott (Devlin, a kind of Utterson), Leo Genn (Dr. Lanyon), Oscar Homolka (Dr. Stryker),

Gillie Fenwick (Poole), Billie Whitelaw (Gwyn, a prostitute), Tessie O'Shea (Tessie O'Toole), Torin Thatcher (Sir John Turnbull), Gillie Fenwick (Ivy Peterson), available on video cassette from Artisan Entertainment.

Dr. Jekyll and Mr. Hyde (NBC, March 7, 1973), c, 90 minutes.

CREDITS: Prod.: Burt Rosen and David Winters; dir.: David Winters; tel.: Sherman Yellen, based on the novella *Strange Case of Dr. Jekyll and Mr. Hyde* by Robert Louis Stevenson; mus. and lyrics by Lionel Bart, Mel Mandel, and Norman Saches.

CAST: Kirk Douglas (Dr. Jekyll and Mr. Hyde), Michael Redgrave (Danvers), Donald Pleasance (Smudge), Susan Hampton (Isabel), Susan George (Annie), Stanley Holloway (Poole), Judi Bowker (Tupenny), Nicholas Smith (Hastings), Geoffrey Chater (Lanyon), John T. Moore (Utterson), Geoffrey Wright (Wainwright).

The Strange Case of Dr. Jekyll and Mr. Hyde (British BBC, November 20, 1980; American PBS—*Mystery!* series, January 6 and 13, 1981), c, 120 minutes.

CREDITS: Prod.: Jonathan Powell; dir.: Alistair Reid; tel.: Gerard Savory, based on the novella *Strange Case of Dr. Jekyll and Mr. Hyde* by Robert Louis Stevenson.

CAST: David Hemmings (Dr. Henry Jekyll and Mr. Edward Hyde), Ian Bannen (Oliver Utterson), Lisa Harrow (Ann Coggeshall), Roland Curram (Poole), Toyah Wilcox (Janet), Diana Dors (Kate Winterton), Roger Davison (Bradshaw), Clive Smith (Hastie Lanyon), Gretchen Franklin (cook), Jane Slaughter (Gwen), Anna Faye (Mary), Gaye Brown (Diane), Tim Calver (pimp), Kenteas Brine (prostitute), Sevilla Delfski (Fifi), Sheelah Wilcocks (Mrs. Willoughby).

ABC Weekend Special "O. G. Readmore Meets Dr. Jekyll and Mr. Hyde" (ABC, September 13, 1986), c, 30 minutes.

CREDITS: Prod. and dir.: Rick Reiner; tel. Malcolm Marmorstein; based on the novella *Strange Case of Dr. Jekyll and Mr. Hyde* by Robert Louis Stevenson; dir. of animation, Dave Bennett; mus.: Steve Zuckerman; ed.: Chuck Gladden.

CAST: Voices: Lucille Bliss, Stanley Jones, Ilene Latter, Neil Ross, Hal Smith.

Special "Dr. Jekyll and Mr. Hyde" (Syndicated, 1986; Australia), c, 75 min.

CREDITS: Prod.: Roz Phillips and Tim Brooke-Hunt; animation dir: Warwick Gilbert; tel.: Marcia Hatfield: based on the novella *Strange Case of Dr. Jekyll and Mr. Hyde* by Robert Louis Stevenson; mus. John Stuart; ed.: Leonard Lee.

CAST: Max Meldrum (Dr. Jekyll), David Nettheim (Mr. Hyde), John Ewart (Utterson), Carol Adams, Simeon Hawkins, Phillip Hinton, Andrew Inglis, Jill McKay, David Roach-Turner.

Shelley Duvall's Nightmare Classics "The Strange Case of Dr. Jekyll and Mr. Hyde" (October 29, 1989, showtime), c, 55 minutes.

CREDITS: Prod.: Bridget Terry; executive prod.: Shelley Duvall; dir.: Michael Lindsay-Hogg; tel.: J. Michael Straczinski, based on the novella *Strange Case of Dr. Jekyll and Mr. Hyde* by Robert Louis Stevenson; mus.: Stephen Barber; cam.: Ron Vargas; ed.: Roy Watts.

CAST: Anthony Andrews (Dr. Henry Jekyll and Edward Hyde), Laura Dern (Rebecca Laymon), Gregory Cooke (Richard Utterson), Nicholas Guest (Fred Morley), George Murdoch (Professor Laymon), Rue McClanahan (madam), Mary Kohnert (Julie), Elizabeth Gracen (prostitute #1), Lisa Langlois (woman in Pub), I. M. Hobson (Poole).

Special "Jekyll and Hyde" (January 21, 1990, ABC), c. 120 minutes.

CREDITS: Prod.: David Wickes and Patricia Carr; dir. and tel.: David Wickes, based on the novella *Strange Case of Dr. Jekyll and Mr. Hyde* by Robert Louis Stevenson; mus.: John Cameron; sp. mak. eff.: Image Animation; cam. Norman G. Langley; ed. John Shirley.

CAST: Michael Caine (Dr. Henry Jekyll and Edward Hyde), Cheryl Ladd (Sara Crawford), Joss Ackland (Dr. Lanyon), Ronald Pickup (Jeffrey Utterson), Kim Thomson (Lucy), Kevin McNally (Sergeant Hornsby), David Schofield (Edward Snape), Lee Montague (Inspector Palmer), Miriam Karlin (Mrs. Annabelle Schneider), Joan Heal (Mrs. Clark), Frank Barrie (Poole), Diane Kean (Mrs. Hackett), Lionel Jeffries (William Jekyll), Martyn Jacobs (young man); Duncan Gold (businessman), John Scarborough (auctioneer), Ray Armstrong (head groom), Nina Kennedy (Victoria Wyatt), Peter Gale (Lanyon's brother), Andrew Castell (Dr. Lloyd).

Deacon Brodie (BFS Video, 1996; Great Britain), c, 90 minutes.

CREDITS: Dir.: Philip Saville; scr.: Simon Donald.

CAST: Billy Connolly (Deacon Brodie), Catherine McCormack (Anne Grant), Patrick Malahide (William Creech).

RADIO

Special "Dr. Jekyll and Mr. Hyde" (Station WGBS, New York, October 31, 1926).

CREDITS: Dir. and writer Dailey Paskman, based on the novella *Strange Case of Dr. Jekyll and Mr. Hyde* by Robert Louis Stevenson.

CAST: Howard Kyle (Dr. Jekyll and Mr. Hyde).

Favorite Story "Dr. Jekyll and Mr. Hyde" 1946. (Syndicated, August 20, 1946).

CREDITS: Radio play by Jerome Lawrence and Robert E. Lee; based on the novella *Strange Case of Dr. Jekyll and Mr. Hyde* by Robert Louis Stevenson.

Short Stories "Dr. Jekyll and Mr. Hyde" (NBC, 1948).

CREDITS. Based on the novella *Strange Case of Dr. Jekyll and Mr. Hyde* by Robert Louis Stevenson.

CAST: Not known.

Story Time "The Strange Case of Dr. Jekyll and Mr. Hyde" (Radio 4, 1977; Great Britain).

CREDITS: Based on the novella *Strange Case of Dr. Jekyll and Mr. Hyde* by Robert Louis Stevenson.

CAST: A five-part reading of the novella, reader: Leonard Maguire.

Best Seller No. 4 "Strange Case of Dr. Jekyll and Mr. Hyde" (Radio 4, 1978; Great Britain).

CREDITS: Prod.: Stanley Williamson; based on the novella *Strange Case of Dr. Jekyll and Mr. Hyde* by Robert Louis Stevenson.

CAST: Not known.

Mystery Theater "Strange Case of Dr. Jekyll and Mr. Hyde" (Syndicated, 1998).

CREDITS: Prod. and dir.: Michael Sollazzo; adapted by John McKinley; based on the novella *Strange Case of Dr. Jekyll and Mr. Hyde* by Robert Louis Stevenson.

CAST: The St. Charles Players (Jim Barker, Terry Fishman, Linda Livingston, Allan Poe, Robert Reynolds, Ron Rezac, Michael Sollazzo).

AUDIO

Dr. Jekyll and Mr. Hyde (Spoken Arts SA 3005, date unknown).

CREDITS: Dir.: Christopher Casson; based on the novella *Strange Case of Dr. Jekyll and Mr. Hyde* by Robert Louis Stevenson.

CAST: Read by Robert Somerset; with: Aiden Grennell (Dr. Jekyll and Mr. Hyde), Peter O'Connell (Lanyon).

The Strange Case of Dr. Jekyll and Mr. Hyde (London Decca Records, date unknown).

CREDITS: Prod.: Sound Recording Committee; based on the novella *Strange Case of Dr. Jekyll and Mr. Hyde* by Robert Louis Stevenson.

CAST: Read by Major J. R. T. Mathews on three records.

The Strange Case of Dr. Jekyll and Mr. Hyde (RCA Records, 1944).

CREDITS: Prod.: The American Foundation for the Blind; based on the novella *Strange Case of Dr. Jekyll and Mr. Hyde* by Robert Louis Stevenson.

CAST: Read by John Brewster on six records.

Dr. Jekyll and Mr. Hyde (Metacom, P.O. Box 11041, Minneapolis, MN 55411, 1948).

CREDITS: From the 1948 NBC radio network *Short Story* series broadcast of "Dr. Jekyll and Mr. Hyde"; based on the novella *Strange Case of Dr. Jekyll and Mr. Hyde* by Robert Louis Stevenson.

CAST: Unknown.

The Strange Case of Dr. Jekyll and Mr. Hyde (Caedmon Records TC 1283, 1969).

CREDITS: Based on the novella *Strange Case of Dr. Jekyll and Mr. Hyde* by Robert Louis Stevenson.

Cast: Read by Anthony Quayle.

The Strange Case of Dr. Jekyll and Mr. Hyde (Mystery Theatre, 1998).

CREDITS: Prod. and dir.: Michael Sollazzo; adapted by John McKinley; based on the novella *Strange Case of Dr. Jekyll and Mr. Hyde* by Robert Louis Stevenson.

CAST: Read on two audio cassettes by the St. Charles Players (Jim Barker, Terry Fishman, Linda Livingston, Allan Poe, Robert Reynolds, Ron Rezac, Michael Sollazzo).

Internet Sites

www.bibliomania.com/Fiction/stevenson/drjekyll/index.html—*Strange Case of Dr. Jekyll and Mr. Hyde,* the text online.

www.drjekyllandmrhyd.com—*Dr. Jekyll and Mr. Hyde,* not the Broadway musical.

www.eerie.com—Jekyll and Hyde Clubs in New York, Chicago, and Dallas, "restaurants and interactive entertainment centers."

www.Jekyll-hyde.com—*Jekyll and Hyde,* the Broadway musical.

www.sc.edu/library/scotlit/rls.html—R. L. S. at the Thomas Cooper Library at University of South Carolina.

www.staff.uiuc.edu/~hcahndle/RLSdream.htm—The writing of the *Strange Case of Dr. Jekyll and Mr. Hyde.*

www.users.globalnet.co.uk/~crumey/scot.htm—Scottish writers.

About the Authors

RAYMOND T. MCNALLY is the co-author of the bestselling *In Search of Dracula* (1972 and revised edition 1994) and *Dracula, Prince of Many Faces* (1989), both still in print. He has taught history at Boston College for more than forty-two years. He has been awarded Fulbright Research Fellowships to Russia, Romania, and Turkey. He has authored six scholarly books and more than twenty articles. His children Michael, Tippy, Brigit, and Tara are grown up. Professor McNally currently lives with his wife, Carol, and Patrick, their teenaged son, in Newton, Massachusetts, and teaches a course on "The History of Horror," a comparative study of classic horror literature and movies, at Boston College. Dr. McNally is a horror movie buff.

RADU R. FLORESCU is Professor Emeritus at Boston College, director of the East European Research Center, and fellow of St. Anthony College Oxford. He is currently honorary consul of Romania for New England. Together with Professor McNally he co-authored the bestseller *In Search of Dracula* (1972 and revised edition 1994), which was translated into more than a dozen foreign languages. He also co-authored *Dracula: A Biography* (1974) and *Dracula Prince of Many Faces* (1989), in addition to three other books on the subject. His other works include *In Search of Frankenstein* (1973 and 1996), two major publications on Romanian history, and specialized articles on Eastern Europe. He is listed in the millennium edition of *Marquis's Who's Who in the World* and has recently been awarded an Honoris Causa diploma by the Romanian Academy.